Ai-Ling Tsai

Strategically Integrated HRD

Other Titles by Jerry W. Gilley

Principles of HRD
Stop Managing, Start Coaching! (coauthor)
Internal Consulting for HRD Professionals
Marketing HRD within Organizations
Improving HRD Practice

Strategically Integrated HRD

Partnering to Maximize Organizational Performance

JERRY W. GILLEY
and ANN MAYCUNICH

Addison-Wesley
Reading, Massachusetts

Many of the designations used by manufacturers and sellers to distinguish their products are claimed as trademarks. Where those designations appear in this book and Addison-Wesley was aware of a trademark claim, the designations have been printed in initial capital letters.

Library of Congress Cataloging-in-Publication Data
Gilley, Jerry W.
    Strategically integrated HRD : partnering to maximize
organizational performance / Jerry W. Gilley and Ann Maycunich.
        p.   cm.
    Includes bibliographical references and index.
    ISBN 0-201-33980-3
    1. Personnel management.   2. Partnership.   3. Organizational
effectiveness.   I. Maycunich, Ann.   II. Title.
HF5549.G5133   1998
658.3—dc21   98-14117
                                                                        CIP

Addison-Wesley is an imprint of Addison Wesley Longman, Inc.

Jacket design by Suzanne Heiser
Text design by David C. denBoer
Set in 11/13-point Meridien by Nighthawk Design

123456789-MA-0201009998
First printing, May 1998

Addison-Wesley books are available at special discounts for bulk purchases in the U.S. by corporations, institutions, and other organizations. For more information, please contact the Corporate, Government, and Special Sales Department at Addison Wesley Longman, Inc., One Jacob Way, Reading, MA 01867, or call 1-800-238-9682.

Find us on the World Wide Web at
http://www.aw.com/gb/

Contents

Figures

Acknowledgments

I would like to acknowledge Nick Philipson, our editor, for his constant support and encouragement, and for championing this project. I'm extremely grateful for the opportunity to work with my co-author and friend, Ann Maycunich. I would like to thank her for her encouragement, support, determination, and perfectionism. Finally, I would like to thank my mother, Lottie V. Gilley, for a lifetime of patience, encouragement, and love, for which I am eternally grateful. She has been my anchor in the sea of life, my beacon on moonless nights, and my co-pilot through my life's journey.

Jerry W. Gilley

I would like to thank my family, particularly my parents, Ken and Connie Maycunich, for their neverending love and support. I offer thanks to Nora Ruder, VP of Foremost Insurance and mentor extraordinaire, for unselfishly allowing me to pursue my dreams in spite of the hardship placed upon her by doing so. Finally, I'm particularly grateful to Jerry Gilley for allowing me to be a part of this project. Mere words cannot describe the depth of this experience.

Ann Maycunich

Strategically Integrated HRD

CHAPTER 1

Strategically Integrated HRD: Blending Philosophy, Strategy, Partnerships, and Practice

Many human resource development (HRD) professionals spend much of their time designing classroom-based training events; others behave as if their mission were to conduct workshops, seminars, meetings, and conferences. Consequently, they view training as an end unto itself. This belief is reinforced by management when they do not use HRD as a strategic tool in improving organizational performance and effectiveness. Moreover, training vendors, professional associations, and direct mail distributors reinforce this belief when they guarantee that they can fix every possible organizational ill using the latest ten-step format, the newest training games, or the "four-quadrant anything." With this type of reinforcement, <u>it is not surprising that HRD professionals fail to understand the importance of becoming strategic partners within an organization.</u>

When HRD professionals believe that the business of HRD is to deliver *training for training's sake,* all their energy is directed toward the number of training courses they deliver and the number of employees they train. Consequently, they rely on employees' responses to training as a means to justify HRD's existence rather than focusing <u>on learning transfer or the impact of training.</u> Is this philosophy of HRD the most appropriate way of helping improve organizational performance and effectiveness? Let's consider the parable of the sower as a way of examining this question.

THE PARABLE OF THE SOWER

As the story goes, the sower threw his seed indiscriminately on top of the soil. Some of the soil was stony, and the seeds had difficulty producing a consistent crop. Some of the soil was full of thorns, which prevented the seeds from growing to maturity. Some of the soil was shallow, which allowed the seeds to take root but prevented the development of a strong root system; the crop soon withered away under the hot August sun. Some of the soil was hard, preventing the seeds from taking root at all. However, some of the soil was fertile and prepared to accept the seeds, and consequently, produced a bumper crop.

How does this parable relate to the field of HRD? The sower is the HRD professional. The seeds are HRD interventions that are designed to improve organizational performance and effectiveness. The different types of soil represent two things: the organization's readiness to provide growth and development opportunities, and the organizational barriers that prevent performance improvement, growth, and development.

Stony soil represents an organization that has a hot and cold relationship with HRD. Some divisions embrace HRD while others avoid it. Thorny soil is representative of organizations that allow their managers, structure, operations, and reward systems to get in the way of performance improvement and growth. Shallow soil represents organizations that do not encourage learning transfer. When learning does occur, it only improves job performance temporarily before it gets lost among hundreds of competing events. Hard soil is representative of organizations and people who believe that they have nothing to learn. Consequently, they resist learning altogether. Fertile soil represents organizations that are prepared to accept growth and development opportunities and are willing to support and encourage them.

Productive sowers have learned they cannot just throw their seed indiscriminately on top of the soil, go home, and wait for a bumper crop. They must prepare the soil for planting by removing the stones and thorns and tilling it. They must plant their seeds deep in the earth, fertilize the soil soon after planting, irrigate if Mother Nature does not cooperate, weed the growing crop to ensure maximum growth, continue to fertilize and water the crop during the long hot summer months, and, finally, harvest the crop and prepare the soil for winter.

Which sower is the most productive? The answer is obvious: the one who is willing to carefully prepare the soil to produce maximum yields. Likewise, improving organizational performance and effectiveness is not about better products, more capital, or even better business processes, but about growing and developing human resources. Unfortunately, even though they are the heart of every organization, people are the organizational asset least developed and cared for. Without their people, organizations will not be able to operate or serve their customers. In essence, organizations will not be able to produce products or provide services without the input and effort of their employees.

Organizations are people, so why are people treated so poorly so much of the time? The answer is simple. Many organizations have an HRD philosophy similar to the planting strategy of the sower in the parable. They think that developing their human resources requires no effort. Their philosophy goes something like this: "We'll throw some training at our employees and hope that performance improves"; or, "We really don't have the time to train and develop our people because we're so busy"; or, "We'll get around to it as soon as we can; remember, the customer comes first"; or, "If they don't develop fast enough or produce well enough we will find someone else who will" (Gilley & Boughton, 1996, p. 48).

Many HRD professionals simply cannot see the damaging effects of the old HRD philosophy. Gill (1995) believes that the old HRD philosophy is contributing to the destruction of organizations. He states: "at the end of the 20th century, our 17th century organizations are crumbling because the changes which are required to improve performance and productivity are simply not being made" (p. 26). High-performance organizations require a shift from the old HRD approach to a new philosophy of HRD, one that enables HRD professionals to become strategic partners responsible for improving organizational performance and effectiveness.

THE SIX TRAINING ANCHORS THAT LEAD TO DISASTER

Six deeply held beliefs contribute to the "training for training's sake" philosophy of HRD. These beliefs appear to anchor HRD professionals into this philosophy. Consequently, these beliefs affect their behavior and actions as well as the decisions they make. The anchors are as follows:

1. Training makes a difference.
2. Training is an HRD practitioner's job.

3. The trainer's purpose is to manage training programs.
4. Training's purpose is to achieve learning objectives.
5. Employees should enjoy the training they receive.
6. Training is designed to "fix" employees' weaknesses (Gill, 1995).

Training Makes a Difference

Many HRD practitioners are true believers. They honestly think that training by itself can change an organization and improve its performance and effectiveness. When this belief is held, HRD practitioners think there is a direct cause-and-effect relationship between training and improving performance in the workplace. Yet nothing could be further from the truth! Employees are so bombarded with problems, circumstances, and decisions that little of the training they receive can penetrate their mental shields. Without careful and deliberate reinforcement on the job, most of what employees learn is forgotten and never applied.

Training Is an HRD Practitioner's Job

Many HRD practitioners have the attitude that training is their responsibility. Managers reinforce this belief by allowing their training responsibilities to be delegated to professional trainers. In other words, managers wash their hands of the responsibility of developing their employees.

Who should be responsible for training? Gilley (1998) believes that the person held accountable for employee performance and productivity ultimately should be responsible for training. This individual should also be responsible for conducting employee performance reviews, providing feedback, and confronting poor performance. The person responsible for training should be held accountable when productivity declines or when the organization fails to meet its goals and objectives. The person an organization holds accountable for each of these activities is the "manager." Managers lacking the skills essential to adequately train employees should be relieved of their managerial duties and responsibilities.

Because HRD practitioners are not truly responsible for employee performance and productivity, should they be responsible for providing employee training? The answer is no. Training should be the primary responsibility of managers because they are the only organizational players truly held accountable for employee performance and productivity. Organizations need to allow people who have real-world experience—managers—to deliver training. This is the only way learning transfer will be successful. Organizations must use managers' performance coaching skills to improve performance and manage change (see Chapter 6). In this way, managers will become the champions of training rather than its gatekeepers.

If managers take over the role of trainer, what will HRD professionals do? HRD professionals should evolve from trainers into organizational development consultants (see Chapter 7). In this role, HRD professionals would support and supplement the efforts of managers as trainers by training *them*. Organizational development (OD) consultants should also provide managers with predesigned training programs that can be used in a short-course format.

The Trainer's Purpose Is to Manage Training Programs

Many HRD practitioners spend a great deal of their time managing the training event. They schedule courses, select training materials, manage enrollments, arrange conferences and workshop logistics, and collect and analyze evaluation forms. In fact, so much of their time is spent doing these types of activities that they have little time to spend on the critical issues facing their organizations, such as business process improvement, strategic planning, performance management systems, and change management. HRD practitioners operate as though business issues have little effect on training. They are happy managing training and behave as if their department is tangential to other operational units.

Training's Purpose Is to Achieve Learning Objectives

This belief can be termed the "Curse of Bob Mager" because, as the father of instructional systems design, he has convinced a generation of HRD practitioners of the importance of well-written learning objectives—so much so, that many HRD practitioners believe accomplishing learning objectives is the primary purpose of training. Learning objectives do provide structure and direction for a training program, and they help define the purpose of training. Yet while they are important, they are not an end unto themselves. Professional trainers rely too much on them. Learning objectives cannot assure performance improvement or add value to an organization. Only HRD interventions that help an organization achieve its strategic business goals can.

Employees Should Enjoy Training

Many HRD practitioners believe employees should enjoy training. Such a belief is evident by the type of training evaluations used. Most HRD practitioners rely on evaluations of responses to determine if employees enjoyed training. Consequently, training programs that produce stress or cause employees to feel uncomfortable may not be viewed as positively as those designed for enjoyment. Is it any wonder that most training programs are designed to satisfy employees?

Training should be free from negative feedback that reduces employees' self-esteem. However, training has a greater purpose if done correctly. It should be designed to improve organizational performance and effectiveness. Sometimes this requires painful experiences, the types that develop employees as well as the organization.

Training Is Designed to Fix Employees' Weaknesses

One of HRD practitioners' biggest problems is that they believe they are in the business of "fixing" employees. As a result, training is remedial in nature, giving employees the impression that something is wrong with them. Therefore, training interventions are designed to correct employees' weaknesses rather than building on their strengths and managing their weaknesses. Such a philosophy undermines the efforts of HRD professionals and conditions employees to enter training with a negative and defensive attitude. Consequently, organizational performance and effectiveness do not improve.

TWENTY-FIVE DEADLY SINS
OF HRD PROFESSIONALS

Every day HRD professionals commit several conscious and unconscious transgressions that prevent organizations from achieving strategic business goals and objectives. Each of these deadly sins prevent HRD professionals from becoming influential partners within organizations and continues to lock them into the "training for training's sake" philosophy. The twenty-five deadly sins of HRD professionals are:

1. failing to develop a philosophy of HRD dedicated to achieving organizational results

2. failing to adopt a strategic approach to improving organizational performance and development
3. failing to think strategically before responding to a client's request for training
4. failing to develop an understanding of an organization and its businesses
5. failing to design, develop, and implement an organizational effectiveness strategy
6. failing to develop a systems approach to organizational change and development
7. failing to develop performance management systems
8. failing to become strategic business partners within organizations
9. failing to link HRD interventions and initiatives to an organization's strategic business goals and objectives and its business and performance needs
10. failing to adopt a customer service approach with internal clients
11. failing to let managers develop their employees
12. failing to develop a management development partnership to improve organizational performance capacity and effectiveness
13. failing to encourage managers to use performance appraisals as a vehicle for providing their employees with meaningful, specific, and timely feedback
14. failing to help managers develop performance coaching skills
15. failing to implement organizational development partnerships that will transform organizational effectiveness
16. failing to make the transition from trainer to internal organizational development consult
17. failing to identify organizational and performance needs
18. failing to use organizational and performance needs as the foundation of all HRD interventions and initiatives
19. failing to design and develop performance improvement and change interventions that maximize organizational performance
20. failing to create a learning acquisition strategy
21. failing to eliminate barriers to learning transfer
22. failing to implement transfer of learning strategies
23. failing to measure the impact of performance improvement and organizational results achieved through HRD
24. failing to improve the image and credibility of HRD within an organization

25. failing to develop a promotional strategy for the HRD program

STRATEGICALLY INTEGRATED HRD

In order to overcome each of these twenty-five sins as well as to maximize organizational performance, HRD professionals should:

1. develop a new philosophy of HRD (Chapter 2).
2. apply two organizational transformation techniques to improve organizational effectiveness (Chapters 3 and 4).
3. create three performance partnerships as a way of executing organizational change and learning (Chapters 5, 6, and 7).
4. change HRD practice as a way of unleashing continuous improvement and quality (Chapters 8, 9, 10, and 11).
5. apply tools and technologies to improve HRD and organizations (Chapters 12 and 13).

We refer to this five-phase framework as *strategically integrated HRD* (Figure 1.1).

The following chart illustrates the phases of strategically integrated HRD and the deadly sins that they address.

Deadly Sin	Phases of Strategically Integrated HRD
1, 2, 3	Developing a strategically integrated HRD philosophy (Chapter 2).
4, 5, 6, 7	Improving organizational effectiveness (Chapters 3 and 4).
	Creating performance partnerships
8, 9, 10	Strategic business partnerships (Chapter 5).
11, 12, 13, 14	Performance coaching partnerships (Chapter 6).
15, 16	Organizational development partnerships (Chapter 7).
	Unleashing HRD practice
17, 18	Identifying organizational and performance needs (Chapter 8).
19	Designing and developing performance improvement and change interventions (Chapter 9).
20, 21, 22	Facilitating learning acquisition and learning transfer (Chapter 10).
23	Measuring performance improvement and organizational results (Chapter 11).

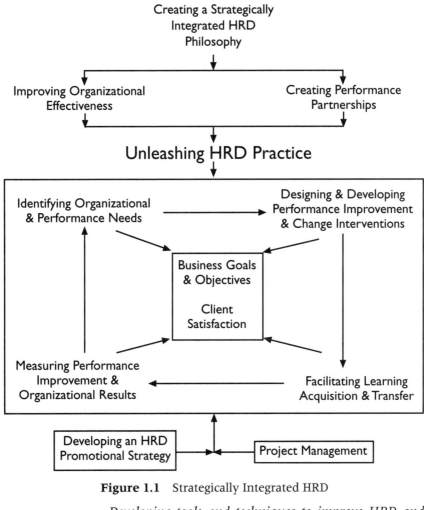

Figure 1.1   Strategically Integrated HRD

Developing a Strategically Integrated HRD Philosophy

HRD professionals' lack of vision is one of their biggest problems. Many HRD professionals believe that training is the answer to all organizational ills. Yet training can only correct problems caused by the lack of knowledge or skill. Training cannot by itself ensure improved organizational performance or effectiveness.

Many HRD programs are not linked to the strategic business goals of the organization (Brinkerhoff & Gill, 1994). When this occurs, training is conducted in a vacuum. Little attention is paid to the problems facing the organization and how training can be used to address them. As a result, employees fail to receive the type of training and reinforcement needed to improve performance. Organizational performance cannot improve because training is not focused on the business needs of the organization. Gilley and Boughton (1996) call this type of training the "hit or miss" approach. Some training is on target, but most is not.

HRD professionals can choose an activity strategy where training is the cornerstone or a results-driven strategy that is performance-centered (Gilley & Coffern, 1994). These strategies differ in their outcomes and in their contribution to an organization. The former will lead to training for training's sake while the latter will help organizations achieve their strategic business goals and objectives.

HRD professionals must choose which path they wish to follow. An activity strategy leads to business as usual. Result-driven strategies such as strategically integrated HRD enable HRD programs to maximize organizational performance.

Strategically integrated HRD is a philosophy that describes what HRD professionals believe to be true about the field of HRD. It describes their fundamental beliefs about HRD and helps them conceptualize and translate practice into action. A strategically integrated HRD philosophy is a system of values and guiding principles by which HRD professionals operate. In short, a strategically integrated HRD philosophy is one's basic theory or viewpoint of HRD (Chapter 2).

A strategically integrated HRD philosophy is also a set of operational guidelines used in improving organizational effectiveness. This is accomplished by developing an organizational effectiveness strategy, forming performance partnerships, and unleashing HRD practice.

Improving Organizational Effectiveness

HRD professionals cannot develop a strategically integrated HRD program unless they also create a comprehensive and organization-wide strategy for improving organizational effectiveness (Fallon & Brinkerhoff, 1996; Gilley & Coffern, 1994). As a way of achieving this outcome, HRD professionals can use two organizational transformation techniques: the organizational effectiveness framework (Chapter 2) and strategic planning (Chapter 4).

The organizational effectiveness framework can be used as a troubleshooting guide to identify possible breakdowns within an organization. It consists of two critical parts: the organizational system and the performance management system. These two major components consist of fifteen critical functions that work in concert to help organizations produce products and services for their clients. They are as follows:

Organizational System

- leadership
- mission and strategy
- organizational culture
- structure
- work climate
- policies and procedures
- management practice (Chapter 3)

Performance Management System

- human resources
- compensation and reward system
- learning system
- career planning
- work design
- recruiting and selection
- performance coaching
- performance appraisal process (Chapter 3)

HRD professionals can also improve organizational effectiveness through strategic planning activities (Chapter 4). "Strategic planning is a bit different from casual planning efforts because a strategic plan usually draws the boundaries within which organizations can operate" (Hale & Westgaard, 1991, p. 18). Strategic planning helps organizations set priorities, which enable them in turn to direct their energies and efforts. Strategic planning consists of five phases:

1. scoping
2. analyzing
3. visualizing
4. planning
5. implementing and evaluating

Creating Performance Partnerships

Performance partnerships must be formed at three levels. First, HRD professionals must be willing to become strategic business partners with clients from different business units, divisions, and departments so that they can provide them with better service (see Chapter 5). Such partnerships require HRD professionals to become responsible for providing customer service, helping their clients make performance improvement and organizational development decisions, and identifying demands facing their clients and how they should respond accordingly.

HRD professionals must also create management development partnerships with managers and supervisors as a way of improving organizational performance. Such partnerships can be best accomplished by helping managers and supervisors make the transition to performance coaching (see Chapter 6). In this way, managers and supervisors become responsible for the lion's share of training and development for their employees. This frees HRD professionals to help facilitate organizational change and development. This type of partnership is referred to as a *micro approach,* where performance improvement occurs one manager and one employee at a time.

A final performance partnership is known as the *macro approach* (Chapter 7), which occurs when HRD professionals begin focusing their attention on improving organizational effectiveness by altering the organizational and performance management systems (see Chapter 3). This type of partnership can only be formed when HRD professionals have access to organizational leaders and decision-makers. Its focus is on improving the organization through change and organizational development interventions that directly maximize organizational performance.

There are several behaviors that HRD professionals must be willing to demonstrate in order to create performance partnerships within the organization. HRD professionals must:

- maintain a strategically integrated HRD philosophy.
- develop an organizational effectiveness strategy.
- shift from designing, developing, and implementing "training events" to creating interventions that are targeted at improving organizational performance and effectiveness through learning transfer.
- help organizations achieve their strategic business goals and objectives.

- think strategically before responding to requests for training.
- operate as though performance improvement is the responsibility of everyone in the organization.
- develop transfer of learning strategies that foster organizational improvement.
- improve the image and credibility of HRD within the organization.
- accept the role of organizational development consultant as a way of helping organizations improve their performance.
- relinquish training responsibility to managers.

Unleashing HRD Practice

HRD professionals need to adopt a new approach to maximizing organizational performance, one that addresses the real problems of an organization and that enables it to achieve needed results. HRD professionals need to develop an approach that helps them connect performance improvement and change interventions to the strategic business goals of organizations. Such an approach must focus on learning transfer strategies rather than on training activity. In short, HRD professionals must redesign the performance improvement and organizational change process in order to develop a strategically integrated HRD program. The process consists of four phases. These are:

1. identifying organizational and performance needs (Chapter 8)
2. designing and developing performance improvement and change interventions (Chapter 9)
3. facilitating learning acquisition and learning transfer (Chapter 10)
4. measuring performance improvement and organizational results (Chapter 11)

Identifying Organizational and Performance Needs

The first step in the needs analysis process is to clearly identify opportunities for performance improvement and organizational development. This requires HRD professionals to examine, analyze, and evaluate possible sources of opportunity. Managers' and supervisors' expectations regarding employee performance can help HRD professionals identify organizational and performance needs. The strategic direction of the organization can also identify critical organizational and performance needs. Customers who use the organization's products and services can provide feedback about their quality, performance, and effectiveness, further helping identify organizational and performance needs.

Designing and Developing Performance Improvement and Change Interventions

HRD professionals concerned with identifying learning objectives; choosing, arranging, and sequencing learning objectives; designing or selecting learning activities; writing participant manuals; selecting the location for learning to take place; identifying the target audience; and getting managers and supervisors involved are engaged in the design and development process (Gilley & Eggland, 1989). It is the foundation of all performance improvement and change interventions.

Facilitating Learning Acquisition and Transfer

During the performance improvement process, HRD professionals and managers must do several things to ensure that employees acquire and retain learning. These include: managing learning activities, providing feedback to participants during learning activities, monitoring learning acquisition, and providing a supportive and positive learning environment. Each of these is essential in producing learning that brings about skill development, increased knowledge, and changed attitudes.

Managers and HRD professionals can help foster learning acquisition and transfer by providing practice opportunities both during and after training. In addition, HRD professionals can design peer coaching materials to reinforce on-the-job application and integration. Providing individualized feedback, job performance aids, realistic work-related tasks, opportunities for support groups, follow-up support, timely feedback, and problem-solving sessions are other ways to enhance learning acquisition and learning transfer.

Before learning can be translated into value for an organization, it must be applied to the job. Therefore, no other step in the performance improvement and change process is more important than this one. Unfortunately, too many learners are "on their own" immediately after a training event, struggling to integrate new skills or knowledge on the job. Confused and frustrated, employees often fail to confidently and accurately transfer learned principles to their work. Consequently, much of what is learned during training is lost, never to be applied or used.

*Measuring Performance Improvement
and Organizational Results*

The outcomes of the performance improvement process are ultimately assessed through evaluation. The most common forms of performance evaluation are formative and summative. *Formative evaluation* is intended to provide feedback for program improvement and to facilitate choosing among possible modifications. It should be used as the basis for constructively modifying the HRD effort in the future, not simply as a basis for keeping it alive or, alternatively, completing the process. *Summative evaluation,* on the other hand, is geared to assess the overall outcomes of the performance improvement process and leads to a decision to continue or to terminate the process (Gilley & Eggland, 1989).

One of the reasons HRD professionals do not conduct impact evaluations of their programs is that they do not know how. While they are experts at designing, developing, and implementing training, when it comes to evaluating the results of training many HRD professionals are lost. They do not know the strategic and diagnostic questions to ask when evaluating results from training. This lack of knowledge prevents the discovery of training outcomes. Therefore, they cannot, with any degree of certainty, defend HRD's contribution to organizational improvement.

Impact evaluations are very difficult to perform as they do not provide immediate feedback regarding the effects of training. Therefore, HRD professionals put them off and often never get around to conducting them. In other words, they are not a priority of most HRD professionals.

Some of the questions that perplex HRD professionals about impact evaluations are: "When is the proper time to evaluate the impact or return on investment (ROI) of training?" "Is it an activity to be conducted several months after training, as part of front-end analysis, or both?" The answer to these questions will give HRD professionals direction when they use impact evaluations.

Applying Tools and Techniques to Improve HRD and Organizations

When an organization is growing and expanding, HRD is perceived as important and necessary in the eyes of senior executives. In fact, they sometimes see it as part of the reason the organization is so prosperous. During financially difficult periods, however,

HRD becomes a burden, and commitment to the HRD program is severely reduced and sometimes the program is even eliminated.

This hot and cold relationship with management is caused by HRD professionals' failure to properly demonstrate and communicate the value of HRD. They fail to understand that senior management has a short memory and takes HRD for granted; unless a serious effort is made to demonstrate the virtues of HRD, management will forget its contribution to organizational success (Chapter 12).

Every strategically integrated HRD professional is a project manager responsible for designing, managing, implementing, and evaluating performance improvement, change, and organization development interventions. Such responsibilities include planning, organizing, directing, and controlling project outcomes that are delivered on time, within budget, and to quality specifications (see Chapter 13).

Strategically integrated HRD professionals can better manage projects using an eight-phase process that includes:

1. project definition
2. project planning
3. project visualization
4. project communication and leadership
5. project implementation
6. project controls
7. project termination
8. project evaluation

REFLECTING: THE KEY TO DEVELOPING STRATEGICALLY INTEGRATED HRD

Every morning many of us wake up and wonder how we evolved to our current status in life. We wonder why we do what we do and why we perform the activities and roles we do. We realize that we have charted a career path for ourselves, but cannot remember the decisions that led us to it. Unfortunately, we spend little time thinking about how we got to this point. Consequently, many of us just accept our fate, realizing that the complexity of our lives is one of the reasons for our uncertainty. However, one day curiosity gets the better of us, and we stop and ask a very simple but thought-provoking question, one question that changes our lives forever: "How did I get to this point in life?" When this occurs, we have begun the process of reflection.

Reflection allows us to consider, examine, analyze, critique, or contemplate our past. It allows us to ask "what if" questions and to consider possibilities. As a result, we begin piecing together the fragmented parts of our lives. Reflection allows us to better understand ourselves by examining our beliefs and assumptions. It provides insight into our mistakes, our successes, our failures, and our difficulties. It helps us understand how we evolve.

According to Schwinn (1996), reflection is comprehending the existence or meaning of what was previously unknown or unrecognized, and then acting on the differences between prior and current expectations. Not only is reflection the window to an understanding of our past, but it is also the door to our future. Reflection is the key to change. It allows us to challenge our assumptions and beliefs regarding our lives, which enables us to change our "philosophy" of life. Ultimately, we begin to change our personal philosophy, life strategy, and personal and professional practice. As a result, we become different people, which changes the direction of our lives.

If reflection is critical in our personal lives, it is also important in our professional lives. HRD professionals often struggle with how they evolve within their careers and the field of HRD. Their philosophy of HRD, the strategies they embrace, the partnerships they develop, and their HRD practice have changed dramatically over the years. The interaction of these four elements holds the key to success in HRD (see Figure 1.2). Reflecting can begin in any one of these four places. However, the changes made as a result of our reflection in one area have an impact on the three other areas.

For example, by implementing a performance management system (*organizational effectiveness strategy*) within an organization, employees received specific, timely, meaningful, and positive performance feedback. Consequently, their productivity increases. From this positive experience, HRD professionals begin thinking differently about the purpose of HRD (philosophy). They may begin to believe that the purpose of HRD is more than simply providing training programs. Thus, they begin changing their HRD practice within the organization, which might mean developing a performance partnership with a new department in the organization. This partnership might affect the HRD professionals' strategy, HRD philosophy, or practice. Thus the cycle continues.

The same cycle occurs when HRD professionals begin reflecting on their role (*organizational development consultant*) within the organization. Let's say that HRD professionals believe that they need to initiate significant change in the organization (*organizational*

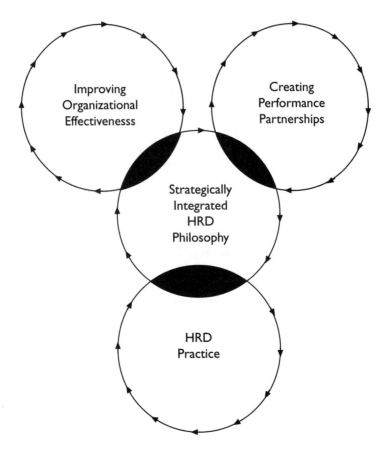

Figure 1.2   Reflective Model of HRD

development partnership). Therefore, they actively look for opportunities to help senior executives and managers in decision-making or problem-solving efforts. As a result, HRD professionals begin thinking about how they can help the organization achieve its strategic mission. Such thinking begins to impact and change their beliefs regarding HRD (*philosophy*). As they rethink their philosophy of HRD, they begin to realize the importance of facilitating a strategic planning activity (*intervention*) within the organization, which reinforces their new role as organizational development consultants.

When we begin reflecting on our philosophy of HRD, it can impact our organizational effectiveness strategy, performance partnerships, and HRD practice individually or simultaneously. For example, several years ago, three senior HRD professionals at William M. Mercer Inc. were in a heated and serious discussion regarding the purpose of HRD (philosophy) in their organization. They were concerned about how to reverse the organization's perception of HRD.

In the past the HRD department was perceived as a "training house" rather than as a program that could transform the organization. As a result of their discussion, they adopted a new philosophy of HRD, one that focused on improving organizational performance, effectiveness, and productivity through organizational development interventions. Over time, Mercer's HRD practice began changing in the organization. They began developing performance partnerships, which reinforced the change in their HRD philosophy. They started conducting high-level performance and organizational needs assessments, designing performance appraisal systems, examining the work climate and culture of the organization, and coaching executives on performance issues. In other words, a change in their HRD philosophy dramatically changed their entire HRD practice, partnerships, and strategic approach.

Let's consider how reflecting on an HRD activity (needs analysis, HRD practice) can affect one's organizational effectiveness strategy, performance partnerships, and HRD philosophy. Remember that when reflecting, we should examine what we do and why we are doing it. The following questions will help HRD professionals consider how conducting needs assessment activities can impact all other elements.

Philosophy of HRD

1. What is the purpose of needs assessment?
2. How has the organization benefited from needs assessments?
3. What have I learned about the practice of HRD from conducting needs assessments?
4. If I never conduct another needs assessment again, how will it benefit/impede the organization?
5. How are needs assessments perceived by the organization?
6. Who benefits the most from needs assessments?
7. By conducting needs assessments, how has my philosophy of HRD changed?
8. How do needs assessments benefit me within the organization?
9. Who "owns" the needs assessment process and its results?

Performance Partnerships

1. What are the primary outcomes of needs assessments?
2. What will we do with the information after it has been gathered?
3. Who typically participates in needs assessments?
4. What have I learned about the organization by conducting needs assessments?

5. How could I get the same information without conducting needs assessments?
6. What have I learned about needs assessments from conducting them?
7. What are other organizational members' roles during needs assessments?
8. Who benefits the most from needs assessments?
9. How does needs assessment improve performance partnerships?

Organizational Effectiveness Strategy

1. How is the organization affected by needs assessments?
2. How will needs assessments affect management practice within the organization?
3. How does the organizational structure, work climate, policies and procedures, and leadership affect needs assessments?
4. How does the performance management system affect needs assessments?

These questions are grouped into three areas of inquiry. Some will help us better understand our philosophy of HRD; some will help us better understand performance partnerships; others will help us better understand our organizational effectiveness strategy when conducting needs assessments. Regardless, reflecting on this activity will provide us with a tremendous amount of useful information that should help us change our assumptions about the activity, our philosophy of HRD, performance partnerships, and organizational effectiveness strategy.

Developing a strategically integrated HRD program is hard work, but it can reap outstanding results. It is important to remember that changing one's philosophy of HRD, organizational effectiveness strategy, performance partnerships, and HRD practice must be well thought out. Every organization is different. Therefore, timing is critical. What works in one organization might not work in another. Be selective and thoughtful.

TWENTY-FIVE OUTCOMES OF STRATEGICALLY INTEGRATED HRD

By applying the principles, techniques, and strategies outlined in this book, HRD professionals should be able to:

1. develop a philosophy of HRD that will help organizations achieve their business results.
2. adopt a strategic approach to improving organizational performance and development.
3. think responsively but responsibly about client requests.
4. develop an understanding of an organization and its business.
5. design, develop, and implement organizational transformation tools and techniques.
6. develop a systems approach to organizational change and development.
7. develop performance management systems.
8. develop strategic business partnerships.
9. link HRD interventions and initiatives to an organization's strategic business goals and objectives.
10. adopt a customer service approach with internal clients.
11. help managers develop their employees.
12. cultivate management development partnerships.
13. help managers link performance appraisals to performance improvement.
14. help managers develop performance coaching skills.
15. implement organizational development partnerships.
16. make the transition from trainer to organizational development consultant.
17. identify organizational and performance needs.
18. use organizational and performance needs as the foundation of all HRD interventions and initiatives.
19. design and develop performance improvement and change interventions.
20. create a learning acquisition strategy.
21. eliminate barriers to learning transfer.
22. implement learning transfer strategies.
23. measure the impact of HRD intervention.
24. improve the image and credibility of HRD within organizations.
25. develop a promotional strategy for an organization's HRD program.

CONCLUSION

Training for training's sake has failed to improve the effectiveness, efficiency, and competitiveness of most of today's organizations. In addition, the nature of the worldwide business environment has forced organizations to look for new solutions to old problems. As a result, the centralized and slow-moving HRD program is being replaced by a streamlined, efficient, fast-moving, and effective HRD function designed to improve organizational performance and effectiveness—one that is strategically integrated into the fabric of the organization.

HRD professionals have a choice: they either help their organizations develop new and innovative ways of improving organizational performance or maintain training for training's sake. They can either become strategic partners within an organization or maintain the centralized HRD department as a separate entity. Regardless, HRD professionals must choose a path.

If HRD professionals choose to champion a strategically integrated HRD approach, they must begin by examining their assumptions and beliefs regarding HRD, adopt techniques to improve organizational effectiveness, develop performance partnerships, reengineer their HRD practice, and apply tools and techniques to improve HRD and the organization.

PART I

Developing a New Philosophy of HRD

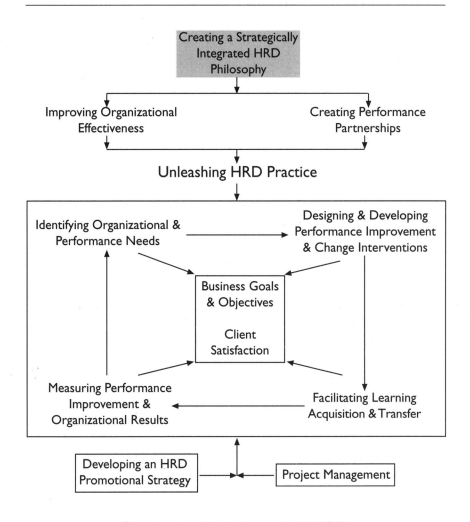

Creating a Strategically Integrated HRD Philosophy

Improving Organizational Effectiveness

Creating Performance Partnerships

Unleashing HRD Practice

Identifying Organizational & Performance Needs

Designing & Developing Performance Improvement & Change Interventions

Business Goals & Objectives

Client Satisfaction

Measuring Performance Improvement & Organizational Results

Facilitating Learning Acquisition & Transfer

Developing an HRD Promotional Strategy

Project Management

Strategically Integrated HRD

CHAPTER 2

Creating a Strategically Integrated
HRD Philosophy

The journey of creating a strategically integrated HRD function cannot begin until we understand *why* HRD professionals behave the way they do. The answer may be found in the assumptions and beliefs that HRD professionals have about HRD. In other words, what is their philosophy of HRD, and how does it affect their behavior and action?

Many HRD programs are perceived to be "outside" the mainstream of the organization, because they are viewed as merely *internal training houses* for employees. Because of this, training is not considered critical to the success of the organization nor are the HRD professionals taken seriously. Moreover, little attention is given to the outcomes of training or the impact it has on employee performance. Another perceptual problem is that HRD professionals are not viewed as credible because "they don't live in the real world, facing the problems other organizational members face." Because of these perceptions, HRD programs are often treated with a lack of respect. Such perceptions cause senior management to seriously question the value of HRD. As a result, HRD programs are the first to be eliminated during periods of financial difficulty. Thus, the image and credibility of HRD remain weak.

The future of many organizations depends on developing a human resource strategy that enables them to remain competitive in a global economy. Therefore, organizations are in search of new ways of developing human resources. In order to accomplish this, organizations must be willing to adopt an innovative approach to HRD practice; one approach that will allow HRD to be "within" the mainstream of the organization, enabling HRD professionals to enhance organizational performance and effectiveness. In other words, HRD programs must become strategically integrated into the organization.

In the summer of 1988, Patricia McLagan, coauthor of ASTD's *Model for Excellence* (McLagan & Bedrick, 1983) and *New Models for HRD Practice* (McLagan & Suhadolnik, 1989), revealed to one of the authors (Gilley) that an HRD program should not be a separate isolated department with an attached budget, but rather should be a function within the organization. What does this statement mean, he thought? Several years later while working on the original evolution of HRD model with Amy Coffern, he began to understand what she was trying to say: HRD programs must be integrated into every aspect of organizational life in order to be effective. HRD programs must be the responsibility of every manager, supervisor, executive, and employee. In other words, an HRD program cannot be a department, it must be a philosophy of operation that is the cornerstone of organizational transformation and development. One way of understanding this phenomenon is by examining the evolution of HRD, which demonstrates how an HRD program transforms from a centralized department to a strategic function within the organization.

THE EVOLUTION OF HRD

According to Gilley and Coffern (1994), HRD programs evolve through six separate phases (see Figure 2.1), each with its own distinctive characteristics, purposes, and approaches. As HRD programs evolve, their focus changes. In addition, management becomes more aware of its role in improving employee performance. As a result, HRD becomes less a separate department and more an integrated function within the organization. The phases of evolution are:

1. no HRD
2. one-person HRD
3. vendor-driven HRD (VD-HRD)
4. vendor-customized HRD (VC-HRD)
5. decentralized performance improvement HRD (DPI-HRD)
6. strategically integrated HRD (SI-HRD)

One clue used in determining the current phase of HRD is the types of intervention being offered. According to Silber (1992),

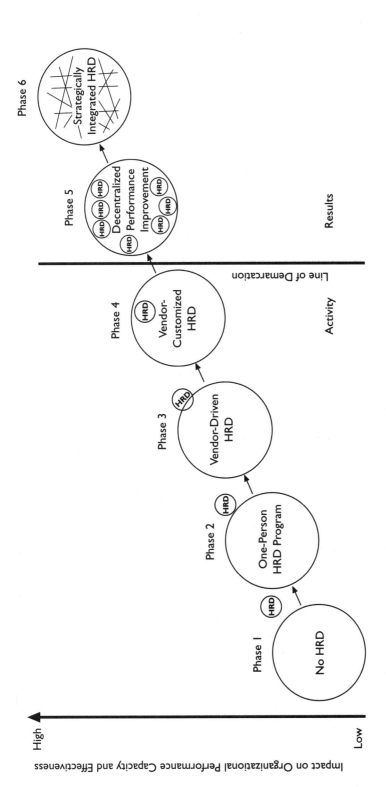

Figure 2.1 Creating a Strategically Integrated HRD Function. Adapted with permission from J. W. Gilley and A. J. Coffern, *Internal Consulting for HRD Professionals*, McGraw-Hill, 1994.

there are five types of intervention that HRD professionals can use. These include isolated training, isolated performance, total training, total performance, and total cultural. Each *can* add value to the organization; however, their impact is drastically different. As each phase of HRD is being examined, we will identify the most common location of each intervention.

Other clues in determining the current phase are:

- the type of organizational effectiveness strategy employed by HRD professionals
- the type of performance partnerships developed
- the way the HRD program is organized
- the application and sophistication of HRD practice within the organization

Each of these clues will be examined more closely as we discuss the evolution of HRD.

Phase 1: No HRD

In many organizations there is no HRD program or activities. Thus, little or no formal training is provided to employees. The reason is that HRD is not valued by management. If training does occur, it is accidental. During this evolutionary period, HRD is not viewed as a way of improving organizational performance or effectiveness. Consequently, there is no organizational effectiveness strategy, performance partnerships, or HRD practice to examine. Employees and managers are on their own to improve organizational performance and quality. Many small businesses and most retail operations (i.e., franchise stores and automotive dealerships) maintain this approach to HRD.

Phase 2: One-Person HRD

When organizations realize that training might help them improve their effectiveness and increase their competitiveness, the HRD program evolves to the next phase. This period is known as One-Person HRD. When an HRD program begins to emerge, it becomes externally attached to the organization in order to sustain itself (see Figure 2.1). At this point, the HRD program is totally dependent on the organization in order to survive (i.e., money, human resources, recognition, and approval).

During this period, HRD professionals are "jacks-of-all-trades." In other words, a single person is responsible for identifying and analyzing employees' needs; designing, developing, and implementing training programs; and evaluating their success (philosophy of HRD). Because each of these tasks is very complex, it is impossible for a single person to do them all well. Therefore, the effectiveness of HRD often suffers. One-Person HRD programs are very common in small- to medium-sized organizations.

To further complicate things, many of the individuals responsible for HRD are not well trained, nor do they understand the true purpose of HRD. Many are former line managers, salespersons, customer service representatives, or office managers who have demonstrated they can work well with people. Such experience will help them understand the day-to-day operations of the organization, but it is inadequate preparation for improving organizational performance and effectiveness through learning transfer. Such a practice may harm the credibility of HRD, prevent its acceptance within the organization, or prevent HRD's evolution to the next phase.

Isolated Training

Isolated training is the simplest form of intervention. It is used to fix an isolated performance problem such as time management, planning skills, scheduling skills, or writing skills. Isolated training is very common among activity-driven HRD programs such as One-Person (Silber, 1992).

Strategy, Partnerships, HRD Practice, and Structure

During this phase of evolution, neither an organizational effectiveness strategy nor performance partnerships are present. HRD practitioners are not concerned about them because they are so busy trying to provide training that they have little time for any other activities. Consequently, HRD practice is activity based. Training is based on the experience of the HRD practitioner and is delivered in an informal manner during sales meetings or on the job.

Sometimes formal training sessions are conducted and are informational in nature, even though they are not designed to change performance, improve quality, or enhance organizational competitiveness. Patrick A. Combs, general manager of Warner Communications in Lincoln, Nebraska, said this phase of HRD is at best "a starting point for organizational improvement but fails to capture the energies of the organization or help develop people or the organization."

The HRD program is often housed as a part of a small human resource department generally staffed by a part-time HR specialist. The structure, while recognized, is not seriously or formally considered a part of the strategic focus of the organization. A part-time trainer is usually assigned to fulfill all the duties and responsibilities of the program while balancing other assignments.

Phase 3: Vendor-Driven HRD (VD-HRD)

As the HRD program grows stronger, it begins to penetrate the organization. Over time it develops a firm grip on the organization but is still perceived as outside the mainstream. The HRD program is, however, still very weak and cannot sustain itself without organizational support. Management can easily eliminate the HRD program by cutting its budget, and often does. If the HRD program survives this period, it often completely penetrates the organization and becomes a full-fledged department within the organization.

At this point, the HRD program has evolved to the vendor-driven HRD level. It has a healthy budget and its practitioners are busy selecting and delivering training programs. Through its activity, the HRD program often provides isolated value to the organization, thus enabling HRD to become more important. Consequently, the HRD program picks up important sponsors and advocates that help improve its image within the organization. But this is a very, very critical time for the HRD program. Its budgets can still be eliminated because it has yet to become an essential tool used to improve organization performance and effectiveness. Unfortunately, the HRD program is still not viewed by management as a business partner.

Many HRD professionals believe their job is to provide employees a comprehensive and complete list of training courses. Little attention is paid to *why* employees participate in training as long as they attend some training class each year. In addition, training is sometimes viewed as a reward for a job well done. Such an approach is referred to as the "activity strategy" of HRD. During this evolutionary phase—"training for training's sake"—is an HRD practitioner's philosophy.

One of management's favorite forms of HRD is vendor-driven HRD due to its ease of administration and management. Tremendous training activity is characteristic of vendor-driven HRD, although organizational performance seldom improves. During this period, the primary responsibility of HRD practitioners is to identify, evaluate, and select training programs from a myriad of outside "training houses." Gilley and Coffern (1994) refer to HRD practitioners who operate in such a manner as "brokers of training programs." Wendy Male, professional development specialist at William M. Mercer Inc., believes that this is the primary responsibility of HRD practitioners because they are accountable for selecting training programs that help improve employees' skills, knowledge, and attitudes. She adds "anyway, training programs provided by vendors are often better than the ones designed internally, and since our (HRD practitioners) job is to provide as much training as possible it appears to be the most efficient way of achieving this goal." This clearinghouse approach is primarily what is wrong with the HRD profession because it allows *training activity* to become the focus of HRD, which produces long-term damage to the image and credibility of HRD.

Vendor-driven HRD programs do force HRD practitioners to ask more sophisticated and critical questions, such as, "What skills or knowledge are preventing optimal performance?" However, HRD practitioners have not yet addressed the most important question, which is, "How can HRD help the organization accomplish its strategic business goals and objectives?" Vendor-driven HRD is, however, a move along the continuum, and in the right direction.

Isolated Performance

Common during this evolutionary phase of HRD is a more sophisticated type of intervention known as isolated performance, which requires minor environmental redesign, incentive/motivation system changes, and job aids to fix isolated performance problems. The effects of most isolated performance interventions are short lived because the "system" has not really changed enough for real performance improvement to occur. Examples of isolated performance interventions include training in supervisory skills, time management, meeting management, and interpersonal skills. These are most common during the vendor-driven HRD phase.

Strategy, Partnerships, HRD Practice, and Structure

During this phase, an HRD professional's organizational effectiveness strategy is isolated to improve individual employee performance. Little attention is given to how training enhances organizational performance, competitiveness, or efficiency. In other words, vendor-driven HRD is focused on improving employees' skills and knowledge in hopes that such development can and will help maximize organizational effectiveness and performance.

During this phase, HRD practitioners are beginning to develop performance partnerships. These occur because HRD practitioners are providing as much training to as many departments and divisions as possible. As a result, HRD practitioners are becoming more customer oriented. Natural outcomes of this approach include better customer relationships and improved organizational awareness of HRD, its interventions, and services. It is important to understand that developing formal performance partnerships is not an HRD practitioner's primary objective but a natural by-product of increasing training activity.

HRD practice becomes more formalized during this phase. HRD practitioners are conducting more needs assessment activities designed to uncover skills and knowledge deficits as well as identifying areas of training interest. Needs assessment activities are still not seen as a way of developing performance partnerships or as a way of providing direction for the HRD program. They are seen merely as ways of identifying the next series of training activities that organizational leaders perceive to be of value.

Providing formal training activities is the only objective of vendor-driven HRD programs. Naturally, this becomes the principal focus of HRD practice. In order to "keep up" with ever-increasing training demand, organizations begin to hire more and more trainers whose primary job responsibility is to provide training. Little if any effort is made in ensuring that training is being transferred to the job by employees. In fact, managers and executives often refer to training as "something that those trainers do" and do not see employee development as their responsibility. This attitude becomes the Achilles heel of vendor-driven HRD programs. Finally, identifying employees' reactions to training is the only type of formal evaluation being conducted during this phase.

During the VD-HRD phase, the HRD program begins to separate itself from the HR department and to establish its own structure. Sometimes the HRD program remains in the HR department but is a separate operating unit with a coordinator (broker of training) and a few full- and part-time trainers assigned. As we said previously, the program is only loosely attached to the organization (Figure 2.1) and can be eliminated at any time. But it is emerging and beginning to be recognized as a potential source for improving employees' knowledge and skills.

Phase 4: Vendor-Customized HRD (VC-HRD)

The next evolutionary phase of HRD is similar to the vendor-driven phase. The principal difference is that HRD practitioners are customizing training programs to align with the organization's environment and culture (Gilley & Coffern, 1994). As a result, formal instructional design activities emerge during this phase. Consequently, HRD practitioners become responsible for redesigning and redeveloping training programs to fit the organization.

Again, HRD practitioners are asking more sophisticated questions in their effort to address the critical issues facing the organization, the most essential of which is, "How can training become more organizationally focused?" The answer to this question motivates HRD practitioners to customize vendors' programs so that they compliment and match their organizational culture. Gloria Regalbato, Director of HRD for Bath and Bodyworks Inc., said, "HRD programs which are in the vendor-customized HRD phase are beginning to examine the critical issues facing the organization. Once determined, HRD practitioners can begin customizing training programs in order for them to become organizationally focused."

The philosophy of HRD is the same during the vendor-customized phase as it was in the previous phase, except that the "training house" approach is brought inside the organization. This slight philosophical shift allows the instructional design role of HRD to become paramount. HRD practitioners begin spending a majority of their time as instructional designers rather than taking the opportunity to help executives change the organization or improve its performance.

During this phase of evolution the HRD program has developed to full departmental status within the organization. The HRD program has a comprehensive and complete budget, a mission statement describing its purpose, a manager responsible for overseeing its internal affairs and providing direction within the organization, a complete staff including trainers and institutional designers, and a formal reporting relationship and position on the organizational chart. In other words, the HRD program has finally "arrived" and is considered a viable and productive department within the organization.

Total Training

This intervention requires HRD professionals to take a broader view of performance problems. Rather than looking at a single skill to be changed, the performance problem is addressed holistically. Consequently, employees may attend training programs that address a *set* of skills that contribute to their performance. Employee "isolated training" programs address sets of skills including time management, planning, scheduling, and writing. Total training blends each of these skill areas into a single performance activity.

For example, managing projects requires employees to develop time management, planning, scheduling, and writing skills. Therefore, employees receive total training in project management instead of attending four separate training programs that on the surface may appear to be unrelated. However, "total training is limited in the solution set it considers: it is still only using training as a vehicle for change" (Silber, 1992).

Total training is very common during the early part of the vendor-customized HRD phase because HRD professionals recognize "potential" to improve the organization; however, they often fail to focus on transfer of learning, and managers often fail to properly conduct performance appraisals and provide feedback (see performance coaching, Chapter 6). Learning, then, is rarely applied to the job. Consequently, the total training approach seldom improves organizational performance. The primary limitation to this approach is the heavy reliance on "training activity" as the solution to complex performance problems. Employees will return from training and most likely fail in integrating what they have learned on the job because the organizational system has not been altered to support the new learning.

Strategy, Partnerships, HRD Practice, and Structure

As HRD practitioners begin providing more and more total training activities their organizational effectiveness strategy begins to mature. The strategy becomes more performance focused and begins to incorporate organizational issues such as the organization's culture, work climate, structure, mission and strategy, leadership, policies and procedures, and management practices (see Chapter 3). The process of customizing training programs also focuses HRD practitioners on these issues. Consequently, HRD practitioners begin developing an awareness of both the organizational system and the performance management system approaches that increase performance improvement and organizational development. Such knowledge will be very important if the program is to evolve to the more advanced phases of HRD.

Because HRD practitioners are required to customize training programs to fit the organization, they must further develop relationships with their internal clients. Such relationships are more formalized than in the previous phase because clients are expected to help HRD practitioners customize training programs.

It could be said that the most important part of the vendor-customized HRD phase is that HRD practitioners are being forced outside of their isolated departments and required to work directly with the people they are trying to serve. Because of this opportunity, HRD practitioners begin developing an understanding of the organization and its business. Over time, such interaction will help HRD practitioners understand that their real purpose is to help the organization achieve its business goals and objectives through management and organizational development partnerships.

One of the biggest changes in HRD practice occurs during this evolutionary phase as practitioners become instructional designers responsible for customizing training programs. Organizations such as Arthur Anderson & Co., Motorola, Waste Management, and AT&T employ entire departments of instructional designers. Such a shift is critical to the future evolution of HRD because designing performance improvements and change interventions will be essential to maximizing organizational performance and will continue to be a useful service during the next two evolutionary phases.

Training activity remains the central focus of vendor-customized HRD programs. Therefore, training conducted by full-time trainers continues to be viewed as an important activity. During this phase, managers and supervisors are rarely used to provide training. The HRD manager's role emerges as critical here because increasing training activity is of paramount importance. Thus, an HRD manager is needed to increase the HRD budget, which becomes one of the most important battles fought during the vendor-customized HRD phase, and the HRD manager's primary responsibility.

Another major evolutionary change is in the way HRD programs are structured. During the VC-HRD phase, HRD programs are separate operating departments with a complete staff and budget. Departmental status includes an HRD manager, trainers, instructional designers, and one or two quasi-internal consultants— generally senior trainers responsible for client relationships or needs analysis activities. Typically, HRD departments are centralized in the organization's head office or headquarters as a way of improving "training coordination and design and development activities" (Gilley & Coffern, 1994). In many organizations, VC-HRD programs are separate from the HR departments but generally report to the same person within the organization (i.e., vice president or director of human resources).

Line of Demarcation: Moving from Activity
to Results-Driven HRD

HRD programs that are below the vendor-customized level focus primarily on activity (see Figure 2.1). Their HRD practitioners operate as though training by itself could improve organizational performance and effectiveness. Little thought is given to training impact or achievement of the organization's strategic business goals.

Moving from vendor-customized HRD toward strategically integrated HRD is the most difficult part of the evolution process. In order to evolve to the highest level, HRD professionals must begin to think strategically about how HRD interventions can and will positively impact the organization. They must determine which interventions add value to the organization and which do not, always striving to improve organizational performance in everything they do. HRD professionals must understand that organizational decision-makers are not interested in "training" but in what training can do for them. Such an understanding should force HRD professionals to change their practice. They should be cautious. It is easy to generate a lot of training activity and claim that it makes a difference; it is much harder to identify the organizational results needed and to determine whether they have been accomplished. When HRD professionals begin providing interventions that help the organization accomplish its strategic business goals, then HRD has crossed over from the activity zone into the results-driven zone.

The new HRD philosophy must be "learning and change for organizational results and impact." Such a strategy communicates the intention of an HRD program and what it is really trying to accomplish. In other words, HRD is about achieving organizational results rather than training. A total shift in emphasis is required in order to accomplish this strategy. As a result, HRD interventions must produce specific outcomes upon which the organization can rely in order to achieve its strategic business goals.

As a way of developing a results-driven strategy for their HRD programs, HRD professionals should answer several questions that will help them eliminate training for training's sake. The questions are as follows:

- Why is training needed?
- Where is training headed?
- What good will it do?
- How will we know whether it worked?
- Who should receive the training intervention?
- What kind of training interventions fit the business strategy?
- How will the impact of training be evaluated?
- When should the training be delivered?
- Who should be involved in delivering the training?

Phase 5: Decentralized Performance Improvement HRD

As HRD professionals customize their training programs, they begin directing their attention toward a very critical question, one that changes the entire focus of HRD. This question, when asked and answered, demonstrates that the HRD program has moved into the next evolutionary phase of HRD. It is an important question because it forces HRD professionals to consider the issue of employee performance improvement and its impact on the organization. It is a question that helps HRD professionals move from an activity to a results-driven HRD approach. The question is: "How can HRD maximize organizational performance and improve the effectiveness of the organization?" In other words, how HRD can make a difference in the organization becomes an HRD professional's overriding passion, the philosophy of HRD, during this phase.

In order to evolve into the decentralized performance improvement phase, HRD professionals will have to make a very important strategic decision. To move forward, HRD professionals must have the courage to make some fundamental changes, to question their organizational mission and its impact on the organization, and to abandon all they have achieved up to this point. They must be willing to decentralize their department and focus on helping operational divisions improve their performance, thus allowing HRD to become strategically placed throughout the organization rather than centrally located. Then several smaller operationally focused HRD units will be in place.

Decentralized performance improvement HRD requires a much different HRD effort. Gone are the days of delivering training as an activity. Gone are the days of relying on employees' reactions to training in order to validate the value and importance of HRD to the organization. Gone are the days of unprofessional HRD practitioners. In their place is an HRD program with qualified professionals focused on improving organizational performance and effectiveness through learning and change.

During this period performance measurement becomes a strategic weapon used to help determine whether or not HRD interventions improve employee performance and have a positive impact on organizational effectiveness. Interventions that produce the desired results are continued while others are not. HRD professionals are also building collaborative relationships with management to help improve learning transfer and on-the-job performance. Such relationships make it easier for management to share critical information about the organization, including changes in management, new product developments, changes in the compensation and incentive system, and strategic decisions affecting the direction of the organization. This type of information exchange is essential for improving organizational performance and effectiveness.

Total Performance

When HRD professionals use total performance interventions, all aspects of a performance problem are examined before arriving at a solution. Issues under consideration include the compensation and rewards system, managers' and supervisors' skills and techniques, barriers to performance improvement, transfer of learning issues, environment/work design, feedback systems, organizational structure and design, and job processes. These types of factors are examined to help determine the exact cause of the performance breakdown. A systematic approach enables the design and implementation of a more comprehensive and complete performance intervention.

When total performance interventions are used, HRD professionals are examining the cost effectiveness and return on investment for the solutions implemented. In other words, the evaluation process is no longer simply an employee's reaction to training but is used in determining if HRD is adding value to the organization, and if so, where and how much.

Total performance interventions, by their very nature, are results-driven, and are most commonly found during the last two phases of HRD. In fact, this type of intervention is what separates activity HRD programs from results-driven ones.

Burning the Mothership: An Operational Reality

Much like Cortez, the Spanish explorer, HRD professionals must burn the mothership and venture into uncharted lands in search of better ways of helping their organizations improve their effectiveness and performance capacity. HRD professionals must be willing to embrace rapid change by becoming part of their organizations' operational units, rather than retreating to the safety of their own centralized department (the mothership). Finally, decentralized performance improvement HRD can *NOT* survive alongside the old centralized HRD department because theirs is a philosophy of "training for training's sake," while DPI-HRD's philosophy is one of helping to improve organizational performance.

When decentralized and centralized HRD programs coexist, a situation is produced where two completely incompatible philosophies are in a constant struggle for control. This creates a psychotic atmosphere within the organization resulting in confusion and frustration on the part of decision-makers. Consequently, HRD professionals must choose. Either return to the mothership and sail back across the line of demarcation to produce training activity, or go forward and help the organization achieve its strategic business goals by applying an organizational effectiveness strategy, creating and implementing performance partnerships, and unleashing HRD practice.

During the early stages of this phase it may be necessary to maintain a small group of HRD professionals who are responsible for instructional design and coordinating organization-wide projects. Traditional training activities may even continue as HRD professionals make the transition from trainers to organizational development consultants, and as managers begin to shoulder more and more training responsibility. As HRD professionals make the successful transition into other operational units, the centralized HRD department begins to disappear as it is reduced to a support unit responsible for intervention design and development.

What really enables HRD programs to become performance improvement oriented is their willingness to leave the mothership and venture into uncharted lands. This requires HRD professionals to be permanently assigned to business units and to become responsible for improving their productivity and performance. In other words, they become members of an operational group rather than part of a centralized HRD department. Such a departure is often quite difficult for HRD professionals because they must become "accountable" for results, no longer able to hide behind an avalanche of training activity.

The movement from a centralized department to a decentralized unit requires a shift in thinking on the part of HRD professionals. They must begin thinking like their clients instead of like HRD practitioners. As business persons, HRD professionals must understand the revenue and cost implications of their recommendations, and filter their suggestions through the prism of practical reality and operational priorities. They must think strategically about the long-term implications of change prior to implementing interventions. In short, HRD professionals must become strategic business partners (see Chapter 5). For some the transition is easy because they have always operated from this perspective or were part of an operational group prior to joining HRD. For others the journey is a road less traveled, full of uncertainty and insecurity. As always,

HRD professionals must establish credibility by demonstrating their professional competence, integrity, and sincerity.

Organizational Effectiveness Strategy

During this phase, HRD professionals' organizational effectiveness strategy is to maximize organizational performance through performance management systems (see Chapter 3), rather than improving individual employee skills and knowledge. While this approach only embraces half of the organizational effectiveness framework, development of the entire organization occurs during phase six (strategically integrated HRD). Better business results and organizational performance are achieved under DPI-HRD than within the activity strategy based VC-HRD and VD-HRD programs. Consequently, improving organizational performance capacity through such systems is the adopted strategy.

Performance Partnerships

While performance partnerships were emerging during the last phase, they now become formal alliances. Decentralized HRD programs require working relationships with business units. In fact, the decentralized performance improvement HRD approach cannot succeed unless performance partnerships are formed and are functioning effectively.

Each of the three types of partnerships discussed in Chapter 1 (strategic business, management development, and organizational development partnerships) are needed during this evolutionary phase. Strategic business and management development partnerships are the most important during this phase because they help HRD professionals develop the relationships needed to improve organizational performance. Organizational development partnerships are primarily developed during phase six, but they can be developed during this phase.

HRD Practice

During this phase, HRD practice makes a serious shift that allows for the birth of the performance consulting role (see Chapter 3). HRD professionals are beginning to relinquish their training responsibility to managers and supervisors who are ultimately responsible for improving employee performance and organizational productivity (Gilley, 1998). By doing so, organizations are allowing the only organizational players accountable for performance appraisal and employee development to become the champions of HRD, rather than its gatekeepers.

As performance consultants, HRD professionals are responsible for implementing performance management systems designed to maximize organizational performance (see Chapter 3). This includes improving work design, learning, and compensation and reward systems. In addition, HRD professionals are responsible for helping managers make the transition to performance coaching and for implementing performance appraisals that bring about lasting change.

HRD interventions also begin to change during this phase. Instead of simply designing performance improvement programs as a way of improving employees' skills and knowledge, HRD professionals are beginning to develop interventions focused on improving the performance capacity and effectiveness of organizations. While these interventions are more common during phase six, they are becoming more familiar during the decentralized performance improvement phase.

Structure

During this phase the walls of the HRD program are beginning to come down. HRD professionals are realizing that to be effective they must be integrated into the organization. As a result, decentralized performance improvement HRD programs are often assigned to operational units within the organization (Figure 2.2). HRD professionals are now held accountable for improving the results of the operational units rather than generating organization-wide activity.

Professional identity during the DPI-HRD phase begins to change. HRD professionals are no longer "trainer types" but are full-fledged strategic business partners responsible for performance management within an operational unit. Reporting relationships will also change since HRD professionals are not members of centralized HRD departments. Consequently, HRD professionals should report to the vice president or director of their unit. Finally, HRD professionals should work cooperatively across operational units in order to maximize organizational performance. But the hierarchy that existed during previous phases has been replaced by a collaborative team approach. Such an approach is project based and requires the creation of shared partnerships among HRD professionals (see Chapter 13).

Phase 6: Strategically Integrated HRD (SI-HRD)

When HRD programs begin to be *blended into the fabric of the organization* they are becoming strategically integrated (Figure 2.1). HRD

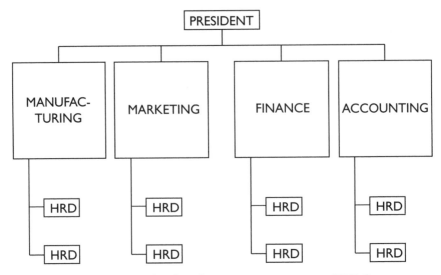

Figure 2.2 Decentralized Performance Improvement HRD Structure

is no longer an individual department but a function within the organization containing several crossover points (see Figure 3.2). HRD professionals must now work collaboratively with management at all levels to improve organizational performance. When this begins to happen, the final phase of the evolution of HRD has begun.

The centralized HRD budget shifts to the operational unit where the HRD program is now housed. This helps the organization and HRD in two ways. First, decentralized HRD programs can demonstrate how they help their units accomplish business objectives, as they no longer hide among a myriad of activities that are commonly found in centralized HRD departments. Thus, HRD professionals are forced to become strategic business partners within their units, and, therefore, produce results.

Second, organizations are compelled to view HRD as an investment rather than as a cost. For example, operational budgets are established to produce results that managers are held accountable for achieving. Staff budgets—those used to support nonrevenue-producing units such as public relations, human resources, and HRD—are established to provide services for the organization. Managers of these departments are held accountable for producing service activity, not producing organizational results. Therefore, the funds made available to a centralized HRD department by definition cannot produce organizational results. Thus, HRD is viewed as a cost to the organization (to provide activity) rather than as an investment (to produce results). By decentralizing HRD and shifting its budget to the operational level, HRD programs become accountable for producing results and will be viewed in the same way as their operational unit.

It is no longer enough for HRD programs to improve performance, they must also improve the overall effectiveness of their organization. In other words, HRD must help the organization achieve its strategic business goals. HRD professionals, therefore, must create interventions that help the organization change. This shift requires HRD professionals to change their philosophy to one of dedication to improving organizational effectiveness, rather than remaining the deliverers of training events. In short, they must become results-driven.

Total Cultural

Total cultural interventions incorporate an examination of problems and solutions in a context that addresses the organization's values and corporate culture (Silber, 1992). During this intervention, HRD professionals use techniques that help them determine the influence of organizational policies, procedures, and culture that can impede performance and prevent the implementation of organizational change. This type of intervention can have the most positive impact on organizational performance and effectiveness.

Only HRD programs that have created an HRD/business partnership can successfully implement total cultural interventions, and this type of partnership is only found during the last evolutionary phase.

Overcoming the Fear of Letting Go

During this phase of evolution, HRD programs seemingly disappear altogether. For some HRD professionals this is an unsettling time, as they believe they have been stripped of their organizational identity and influence. But this is not true; in fact, their influence is at its zenith for two reasons. First, organizational transformation is an everyday reality, and, for the first time in the history of the organization, human resource development is *everyone's* responsibility. Only under these circumstances can organizations maximize their performance or implement lasting change. Second, people support what they create. In other words, when executives, managers, supervisors, and employees accept that human resource development is part of their everyday responsibility, they will support learning and change as a naturally occurring event, rather than resisting it. Gone are the days of trying to convince the organization of the importance and value of HRD interventions. Gone are the days of struggling to implement organizational change and learning transfer. HRD professionals have become facilitators of learning and change by executing an organizational effectiveness strategy, creating performance partnerships, and unleashing HRD practice.

Organizational Effectiveness Strategy

Strategically integrated HRD programs are no longer merely training houses within organizations. They instead help organizations manage change and improve their competitiveness. Several core strategies are commonly used during this phase, including:

Setting Strategic Direction: Helping business units set long-range strategic goals and develop tactical plans in support of those goals (see Chapters 3, 4, 7, and 8).

Leadership Development: Helping clients ensure that current leaders have appropriate performance coaching skills to produce organizational results (see Chapter 6).

Implementing Performance Management Systems: Helping clients improve performance through the use of appropriate development and feedback strategies linked to the compensation and rewards system. This includes identifying competency maps for all job classifications, performance standards, and evaluation methods used to enhance employee and organizational performance (see Chapter 3).

Assessing Organizational Effectiveness: Helping clients determine what their needs are and which services will have the highest organizational impact (see Chapters 3 and 8).

Managing Change: Helping clients develop effective plans for implementing change and understanding the human implications of change (see Chapters 3 and 7).

Another characteristic of this period is the movement from improving employee performance to improving organizational performance and effectiveness. This shift is often subtle, although HRD interventions are now targeted at improving overall performance problems rather than fixing isolated ones. Discussions about installing performance management systems are now commonplace events among HRD professionals and senior management.

Performance Partnerships

Successful evolution to a strategically integrated HRD level requires HRD professionals' complete understanding of the organization, its politics, culture, business, and industry. They must have excellent organizational development skills in order to analyze and evaluate all aspects of the organization. Implementing total cultural interventions also requires a collaborative relationship between HRD professionals and senior management because their support is required in bringing about change. These three competencies will be discussed further in Chapter 5.

The strategically integrated HRD phase requires all three of the performance partnerships previously discussed. During this phase, organizational development partnerships become critical, as HRD professionals are no longer part of a formal HRD department. They work on several projects with various client groups simultaneously (see Chapter 13). Each project is designed to maximize organizational performance, helping to improve the organizational system through change management consulting, the performance management system through performance consulting, or the entire organization through organizational development consulting (see Chapter 7).

A fourth type of partnership is needed in order for strategically integrated HRD programs to be successful. An *HRD partnership,* formed by every HRD professional within the organization, requires HRD professionals to work together as a team on projects. Partnership members must avoid unnecessary political posturing common among professional affiliations, and guard against professional ownership or the gatekeeping of information. Finally, such a partnership should be an attempt to achieve the ultimate goal of strategically integrated HRD: maximizing organizational performance.

Unleashing HRD Practice

HRD professionals do not have to reinvent the wheel to make the transition to strategically integrated HRD. They can rely on the four steps commonly used during the performance improvement process, which is applied every time HRD practitioners design interventions used to improve employees and organizational performance. However, the assumptions, activities, and outcomes of SI-HRD professionals differ from those of VD-HRD practitioners. The performance improvement process consists of:

1. identifying organizational and performance needs
2. designing and developing performance improvement and change interventions
3. facilitating learning acquisition and transfer
4. measuring performance improvement and organizational results

Step 1: Identifying Organizational and Performance Needs

In a strategically integrated HRD program, differing assumptions include the following:

1. The customer is the organization.
2. Performance improvement goals are not the property of the HRD department but are identified in accordance with the business goals and objectives of the organization.
3. The needs assessment process is designed to uncover organizational needs and performance gaps.
4. The needs assessment process is an all-inclusive activity designed to uncover performance problems rather than validate best practices.
5. The needs assessment process requires trust, honesty, and candor.
6. The needs assessment process is an activity designed to improve organizational performance rather than protect the status quo (see Chapter 8).

As a result of these assumptions, the organization and its strategically integrated HRD professionals mutually identify performance needs, rather than simply identify training programs to be delivered. In addition, performance improvement goals are mutually identified and linked to the organization's business goals and objectives. Another major difference between the two approaches is that now *managers* conduct a majority of the needs assessments.

The outcomes are also quite different. Now HRD professionals conduct assessments resulting in the isolation of organizational, managerial, and performance gaps. Once identified, performance improvement and change interventions can be designed that will help improve organizational performance as well as help the organization accomplish its strategic business goals. Since managers participate during this phase, they are more likely to support as well as reinforce future learning efforts.

According to Brinkerhoff and Gill (1994), identifying performance needs helps HRD professionals answer the following questions:

- Is there a performance problem?
- Should performance improvement and change interventions be provided?
- Why should we provide performance improvement and change interventions?

- What performance needs are most important to the organization?
- What value should performance improvement and change interventions provide?

Step 2: Designing and Developing Performance Improvement and Change Interventions

First, SI-HRD professionals assume that performance improvement is based on the business processes that the organization is trying to improve. Second, SI-HRD professionals assume that the design and development of performance improvement and change interventions are a joint effort between management and HRD professionals, and that they are jointly accountable to the organization for its success. Third, SI-HRD professionals assume that performance improvement design is based on the activities required to enhance employee performance rather than on best training practices. Fourth, SI-HRD professionals assume that performance improvement barriers must be identified before the design process begins, in order to ensure that strategies are developed to overcome them. Fifth, SI-HRD professionals assume that performance measures must be identified to ensure learning transfer.

Based on these assumptions, the design and development process is used to create performance improvement and change interventions that "fit" the organization and help it accomplish its strategic business goals. Any performance improvement intervention must fit within the already established performance management system used by the organization. This guarantees that the intervention fits within their overall performance improvement strategy (see Chapter 9).

Many of these activities may seem like mere details or logistics, but they can have a tremendous impact on the quality of the outcomes achieved (Hodges, 1995). The design and development process helps HRD professionals answer the following questions:

- Who should receive performance improvement and change interventions?
- How should learning be facilitated and managed?
- When should performance improvement and change interventions be delivered?
- Who should be involved in the planning and designing of performance improvement and change interventions?
- How should senior management be involved?

- Who should deliver performance improvement and change interventions?
- How will managers and supervisors be prepared to reinforce and support learning on the job?
- How will performance improvement and change interventions be monitored?

Step 3: Facilitating Learning Acquisition and Transfer

SI-HRD professionals assume that facilitating learning acquisition and transfer should be based on the performance objectives of the organization. Performance improvement and change interventions must be performance-focused, allowing time for practice and application, as well as enough content to foster performance improvement. HRD professionals also assume it is important to link performance improvement and change interventions to the strategic business goals of the organization. In order to foster the application and integration of learning on the job, SI-HRD professionals assume that specific job related and organization-specific examples and exercises are critical. Finally, SI-HRD professionals assume that training is not their responsibility, but rather the responsibility of the managers and supervisors accountable for employee performance (see Chapter 10).

In organizations that maintain an SI-HRD approach, performance improvement and change interventions are provided on or close to the job. Managers are used to deliver instruction, utilizing work-related problems to increase application and integration. Performance-based feedback is provided during the program and job performance aids are incorporated to help foster learning transfer. Additionally, support groups are established and action planning is used to help employees integrate and transfer learning.

The principal outcome of SI-HRD's performance improvement and change interventions is that employee performance improves. In addition, employees have job performance aids, support groups, and practical applications needed to apply and integrate learning on the job.

This step in the performance improvement and change process helps HRD professionals determine such things as:

- who is learning and who is not
- what they are learning
- who needs help in learning
- how they should be helped

- is the learning method appropriate
- what else employees have to learn (Hodges, 1995)

The differences between a VD-HRD and SI-HRD approach are most noticeable during this part of the performance improvement and change process. VD-HRD assumes that learning transfer is the responsibility of the employee. Consequently, VD-HRD practitioners do not track the progress or impact of learning on the job, nor do they provide activities that ensure learning is transferred.

SI-HRD professionals assume that learning transfer and reinforcement is everyone's responsibility, including employees, managers, HRD professionals, and senior management. They assume that frequent measurement of progress and impact is essential. They also assume that learning transfer and reinforcement is best managed through an organization's performance management system (see Chapters 3 and 10). SI-HRD professionals assume that employees should participate in transfer related decisions, and that they should have expectations for improvement. Finally, SI-HRD professionals assume that employees will use job performance aids as a way of improving learning transfer.

In Chapter 10, several learning transfer strategies are examined. Briefly, these include the following:

- Managers use positive reinforcement to encourage application.
- Employees are encouraged to form support groups.
- Follow-up activities are used to encourage application.
- Daily logs and journals are used to track progress and application.
- Failure is perceived as a learning activity.
- Barriers to learning transfer are eliminated.
- Performance improvement is recognized and rewarded.
- Managers use the performance management system to improve learning transfer.
- Managers confront poor performance.
- HRD professionals and managers conduct performance evaluations to determine performance impact and improvement (Gilley, 1998).

The SI-HRD approach to learning transfer allows for three outcomes. First, learning is applied to the workplace and employee performance improves. Second, organizational performance and effectiveness is improved. Third, HRD adds value to the organization.

When HRD professionals focus their attention toward transferring and reinforcing learning on the job, they answer these
questions:

- How are skills, knowledge, and attitudes being used on the
  job?
- What prevents learning from being transferred?
- What role do managers and supervisors play in transferring
  and reinforcing learning on the job?
- What should be done before, during, and after a performance
  improvement intervention to enhance learning transfer?
- What role do employees play in learning transfer?
- What role does the organization play in learning transfer?
- What activities should be used to improve learning transfer?
- What can be done to increase learning effectiveness and
  efficiency?

Step 4: Measuring Performance Improvement and Organizational Results

Many HRD practitioners assume that the trainee's reaction to a
training program is the only important consideration. Therefore,
reaction evaluation is only provided immediately after training.
The outcome of this effort is a collection of employees' reactions,
often including information on the value of the content, an analysis of the skills and abilities of the instructor, the quality of the facilities, and an overall rating of the training program. Such information is helpful in improving the quality of the "training event"
and its delivery, but does not help improve employee or organizational performance.

SI-HRD professionals assume that evaluating the impact of performance improvement and change interventions means just that.
They assume every intervention should be measured to determine
if performance improved or change occurred, and to what extent
did it help the organization accomplish its strategic business goals.
They assume that this type of evaluation is the responsibility of
every manager in the organization and is most often performed
during performance evaluation activities (see Chapter 11).

The principal outcomes of evaluation include the value added
by HRD to the organization, the impact of performance improvement on the organization, organizational results realized as a result
of performance improvement, and changes in employee behavior.
Each of these outcomes provides SI-HRD professionals with a

tremendous amount of information regarding the importance and value of HRD to the organization.

Evaluating the impact of performance improvement and change, then, helps answer the following strategic and diagnostic questions:

Strategic Questions

- What difference does HRD make?
- What value is added to the organization as a result of the HRD intervention?
- What impact does HRD have on the effectiveness of the organization?

Diagnostic Questions

- How can HRD be improved?
- How are new skills, knowledge, and attitude being used in the workplace?
- What performance activities and business processes changed as a result of the performance improvement process?

Structure: Creating an Internal Consulting Coalition

Because SI-HRD programs blend into the fabric of the organization, some believe there is no structural framework. Consequently, they assert that HRD does not really exist anymore since a "departmental" structure cannot be found. To the contrary, SI-HRD programs are organized much like management consulting and professional service firms, which become an integral part of an organization during major restructuring or reengineering projects. During these projects, senior management consultants reside within an organization, working alongside executives and managers, analyzing organizational and performance needs, providing recommendations, selecting and implementing change interventions, and evaluating the impact of change (Figure 2.3).

When such a structure is in place, strategically integrated HRD programs operate on a project-by-project basis, assigning HRD professionals (organizational development consultants) to one or more projects at a time (see Chapter 13). Under this operational approach, HRD professionals have three development responsibilities. First, they are free to build strategic business partnerships throughout the organization while bringing about organizational change—which enhances the image of HRD and its professionals (see Chapter 5). Second, HRD professionals are charged with the responsibility of establishing management development partner-

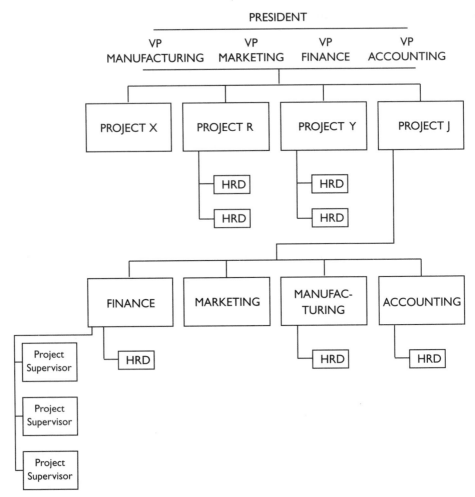

Figure 2.3 Strategically Integrated HRD Structure

ships as a way of improving the professional nature of managers and supervisors (see Chapter 6). Third, HRD professionals function as change agents responsible for organizational development partnerships, which will improve the organization's performance capacity and effectiveness (see Chapters 3, 4, and 7).

SI-HRD: Theory or Practice

Some may argue that the strategically integrated HRD phase is merely a theory and cannot become a reality. They ask for real examples of its existence and application. As with every evolutionary process, it is difficult to determine exactly where one is at any period in time. It is only when an evolutionary phase has been completed that we can provide definitive evidence that we passed through it. In the case of the vendor-driven or vendor-customized phases of HRD, we can provide evidence of their existence. These periods are real transformation phases in the life of HRD and are important steps toward a more progressive, responsive, and responsible HRD program. We can even provide "real" evidence that supports the existence of decentralized-performance improvement HRD. However, the evidence to support the existence of strategically integrated HRD is found only in small bits and pieces within many organizations. Such evidence can be uncovered when organizations like Steelcase, William M. Mercer, and Kellogg embrace the principles and techniques of SI-HRD and reorganize their operations accordingly. Another example of SI-HRD is the formation of organizational development "swat teams" responsible for the continuous improvement of the organization. In fact, most experimental HRD activities are attempts to develop better ways of helping the organization achieve its goals. Many of these are consistent with the principles and techniques outlined in this book, but are not commonly referred to as a strategically integrated HRD approach. These examples, though, are evidence of the emerging existence of SI-HRD.

Countless thousands of HRD professionals in every type of organization are making an effort to change from activity oriented to results driven HRD. To do so, they must first evolve through phase four and five on their way to phase six because it is impossible to jump over a phase. An evolutionary process implies a slow continuous progression. Therefore, HRD programs must progress through every evolutionary phase, though the amount of time spent on any one phase differs from organization to organization. Unfortunately, some HRD programs never progress beyond vendor-driven HRD and the organization suffers accordingly.

The real growth and development of any person or organization is in the journey toward a "perceived end." In other words, learning is a process of becoming and therein lies its benefit. We realize that the strategically integrated phase is *not* the absolute final evolutionary phase of HRD. Once this phase has been closely achieved another, yet unknown, phase will emerge. This is the exciting part of being in a dynamic and ever changing field.

BARRIERS TO STRATEGICALLY INTEGRATED HRD

One of the most difficult questions to answer about the evolution of HRD is "Why do HRD professionals have such a difficult time embracing the obvious advantages of strategically integrated HRD?" There are several reasons HRD professionals resist. First, organizations place extreme pressure on HRD professionals to solve performance problems. As a consequence, they react by providing a simple solution (training) to a set of complex problems. In some rare cases, training is the answer and HRD professionals are rewarded for their immediate and responsive behavior. Thus, they are convinced that training is the answer to all performance problems.

Second, many HRD professionals have a difficult time saying "no" to management when a training solution is requested. Many find it hard to question the authority and wisdom of management and give in to management's demands for training. It requires courage to suggest another alternative—courage that many HRD practitioners lack.

Third, some HRD professionals are afraid to take chances. The strategically integrated HRD approach will place HRD professionals on unfamiliar turf. No longer in their familiar, comfortable classroom, they feel overwhelmed by the complexities of the problems they must solve. There is a tendency to retreat to the classroom (avoidance) or to bring an easy classroom solution to difficult problems (simplification) (Gilley & Coffern, 1994).

Either as trainers or instructional designers, HRD professionals have time to plan, design, and adjust. As performance consultants (change-agents) however, they are often asked to make decisions in seconds. People may not respond or behave exactly the way the textbook model predicts.

Fourth, many HRD practitioners see training as an end in itself. Having entered the field of HRD to be trainers, they believe training will add value to the organization. They are good at delivering training and want to continue, regardless of the organization or type of industry in which they perform.

Fifth, training has a beginning and an end. It begins when the class starts and ends with employees' reactions to the training event. Training is clean and manageable, with no uncertainty or ambiguity to deal with or overcome. HRD practitioners can feel in charge and confident. They strongly resist using a consulting process to identify the causes of poor performance, which is required in strategically integrated HRD.

Sixth, many HRD practitioners make the assumption that performance will improve if learning takes place. Therefore, the emphasis is on classroom activity. But the strategically integrated approach requires HRD practitioners to consider other factors as well, both before and after training. In fact, HRD professionals who embrace the strategically integrated approach believe that the majority of performance improvement occurs on the job as employees struggle to apply what they have learned, with managers providing performance coaching to help encourage success. For many HRD practitioners, however, this is just too difficult a proposition to consider.

Seventh, some HRD professionals simply cannot let go of their fear of losing their "safe and secure" training positions. They are afraid of venturing into the unknown regardless of the positive impact it can have on the organization. These HRD professionals would rather complain about the lack of respect and credibility afforded them by the organization than embrace new ideas and better ways of achieving results.

Eighth, a real and serious problem facing HRD is the lack of qualified and capable HRD professionals willing to make the transition from trainer to organizational development consultant, which is required of SI-HRD programs. To compound this problem, many qualified HRD professionals elect to serve as outside consultants because internal opportunities have been limited. Large management consulting and professional service firms house a majority of the available candidates and are reluctant to give them up.

Finally, some HRD practitioners have spent a lifetime building an HRD "kingdom" within their organization, complete with a large budget, many employees, and perceived organizational respect. Operating like a large university disseminating knowledge, HRD programs charge tuition to operational units and tell others of the value that their department brings the organization. Activity abounds, fostering the belief that HRD is a valuable part of the organizational framework. Changing to a strategically integrated HRD approach would require practitioners (vendor-driven) to give up their kingdoms—a proposition many simply do not want to consider.

Like all great kings and kingdoms, the day of destruction is coming. HRD will be and is being eliminated in many organizations. HRD professionals are losing their kingdoms. Practitioners will wonder, "What happened?" "What could we have done to prevent this?" The answer is to be found in strategically integrated HRD.

CONCLUSION

The activity era has definitely passed. Today, the success of HRD is based on whether or not performance improvement and change interventions enhance organizational effectiveness and performance.

In other words, does HRD add value to the organization? The HRD function must produce specific outcomes that the organization can rely on in helping it accomplish its strategic business goals. Otherwise, organizational decision-makers will not need HRD.

The journey from vendor-driven HRD to strategically integrated HRD cannot begin unless HRD professionals become dedicated to helping the organization achieve its business goals. Each and every HRD professional must accept responsibility for changing the way the HRD community does business. They must become responsible for maximizing organizational performance and change. In short, HRD professionals must accept the challenge of transforming HRD within their organizations and become dedicated to making a difference in their field.

PART II

Improving Organizational Effectiveness

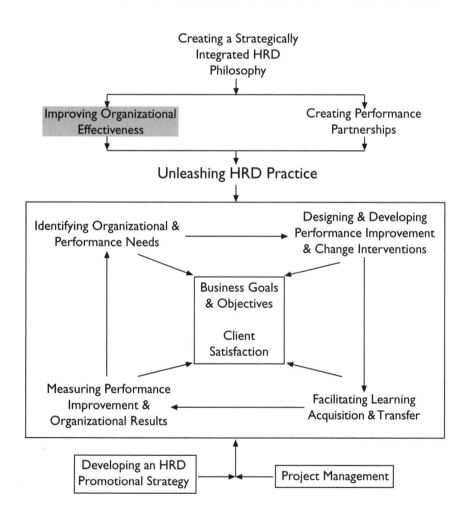

Strategically Integrated HRD

CHAPTER 3

Developing an Organizational Effectiveness Framework to Isolate Performance Problems and Organizational Breakdowns

The primary goal of an HRD professional is to improve the organization and make it more effective, whether this is a large, total system or a small division or department within an organization. Unfortunately, defining organizational effectiveness is not easy. According to Fallon and Brinkerhoff (1996), organizational effectiveness is a company's long-term ability to consistently achieve its strategic and operational goals (p. 14). The goal approach is the oldest and most widely used evaluation approach for measuring organizational effectiveness, but it is by no means the only method.

According to Cameron (1980), there are at least three additional definitions of organizational effectiveness that appear to be appropriate. First, organizational effectiveness can be measured by the ability of an organization to acquire needed resources to accomplish its desired goals. Using this definition, organizations are perceived to be successful when they are able to obtain the quantity and quality of resources appropriate, which could include financial, material, and/or human resources. Second, Cameron believes that organizational effectiveness can be defined in terms of how smoothly the organization functions, especially the degree or absence of internal strain within the organization (Burke, 1992, p. 8). When this definition is applied, it is often referred to as the *process model* of organizational effectiveness. Third, organizational effectiveness can be determined by the extent to which the organization is able to satisfy all of its internal and external clients. Internal clients include employees, managers, and executives, with satisfaction measured in terms of loyalty, motivation, esprit-de-corps, cooperation, and teamwork. External clients obviously include recipients of the organization's products and services. In this scenario, effectiveness can be measured in terms of customer satisfaction with those products and services, as well as their perception of the correctness of their decision to have an ongoing relationship with the organization.

Each of the previous definitions provide insight as to the importance of organizational effectiveness. While it may be difficult to arrive at an agreed-upon definition, it is certainly an important aspect of organizational life. Consequently, HRD professionals must strive to obtain an acceptable definition that relates to their own organization and/or industry. In this way, an agreed-upon target can be identified that all members of the organization strive to achieve.

MYTHS AND ASSUMPTIONS ABOUT ORGANIZATIONAL EFFECTIVENESS

The very notion of organizational effectiveness implies continuous change and development within an organization. However, organizations differ in their ability to recover from or adapt to change. According to Patterson (1997), the capacity of an organization and its members to absorb change without draining energies is referred to as resilience. He contends that resilience is like a personal energy account that consists of things such as time, thought, and effort spent on adjusting to change. In other words, resilience refers to the price people pay for change and their ability to adapt and adjust appropriately to it.

In the face of constant change, employees' energies can be easily depleted over time. To overcome this potential threat, employees must strengthen their skills needed to adapt to change, which will increase their resilience during any particular change activity.

Many HRD professionals proceed with the best of intentions in helping organizations and their employees adapt to change (i.e., improve their resilience). Unfortunately, they often operate under a number of myths regarding organizational effectiveness. This results in the application of faulty strategies that can create a huge drain on organizational resilience. According to Patterson (1997, p. 7), nine myths can prove fatal during organizational change activities:

1. People act first in the best interest of the organization.
2. People want to understand the "what" and the "why" of organizational change.

3. People engage in change because of the merits of change.
4. People opt to be architects of the change affecting them.
5. Organizations are rationally functioning systems.
6. Organizations are wired to assimilate systematic change.
7. Organizations operate from a value-driven orientation.
8. Organizations can effect long-term systemic change with short-term leadership.
9. Organizations can achieve systemic change without creating conflict in the system.

Each of these myths can lead to disaster if not appropriately addressed.

According to Patterson (1997), there are a number of harsh realities facing organizations during times of change. First, most employees act in their own best interests, not in those of the organization. Second, most employees do not really want to know the "what" and the "why" of organizational change—they simply want to know what is in it for them. Third, most employees engage in organizational change to avoid unnecessary difficulties or personal "pain," rather than to implement change based on its merits. Fourth, most employees view change with a great deal of skepticism and cynicism, even though they outwardly appear to be supportive. Fifth, most employees do not participate in a proactive manner when initiating change, preferring instead to be its victims. Sixth, most organizations operate irrationally, and are wired to protect the status quo. Seventh, most organizations do not refer to their guiding principles and values when initiating change, but rather are reacting to outside pressures such as the need for greater revenue, market share, or improved profitability. Eighth, most organizations are unrealistic about the amount of conflict that occurs as a result of change, and naively expect change to be accepted wholeheartedly by employees. Ninth, most organizations unfortunately implement long-term change with short-term leadership. Outside management teams are often brought into the organization to initiate long-term change, instead of using the management team that must live with the ultimate decisions made.

An HRD professional's primary responsibility in implementing organizational change is to help organizations and employees increase their resilience. That is, the organization and its employees must be helped to increase their capacity and ability to adapt to change. Again, Patterson (1997) offers several suggestions that can be used to accomplish this. He believes that ample time must be invested in trying to understand the various group members' self-interests and in finding ways of satisfying those concerns while implementing change.

Another strategy is helping members of the organization to see the connections between the particular change initiatives and the general direction in which the organization is headed. HRD professionals must create a sense of urgency for major change by "selling" the change initiative to critical decision-makers, stakeholders, and influencers. Trust must be established with this group prior to engaging in authentic and potentially redundant communications about the proposed change. Also, the connection between change and the organization's guiding principles must be shown. Establishing trust is accomplished by allowing employees to challenge, without fear of reprisal, the conduct and intentions of those initiating change (Patterson, 1997, p. 46).

HRD professionals must help employees understand that they do indeed have a choice between being a victim or an initiator of change. This effort includes helping employees approach change as an opportunity for advancement and improvement, rather than as an activity perceived as limiting. The urgency of proposed change is underscored when employees realize that their future well-being is at risk if change is not achieved.

HRD professionals are responsible for helping organizational leaders understand and accept the reality that organizational conflict is inevitable, that change will occur continuously, and that creating a safe environment that promotes constructive handling of conflict is the most appropriate action. This type of environment should actively embrace conflict resolution and consensus building as accepted operational practices. HRD professionals can help the organization develop its long-term commitment to change by linking proposed changes to its guiding principles and core values. Finally, the organization must learn to resist the natural tendency to deny the harsh realities of organizational change (Patterson, 1997, p. 47). Instead, HRD professionals should help organizations acknowledge these realities and apply strategies that help the organization become more adaptive to change.

CONDITIONS FOR ORGANIZATIONAL CHANGE

In 1989, Dyer identified the following conditions that must be present if organizational development interventions are to have some chance of bringing about desired change:

1. Management and all those involved must have high invisible commitment to the change.
2. Decision-makers who are involved need to have advanced information to enable them to know what is going to happen and why they are doing what they are doing.
3. The change effort must be connected to other parts of the organization.
4. The effort needs to be directed by managers and assisted by a change-agent (HRD professional).
5. The change effort must be based on an effective diagnosis of the organization and must be consistent with conditions in the organization.
6. Management must remain committed to the change, from diagnosis through implementation and evaluation.
7. Evaluation is essential and must consist of quantitative as well as qualitative data.
8. Employees must clearly see the relationship between the change effort and the organization's mission, goals, and guiding principles.
9. The change-agent must be competent and credible within the organization.
10. Organizations must be at an optimal point of readiness for change in order for it to occur.

When these conditions are present within an organization, HRD professionals will be more successful in implementing interventions that bring about or improve organizational effectiveness.

THE CHANGE PROCESS

The procedures for the change process can be traced back to the original research conducted by Lewin in 1951. While many have attempted to create elaborate change models, the basic premises laid out by Lewin appear to be the most appropriate when initiating organizational change designed to improve effectiveness. Lewin (1951) identifies three steps in the change process that include unfreezing, moving, and refreezing.

The unfreezing phase of the change process involves conditioning organizations for change and establishing ownership within the organization. This effort creates momentum when decision-makers, stakeholders, and influencers align in an effort to introduce change. Once organizational readiness for change has been achieved, HRD professionals can identify possible interventions that will help the organization maximize its developmental opportunities. For Lewin (1951) this means taking action that changes the organizational system from its original level of behavior and operations to its new desired level.

The movement phase is often referred to as a *transformation,* whereby organizations are in the process of redefining and reinventing themselves in order to achieve organizational goals and objectives.

The final phase of the change process is the period of reestablishing equilibrium within the organization. Once change has occurred, the HRD professional's primary focus is to help the organization adjust and begin performing at a higher level.

Formal and Informal Organizations

When implementing change, it is crucial for HRD professionals to consider the scope and intensity of their efforts. French and Bell (1984) liken organizations to icebergs. Formal components of the organization represent that part of the iceberg seen above the water. Informal components lie beneath the water's surface—unseen, unknown, undetected, yet clearly an organizational element. French and Bell believe that the formal organization consists of publicly observable, structural components that include span of control, hierarchical levels, the organization's mission, goals, objectives, policies, procedures, and practices. On the other hand, informal organizational components are not observable and consist of personal perceptions of the organization, the informal power structure, patterns of intergroup and intragroup relationships, perceptions of trust, openness, risk-taking behaviors, and relationships between managers and employees.

When implementing change, HRD professionals must consider both the formal and informal organization. Tichy (1989) believes that the scope and intensity of organizational problems will manifest themselves in the informal components of the organization. He concludes that the depth of intended change refers to how far management is willing to go into the organizational iceberg to solve a problem. Furthermore, real change will only occur when the informal organization and all of its behaviors and practices are radically altered. Changes that occur in the formal organization will rarely penetrate deep inside the organization in such a way as to improve organizational effectiveness and/or performance capacity. He further adds that the greater the depth of the intervention, the greater the risk of failure and the higher the cost of change. Consequently, HRD professionals must be able to condition the organization and establish ownership for change prior to implementing interventions.

THE ORGANIZATION AS A SYSTEM

Organizations have been compared to human organisms. Just as humans have digestive, circulatory, skeletal, and nervous systems, organizations have similar subsystems that enable them to remain alive. Typically, organizations are diagrammed in such a way to describe connections between various departments, both vertically and horizontally. On the horizontal plane, various departments are indicated that represent functions such as finance, marketing, manufacturing, customer service, and so forth. On the vertical plane, organizations are divided into subparts of various departments, usually indicating individual titles and specific reporting relationships.

Rummler and Brache (1995) liken organizations to silos, contending that silos are tall, thick, windowless structures that prevent interdepartmental issues from being resolved between peers at low and mid levels (p. 6). They believe that silo culture forces managers to resolve low-level issues, taking their time away from higher priority customers and competitive concerns (p. 7). Most employees operate within their respective silos, adopting the culture, language, and customs of their department or division. This behavior prevents crossdepartmental interaction, which could improve communications, decision-making, performance, and quality.

The more organizations operate within the silo culture, the more likely they are to produce the organizational "tower of Babel." The tower of Babel is a descriptive metaphor that demonstrates the confusion rampant within organizations that operationalize silo culture. Since employees from different departments fail to communicate or maintain a similar language, they tend to be isolated and operate from a narrow organizational perspective. When the organizational tower of Babel is allowed to flourish, employees are prevented from working across departmental lines to achieve desired goals. Furthermore, organizational decisions are pushed up to higher levels, preventing teamwork and crossdepartmental cooperation.

Altering silo culture remains one of the best ways of improving organizational effectiveness. Rummler and Brache (1995) suggest that organizations must understand their crossdepartmental interactions and dependencies. They provide a methodology known as *relationship mapping* to demonstrate this approach. Figure 3.1 is an example of a relationship map for a medium-sized dental office, reflecting the dependencies of various departments on one another.

A relationship map demonstrates that organizations are indeed systems. Figure 3.1 reveals the grouping of elements that individually establish relationships with each other, as well as those that interact with their environment, both individually and collectively (Gibson, Ivancevich, & Donnelly, 1997). As a system, the organization relies on inputs (resources) and processes (interdependent tasks and activities) to produce the desired results and outputs (products, services, or deliverables). The most important function of relationship mapping is identifying connections between various departments.

According to Rummler and Brache (1995), the greatest opportunity for performance improvement often lies in functional interfaces—those points at which activities are being passed from one department to another (p. 9). Consequently, HRD professionals must help organizations understand their need to create more efficient and effective interdepartmental relationships—ones that improve organizational performance capacity and effectiveness.

Organizations suffering from the tower of Babel syndrome are unable to communicate across departmental lines, make effective decisions, or improve organizational performance and quality. Overcoming this syndrome typically involves adopting a more practical and efficient overall effectiveness strategy—one that helps the organization create a universal, crossdepartmental language that can be used to feed and strengthen the entire firm. This strategy, then, can be used to implement change at both the macro and micro levels.

ORGANIZATIONAL EFFECTIVENESS FRAMEWORK

The human circulatory system serves as a powerful comparison to an organizational effectiveness strategy. As discussed previously, human beings consist of multiple systems such as the digestive, skeletal, and nervous systems. None is more important in keeping humans operational than the circulatory system, which is comprised of major arteries, veins, and capillaries designed to feed all types of cells and tissue throughout the body. This sophisticated network keeps us alive. A blockage in the circulatory system may cause loss of a limb or, in the case of a vital organ, death.

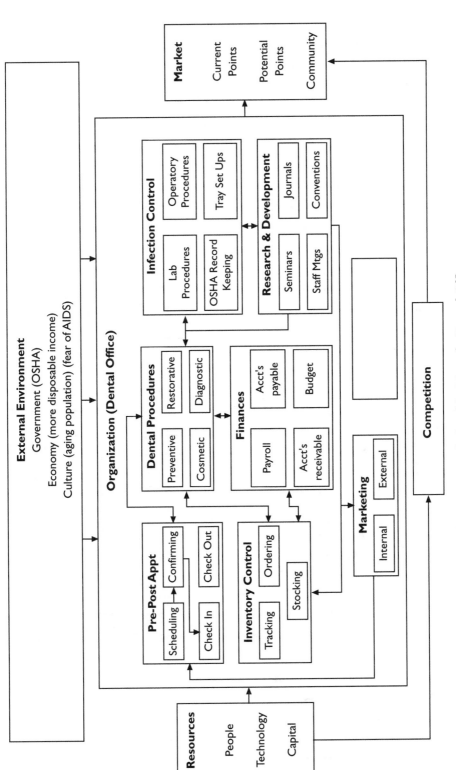

Figure 3.1 Relationship Map of a Dental Office

Similarly, an organizational effectiveness framework consists of both an organizational system and a performance management system (see Figure 3.2). The organizational system consists of interdependent functions on which the organization is dependent in order to remain viable. These seven interdependent functions include:

1. leadership
2. structure
3. work climate
4. organizational culture

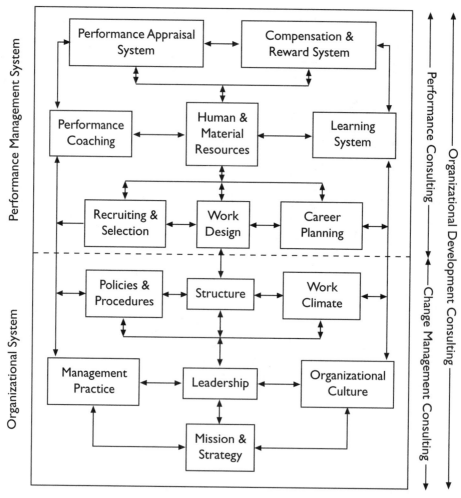

Figure 3.2   Organizational Effectiveness Framework

5. mission and strategy
6. managerial practice
7. policies and procedures

In Figure 3.2, each of these seven functions are dependent on the others, as represented by the arrows. Nevertheless, each function is an independent component of the organization, not unlike the vital organs within the human body.

An organizational effectiveness framework's performance management system is comprised of eight interdependent functions (see Figure 3.2). Once again, both an interdependent and independent relationship exist among these eight functions. They include:

1. human and material resources
2. compensation and reward system
3. learning system
4. work design
5. career planning
6. recruiting and selection
7. performance coaching
8. performance appraisal process

The arrows in both directions convey an open system principle: what changes in one factor will eventually impact the others (Burke, 1992). Connection points exist between the organizational system and performance management system, demonstrating the linkage between the two.

Using an organizational effectiveness framework is important to HRD professionals for many reasons. First, this framework enables HRD professionals to approach organizational change from both micro and macro perspectives. When approaching change from a micro perspective, HRD professionals should rely on the performance management system to enhance organizational performance. Macro level changes require attention to the organizational system, since it is commonly shared across departmental lines and divisions. Second, HRD professionals can analyze the relationships between various functions within the organizational and performance management systems to determine potential breakdowns or areas of weakness. Third, when looking for symptoms of poor performance or quality, a combination of these fifteen functions can be examined to determine whether one, a few, or all are contributing to the breakdown. Fourth, HRD professionals can better develop change interventions by focusing on the most appropriate functions and their interdependencies. Fifth, this framework can be used to identify appropriate layers that consist of groupings either within each respective system or across system lines. Sixth, the organizational system and performance management system may be treated as separate entities requiring completely different interventions. Seventh, depending upon whether their focus is the organizational system, performance management system, or a combination (change management consulting, performance consulting, and organizational development consulting, respectively), HRD professionals will better understand the type of consulting activities in which they will be engaged. We will examine more closely the vertical relationship of this framework and the consulting roles later in this chapter.

Organizational System

As previously discussed, an organizational system consists of seven independent yet interdependent functions, each of which serves as a universal language across departments and divisions. While departments maintain separate identities, languages, and customs, the seven functions are common to all. Members of the marketing and finance departments may have different languages, practices, and customs, but they are unified when taking into account each of these seven functions.

Leadership

A variety of definitions attempt to illustrate leadership. Simply defined, leadership is the process of making decisions regarding how to interact with employees in order to motivate them, then translating those decisions into actions. While this definition does not take into account the various types of leadership within an organization, it does describe its primary purpose. Burke (1992) describes leadership as the behavior of managers and executives that provides direction and encourages others to take needed action (p. 130).

When examined carefully, a host of leadership theories surface that contribute to a better understanding of organizational effectiveness. Gibson, Ivancevich, and Donnelly (1997) identify four major leadership theories applicable in today's organizations:

1. Attribution Leadership Theory—a theory of the relationship between individuals' perceptions and interpersonal behavior;

thus, leaders' perceptions will determine the way they interact with employees and vice versa.

2. Charismatic Leadership—the ability to influence employees due to extraordinary gifts and persuasive powers. Based on this theory, leaders are most effective when they can communicate their vision, build trust, and demonstrate the means of achieving their vision via role modeling, empowerment, and unconventional tactics.

3. Transactional Leadership—a type of leadership that defines what employees want or prefer and helps them achieve the level of performance that results in rewards.

4. Transformational Leadership—the ability to inspire and motivate fellow employees to achieve results greater than originally planned, as well as helping employees to obtain intrinsic satisfaction from their accomplishments (pp. 307–14).

Structure

Structure refers to the arrangement of work functions and employees into specific areas and levels of responsibility, decision-making authority, and relationships in order for the organization to achieve its strategic business goals. When organizations attempt to create a structure, they must consider four important variables:

1. division of labor—the process of dividing work into specialized areas
2. compartmentalization—the process of organizing jobs in accordance with shared characteristics
3. span of control—the number of employees who report to a specific manager or executive
4. authority—the power to make and execute decisions within the organization

Organizations can be divided into centralized and decentralized operations. The fundamental differences are the extent to which the organization relies on formal rules and regulations, and formal and informal communications.

Work Climate

Work climate can be best determined by examining employees' impressions, expectations, and feelings concerning the work environment. Work climate can be affected by organizational leadership, coworkers, the type of organization, economic factors, and departmental stability within the organization. According to Gilley and Eggland (1989), organizations can be divided into four types: passive, hierarchical, competitive, and collaborative according to how employees are viewed and/or the relationship employees have with the organization.

Passive Organizations do not perceive their employees as important and are not committed to their well-being. These organizations fail to rely on the talent, skills, and abilities of their employees to solve problems or make essential decisions and contributions. (Examples: retail operations and small businesses.)

Hierarchical Organizations believe that most employees are committed to the welfare of the organization, but that only a few have the critical talent, skills, and abilities to make informed, critical decisions. Hierarchical organizations are historically large and taller consisting of many layers. (Examples: most Fortune 500 companies, governmental agencies, and universities.)

Competitive Organizations consist of many talented, skilled employees with only a few being loyal to the organization. Employees often possess high levels of education and many years of experience in this type of organization. Most are able to find employment in a number of competitive firms, placing extreme pressure on management and organizational leaders to meet or exceed their needs. (Examples: professional service and consulting firms.)

Collaborative Organizations view employees as important and committed, allowing them to participate in all critical decisions. The firm's culture fosters loyalty and involvement, and management encourages and supports organizational development activities. (Examples: employee-owned organizations and those with unique, progressive leadership.)

Organizational Culture

According to Burke (1992), organizational culture is defined as "the way we do things around here" (p. 130). Culture is often a collection of artifacts, creations, rules, values, principles, and assumptions that guide organizational behavior. Culture is strongly influenced by history, customs, and practices. It could be said that organizational culture is what employees perceive to be the pattern of beliefs, values, and expectations that guide behavior and practice within an organization.

Organizational culture is perhaps one of the most important components of an organizational system. The type of organizational culture that exists often depends upon the type of organization in which one works. Some say that collaborative organizations present the optimal organizational culture. According to Burke (1992, pp. 196–97), collaborative organizational cultures exhibit the following characteristics:

1. Growth and development of organizational members is just as important as making a profit or staying within budget.
2. Equal opportunity and fairness for people within the organization is commonplace—the rule rather than the exception.
3. Managers exercise their authority more participatively than unilaterally or arbitrarily, and authority is associated more with knowledge and competence than role or status.
4. Cooperative behavior is rewarded more than competitive behavior.
5. Organizational members are kept informed or at least have access to information, especially concerning matters that directly impact their jobs or them personally.
6. Members feel a sense of ownership of the organization's mission and objectives.
7. Conflict is dealt with openly and systematically rather than ignored, avoided, or handled in a typical win-lose fashion.
8. Rewards are based on a system of quality, fairness, and equitable merit.
9. Organizational members are given as much autonomy and freedom to do their respective jobs as possible, ensuring both a high degree of individual motivation and the accomplishment of the organization's strategic goals and objectives.

Mission and Strategy

The mission is what executives, managers, and employees believe to be the central purpose of the organization. Establishing an organizational mission is a time-consuming, soul-searching process. Each member of the organization may hold a different perspective of what the organization is attempting to accomplish; however, it is essential that each individual ultimately agrees with and supports the organization's mission. A well-defined mission statement gives everyone a sense of purpose, direction, significance, and achievement.

Strategy refers to how an organization intends to achieve its purposes over an extended period of time. Historically, a long-term strategy attempts to define roles and responsibilities within the organization, thus dictating how work is to be accomplished. Strategy can be considered the organization's game plan, to be embraced and executed by all members while remaining flexible, adaptive, and taking into consideration unique circumstances and events.

Managerial Practices

Managerial practices can be defined as the normal activities used by managers to carry out the organizational strategy, including the utilization of human and material resources and daily contact with employees. Managerial practices can be seen in all interactions with employees, including delegating work tasks, managing projects, implementing organizational change interventions, managing employee conflicts, and confronting poor performance. In short, these practices define the way managers go about accomplishing organizational objectives through people.

Policies and Procedures

Policies and procedures encompass an organization's rules and regulations. Policies are perceived to be the established set of rules that employees must follow, while procedures prescribe how employees will implement daily work activities. Policies and procedures provide structure for the organization, allowing the firm to align employees around its central focus and mission. Policies and procedures govern organizational behavior, providing a means of *norming* practice.

When effectively written, policies and procedures create a sense of group cohesion. They also provide a code of conduct and behavior, developed and shared among employees, which should increase their willingness to participate in projects and assignments. Policies and procedures should be flexible enough to allow for employee input, while at the same time sufficiently structured to provide guidance and direction for employees when uncertainty rules.

Performance Management Systems

According to Gilley (1998), a performance management system is a tool that blends the entire performance improvement process into one cohesive system. A performance management system is designed to link performance to compensation and rewards, as well as to the organization's strategic goals and objectives. This system should be used to improve an organization's recruiting and selection practices, design learning systems that improve employee performance, maintain a formal work design process by which jobs are continuously improved, and develop a performance coaching and appraisal process that provides employees with continuous, ongoing, and meaningful feedback.

Human and Material Resources

Human resources include the people within the organization who accomplish work, while material resources include the tools, equipment, technology, and information necessary for employees to perform their jobs. Both human and material resources should be the center of the performance management system, and should be linked directly to the other seven functions within that system. One of the primary purposes of the performance management system is to continuously develop and improve the organization's human and material resources. In this way, organizational effectiveness can be enhanced on an ongoing basis.

Learning System

Organizational effectiveness strategies prompt HRD professionals to engage in discussions regarding methods of improving employee performance. One of the best ways to facilitate these discussions is to create learning systems within the organization. HRD professionals and managers should mutually design such systems as ways of helping employees with learning acquisition and transfer (see Chapter 10). Learning transfer strategies should be the foundation upon which organizational learning systems are constructed.

A learning system should also be based on the strategically integrated HRD philosophy, which encourages organizations to focus on strengths while managing employee weaknesses. That is, learning systems should encourage employees to continue to develop their strengths via advanced training, new assignments, or challenging projects that increase their skills. At the same time, strategies should be identified and incorporated that help employees manage their weaknesses through partnering, preventing, and delegating (Gilley, 1998).

Career Planning

According to Gilley and Eggland (1989), career planning is "the process of setting individual career objectives and creatively developing activities that will achieve them" (p. 67). Career planning is a long-term effort designed to maximize the skills and abilities of employees. This function differs from career coaching, which is a process used by managers to help employees review and explore their interests, abilities, and beliefs regarding their present and future career paths (Gilley & Boughton, 1996). In other words, career planning is a long-term process that "charts" the employee's career while career coaching helps the employee better understand personal career interests and abilities.

The recruiting, relocation, and training costs associated with turnover can cripple an organization, severely hurting its profitability. Therefore, it is in the best interests of the organization to keep its employees. Career planning enables organizations to hold on to their most important assets, their people. For this reason alone, career planning is worth the effort.

Career planning promotes overall organizational performance through better allocation of human resources. That is, organizations help themselves by placing the right person in the right job. Career planning efforts protect the organization from investing too much time and money in employees who are not suited for specific jobs or responsibilities.

Career planning also benefits the organization by allowing an opportunity to identify employee performance deficiencies, which is normally accomplished via skill and interest inventories as well as observation and performance analysis. Once identified, organizations can recommend developmental strategies designed to overcome deficiencies. As a result, employees will be better trained and more productive.

Providing employees with information about their jobs and other opportunities within the organization is an element of career planning that enables employees to better understand their career choices. Most employees would like to know more about advancement potential, job requirements, activities and duties, and training requirements before selecting a career path. The organization benefits when employees believe that there are career opportunities available to them.

Career planning enables employees to better understand career choices and their associated feelings. This comprehension may help employees make a greater commitment to their career and the organization. Greater loyalty can improve the attitudes of all employees and significantly impact the quality of work produced. Enhanced commitment may have a ripple effect for the organization, resulting in improved customer service, employee relations, and efficiency (Gilley, 1998).

Through career planning employees can gain greater insight into the organization. The more employees know about the organization, the more loyalty they will feel. Such insights allow employees to feel more a part of the organization, rather than just as one of its workers. This could improve teamwork, cooperation, and help foster an ownership attitude.

Finally, career planning allows employees to become more self-sufficient and independent—essential skills for building self-directed and empowered work teams. Also, career planning activities pay off nicely through improved quality, efficiency, and organizational performance.

Work Design

When an organization fails to achieve its strategic business goals and objectives (such as increasing sales revenue), the organization's work and job design require examination to determine whether they impacted the failure. Work design is defined as the series of steps used in producing a product or service (Rummler & Brache, 1995). These steps are performed by employees to achieve unit, departmental, divisional, and/or organizational goals and objectives. When organizations fail to accomplish their objectives, reshaping, reorganizing, redefining, replacing, or improving work design may be in order.

Another step in creating effective work design is identifying the performance outcomes for each job in the organization. In other words, HRD professionals should identify the deliverables produced by every employee in the organization. In most jobs, employees are responsible for the production of several deliverables that collectively define the employee's job. According to Gilley (1998), performance outputs may include the number of sales made per month by sales staff, the service claims satisfied by a customer service representative, the number of successful calls made by telemarketing representatives, the number of packages delivered per day by express mail workers, or the number of orders filled by clerks. Regardless, outputs represent the organization's hourly, daily, weekly, monthly, quarterly, and/or yearly expectations of employees in a specific job classification.

Performance outcomes deemed unacceptable are examined by HRD professionals and managers in an effort to determine if a breakdown is occurring. If a problem is discovered, an intervention can be designed that will help employees demonstrate acceptable performance levels.

Once performance activities have been defined, HRD professionals identify the skills, knowledge, and competencies employees need to accomplish them. This process produces an organizational management tool known as a *competency map* (Gilley, 1998). Competency maps serve as a basis for every job in the organization, while the collective competency map reveals organizational performance capacity.

Competency maps may be developed by asking employees to enumerate the knowledge, skills, and competencies they believe are required for a specific job. Then other employees are challenged to perform the same job to verify and validate the competency map. Finally, an acceptable tool will be created.

Developing a competency map for each job classification serves three purposes. First, maps serve as the foundation for all future HRD interventions. Second, they are used to provide employees with performance feedback, deliver appropriate and timely performance coaching, and evaluate overall employee performance. Third, they are used in organizational recruiting efforts. In other words, once competency maps are identified, organizations can develop interviewing strategies and selection criteria useful in selecting the most appropriate candidates. When used as the foundation of recruiting efforts, organizations benefit by having the right people, with the right skills and competencies, at the right time.

Recruiting and Selection

A core component of performance management systems, recruiting and selection remains the primary tool by which organizations obtain the appropriate human resources necessary to accomplish business objectives and gain competitive advantage. As discussed above, selecting and recruiting activities should be based on an agreed-upon competency map for each job classification within the organization.

Performance Coaching

Performance coaching provides a road map for helping employees become productive and successful. In Chapter 6 we will discuss how managers use performance coaching skills in one-on-one exchanges with employees to improve performance, resolve problems, and achieve results.

Performance coaching encourages managers to establish positive relationships with their employees, enabling them to become active participants as opposed to passive observers. This process requires managers to constantly shift from one role to another, helping employees improve and enhance their self-esteem while achieving appropriate business results.

Performance Appraisal Process

Most organizations have some type of review process designed to give managers an opportunity to judge the adequacy and quality of employee performance and to create performance improvement plans (see Chapter 10). Performance appraisals should be used to:

1. determine whether employees are producing acceptable performance outputs
2. determine whether performance meets or exceeds performance standards
3. determine if employees are performing acceptable activities
4. determine the level of internal and external client satisfaction with outputs generated by employees
5. discuss how employee performance is helping the department and the organization achieve its strategic business goals and objectives
6. design a performance improvement plan for employees
7. confront employee performance and make recommendations for improvement

According to Gilley (1998), a performance appraisal process consists of seven easy steps:

1. gathering employee performance data
2. comparing performance results with performance standards and expectations
3. sharing observations and opinions with employees that include perceptions of their strengths and weaknesses, their record of achieving performance outputs, and their abilities and attitudes toward performance activities
4. allowing employees to respond to managers' critiques
5. discussing manager and employee differences
6. identifying, isolating, and eliminating performance interference
7. identifying performance consequences that will motivate employees to produce adequate, acceptable performance results

Compensation and Reward System

The purpose of any organization is to achieve results, which could include gaining market share, improving quality, and/or increasing profitability. A straightforward, common sense approach useful in enhancing employee performance involves simply notifying employees of results or outputs required, levels of quality needed, and applicable time frames.

Organizations must establish a clear link between producing positive performance outputs and recognition. Properly designed compensation and reward systems build commitment and improve employee motivation. They must reward the right things.

Managers must make difficult decisions regarding each and every employee by judging their performance and making appropriate recommendations. Properly designed compensation and rewards systems gauge employee performance in relationship to performance standards or expectations, directly linking compensation and rewards to actual performance.

On some occasions, employees fail to meet performance standards or expectations. When this occurs, organizations must take action that causes employees to make corrective change. This is called discipline. The purpose of any disciplinary action is to correct a serious performance problem before the organization is forced to suspend or terminate the employee.

Simplified Performance Management Technique

HRD professionals can help managers employ a simple nine-step process that alleviates many performance problems and improves overall employee effectiveness. Managers should:

1. establish a relationship, or rapport, with employees
2. help employees identify their performance problems via performance coaching or performance appraisal activities
3. help employees evaluate their behavior and understand the consequences of continuing in an unacceptable manner. Behaviors may include the execution of steps within a job or the quality of the outputs produced, while consequences include natural outcomes that occur when performance continually fails to meet standards
4. help employees identify ways to change their performance. This may include examining work design, identifying material resources needed to perform more efficiently or effectively, or additional training and development
5. help employees get started by implementing a learning acquisition and transfer plan designed to improve performance (see Chapter 10)
6. not accept employee excuses for failing to successfully accomplish the learning and acquisition plan

7. implement natural consequences agreed-upon in step three if performance fails to improve. Natural consequences are not intended to be a form of punishment, but simply the natural result of failing to improve one's performance
8. never give up on employees, and continue to encourage them to perform to their greatest ability
9. reward performance improvement appropriately, recognizing employees who have achieved desired outcomes in a manner that enhances self-esteem

TYPES OF CONSULTING ACTIVITIES

In Figure 3.2 we identified three types of consulting activities that occur when implementing the organizational effectiveness framework. When HRD professionals are working to improve the organizational system, the most appropriate type of consulting activity is *change management,* which is designed to reshape, redesign, and reengineer the organization. This consulting activity reviews the relationship between the seven functions outlined within the organizational system to see how efficiently and effectively they are working together. Change management consulting examines the impact of the organizational system on the performance management system.

Performance consulting activities involve examination of the overall performance capacity of the organization. Performance consulting studies the interplay between the eight performance management system variables in an effort to determine how employee performance can be improved. This differs from change management consulting in that performance consulting is designed to improve organizational effectiveness by improving the performance management system and the performance behaviors of each and every employee, while change management consulting looks at how the overall organizational system impacts performance.

The most efficient and effective means of improving organizational effectiveness is through *organizational development consulting,* which is the most comprehensive process available to HRD professionals. Organizational development consulting investigates the organizational and management performance systems to evaluate the impact each has on organizational capacity. In Chapter 7, we examine in detail ways for HRD professionals to create organizational development partnerships, and methods for making the transition from the current role to that of organizational development consultant.

APPLYING THE ORGANIZATIONAL EFFECTIVENESS FRAMEWORK

As with every theoretical and conceptual model, the aim is to demonstrate how each can be used to help professionals better do their jobs. In the case of HRD, this includes improving performance capacity, continuous development, and the efficiency and effectiveness of an organization. With that in mind, one only needs to step back and examine the issues, relationships, and logical characteristics of each of the fifteen components of the organization effectiveness framework (see Figure 3.3) in order to employ it. For example, improving organizational performance requires HRD professionals to examine:

- the adequacy of human and material resources
- the hiring and selection practices used to match employees with jobs (recruiting and selection)
- the ability of managers and supervisors to provide formal feedback, and to design corrective action and developmental plans (performance appraisal process)
- the impact of financial and intrinsic rewards on employee motivation (compensation and reward system)
- the effectiveness of learning acquisition and transfer plans used to improve employee knowledge and skill (learning system)
- the long-term growth, development, and achievement potential of employees (career planning)
- the efficiency of work tasks for a specific job and their relationship to other jobs (work design)
- the manager's ability to train, mentor, and provide constructive performance feedback (performance coaching, Figure 6.1)

In other words, the entire performance management system must be examined.

One of the best ways of applying the organizational effectiveness framework is to think of it as a trouble-shooting guide used to isolate performance problems and organizational breakdowns. For example, electronic technicians use electronic diagrams (schematics), automobile mechanics rely on diagnostic tools, and building contractors refer to blueprints to provide them direction and to

Improving Organizational Performance

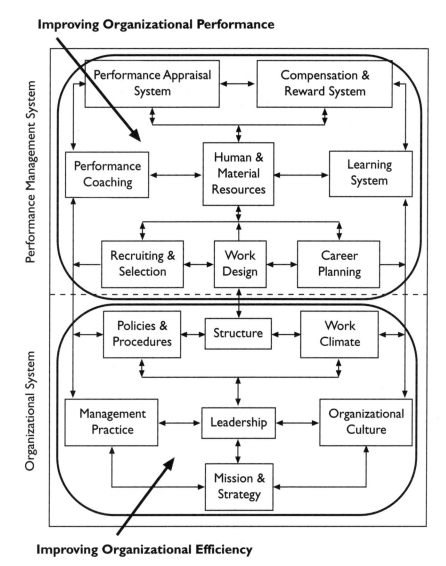

Improving Organizational Efficiency

Figure 3.3 Applying the Organizational Effectiveness Framework

isolate problems or breakdowns. Similarly, HRD professionals employ the organizational effectiveness framework to isolate problems or identify areas that require examination in order to craft a solution for which an intervention can be constructed.

The organizational effectiveness framework is useful during organizational, managerial, performance, and needs analysis activities as a way of identifying gaps between current and desired expectations (see Chapter 8). HRD professionals can use the organizational effectiveness framework to conduct brainstorming activities designed to identify factors that contribute to performance problems or organizational breakdowns. Additionally, the framework can be used to assign areas of inquiry during the problem identification phase of a project. When used to isolate potential problems, define relationships between and among various components, or identify intervention possibilities, the applications are endless.

When applying the organizational effectiveness framework, the following seven steps should be used:

1. Identifying the *most logical components* that should be taken into account in determining the extent of a performance problem or organizational breakdown. (Remember to identify only those components that have a "direct" impact on the problem. Recommendations and interventions may require addressing additional components).
2. Defining each component and identifying its importance within one's organization.
3. Identifying the relative strengths and weaknesses of each component.
4. Examining the relationship among components.
5. Determining any negative impacts that components have on each other.
6. Isolating areas of concern or breakdowns.
7. Identifying recommendations and/or interventions that should be used to neutralize negative impacts.

APPLYING THE SEVEN STEPS

In the following diagram, we demonstrate how the organizational effectiveness framework can be used to identify the most logical components (Step 1) to be examined.

Performance Problem or Organizational Breakdown	Components
Improving Organizational Efficiency	Leadership, Structure, Work climate, Organizational culture, Mission and strategy, Management practice, Policies and procedures (Figure 3.3)
Inadequate Employee Motivation	Performance coaching, Performance appraisal process, Compensation and

	rewards, Human and material resources (Figure 3.4)
Applying Process Reengineering	Learning system, Career planning, Work design, Recruiting and selection (Figure 3.4)
Negative Employee Perceptions	Work climate, Organizational culture (Figure 3.4)
Creating Collaborative Organizations	Management practices, Leadership, Mission and strategy (Figure 3.4)
Improving Teamwork	Performance appraisal process, Compensation and reward system, Human and material resources, Performance coaching, Work design, Structure, Work climate, Leadership, Organizational culture, Management practices (Figure 3.5)
Improving Organizational Communication	Performance appraisal process, Human and material resources, Performance coaching, Work design, Structure, Work climate, Leadership, Organizational culture, Management practices (Figure 3.6)

These are only a few of the possible applications of the organizational effectiveness framework; however, they should prove adequate in demonstrating its use.

The organizational effectiveness framework demonstrates how difficult it is to solve common problems like teamwork and organizational communication—which require comprehensive analysis of most of the organizational effectiveness components and examination of both the organization and performance management systems. Unfortunately, most organizations attempt to resolve these complex problems via skill development or simple training activities designed to heighten employees' awareness of the problem. In reality, such knowledge and/or skill cannot help overcome the difficulty. Is it any wonder these problems never really get solved?

Once the most logical components have been identified, each of the next six steps should be completed. Let us illustrate, using inadequate employee motivation as an example. First, determine the most logical components to be examined. They are performance coaching, the performance appraisal process, compensation and

Inadequate Employee Motivation

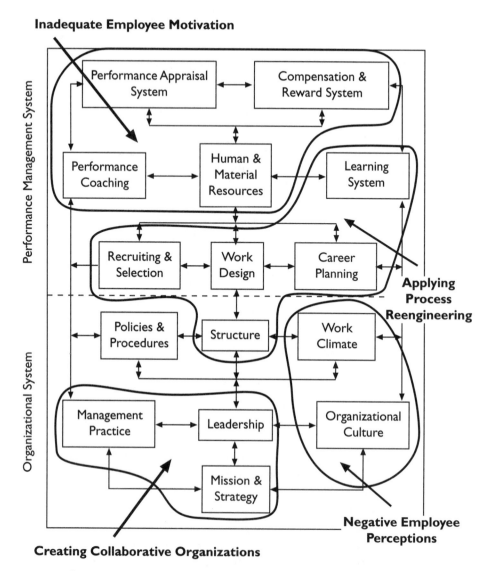

Figure 3.4 Applying the Organizational Effectiveness Framework

reward system, and human and material resources. Second, define each of these components and identify their importance in the organization. This way, one develops a working definition of each component and prioritizes them. The organizational effectiveness components now have been customized to fit the organization.

Third, HRD professionals must identify the strengths and weaknesses of each component. For example, if performance appraisals are conducted infrequently or managers treat them as a waste of time, this would be a significant weakness and could contribute to inadequate employee motivation. Managers may not possess performance coaching skills and, therefore, employees may not be receiving daily feedback regarding their performance, which could also be considered a weakness. The compensation and reward system, however, may be the best in the industry, which would be an important strength. Regardless, each component must be examined.

Fourth, the relationships among components must be examined in order to determine how they impact each other. In our example, the four components are closely grouped together. Consequently, there is tremendous interplay between components. Thus, a slight

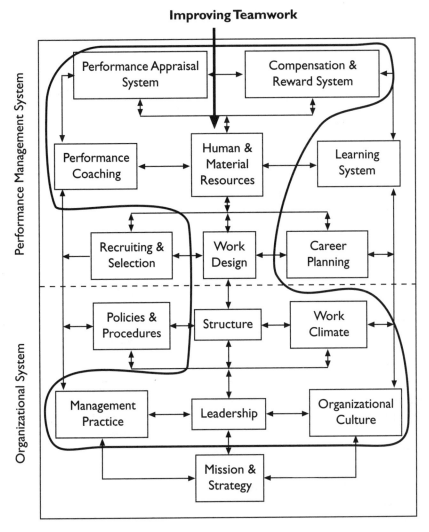

Figure 3.5 Applying the Organizational Effectiveness Framework

Improving Organizational Communication

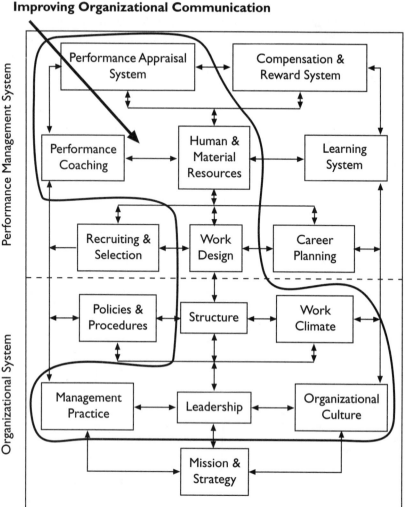

Figure 3.6   Applying the Organizational Effectiveness Framework

change in one component will dramatically affect each of the others. In other words, failure to execute a key component will significantly impact the effectiveness of the other components. For example, if the number of human resources are inadequate to properly produce the results needed by the organization, overall employee motivation may be significantly impacted. Such a condition may negate the effectiveness of other components such as performance appraisal and the compensation and reward system. If this is the case, the only possible solution is to increase the number of human resources used to achieve acceptable business results.

In the previous example, we have demonstrated the last two steps of the process, which are to isolate areas of concern or breakdown and to identify recommendations and/or interventions used to overcome negative impacts. Once this has been achieved, HRD professionals should seek support for implementing the proposed recommendation or intervention.

Every performance problem or organizational breakdown is different. However, using the seven step analysis process will help HRD professionals isolate areas of concern so that appropriate action can be taken. We believe the key to this process is determining the negative impact among components. Once this has been accomplished the "real issues" begin to emerge, thus eliminating hidden agendas and "zealot" behaviors.

In the next diagram, we have identified six common performance problems. Take a few minutes and identify the most logical components to be considered for each. Once this has been accomplished, select one problem and complete the remaining six steps as they would apply in a "real" organization. Repeat this activity until a level of mastery has been achieved.

Performance Problem or Organizational Breakdown	*Components*
Poor Performance Quality	
Managerial Malpractice	
Negative Employee Attitudes	
Improving Long-term Employee Development	
Inadequate Succession Planning	
Lack of Career Development	

CONCLUSION

Blending the organizational and performance management systems into a comprehensive organizational effectiveness framework provides HRD professionals with a blueprint that guides and directs decision-making. The organizational effectiveness framework provides insight into operations at both the macro and micro levels. This framework provides the organization with a universal language that crosses departmental, division, and unit lines, thereby improving organizational performance capacity and effectiveness. Finally, the organizational effectiveness framework is useful in helping improve organizational communications, in fostering organizational change, and in developing improved organizational operations.

CHAPTER 4

Improving Organizational Effectiveness through Strategic Planning

Strategic planning is a forward thinking process that helps organizational leaders shape the future via intelligent, informed, and innovative actions. Strategic planning gives purpose and direction to an organization by allowing it to ascertain, in advance, what it wishes to accomplish and the means by which it can achieve its ends. *Webster's New American Dictionary* defines *strategy* as the "skillful employment and coordination of tactics" and "artful planning and management." Strategic planning provides focus and unity within an organization. It is also the best means to handle external pressures and center customer service activities.

Strategic planning allows everyone in the organization the opportunity to participate in decision-making, and thus to make a personal impact on the organization's future (Simerly, 1987). Consequently, strategic planning can be viewed as a way of improving and enhancing the self-esteem of employees. Make no mistake, strategic planning activities are designed to recreate and reinvent organizations by helping them establish a new vision and purpose. Nevertheless, it can greatly improve organizational effectiveness.

When HRD professionals engage in strategic planning they produce an end product—usually a written document that enables all decision-makers, stakeholders, and influencers to comprehend, analyze and critique the organization's mission, goals, objectives, and strategies. HRD will use this document to help the organization achieve its desired business results. Consequently, strategic planning is both a process and a product. The two are interrelated in such complex ways that it is almost impossible to analyze one without considering the other (Michael, 1973).

For us, the best example illustrating the importance of strategic planning was offered in the book *Alice in Wonderland.*

"Cheshire puss," she began, rather timidly, and she did not at all know whether it would like the name; however, it only grinned a little wider. It's pleased so far, thought Alice and she went on, "Would you please tell me, please, which way I ought to go from here?" "That depends a good deal on where you want to get to," said the cat. "I don't much care where," says Alice. "Then it doesn't matter which way you go," says the cat. "So long as I get somewhere," Alice added as an explanation. "Oh, you're sure to do that," says the cat, "if you only walk long enough."

This simple passage demonstrates a lack of strategic planning, without which an organization is certain to end up somewhere, though it may not be the destination desired.

The strategic planning process is simply a systematic way of organizing the future. Strategic planning is instrumental in helping an organization identify the direction it wants to go, define the outcomes it wants to achieve, and outlining how to get there.

CHARACTERISTICS OF EFFECTIVE STRATEGIC PLANNING

As a way of positioning strategic planning as both a process and a product, we will identify a number of its major characteristics. These components, which serve as the ingredients of a properly designed, implemented, and evaluated strategic plan, include: identifying the nature and scope of the business problem(s) facing an organization; examining the strengths, weaknesses, opportunities, and threats (SWOT) of an organization; formulating the organization's ideal vision; identifying organizational problems and needs; comparing current performance results with desired results in order to ascertain performance gaps; identifying an organizational mission; identifying organizational values and guiding principles; filtering an organization's ideal vision through its mission, values, and guiding principles; establishing organizational goals and objectives; developing action plans that bring about lasting, meaningful change; locating places within the organization where readiness for change is acute; conducting reality testing activities to make certain that strategic plans are attainable and practical; implementing strategic plans in a timely, efficient manner; establishing a formal feedback system that gathers immediate reactions from decision-makers and employees; conducting formative and summative evaluations as a way of determining the overall success of a strategic plan; and implementing continuing revisions to make certain that the strategic plan achieves its desired ends. These characteristics combine to make up five independent but interrelated phases of the strategic planning process: scoping, analyzing, visualizing, planning, and implementing and evaluating. Each will be examined in greater detail later in this chapter.

WHY IS STRATEGIC PLANNING IMPORTANT?

Some believe strategic planning is as much a process as it is a plan (Gilley & Coffern, 1994; Simerly, 1987). Many organizations view strategic planning as a once-a-year activity done to formulate well-written and well-meaning mission statements that, sadly, are quickly forgotten in the heat of organizational competition. When strategic planning is treated in this manner it is not part of the organization's management philosophy. Strategic planning should be a minute-by-minute, day-by-day process of planning and managing financial, material, and human resources. Furthermore, it should be used as a tool to help organizations maintain viability. In short, the strategic planning process provides a vehicle to improve current and future organizational effectiveness.

When organizations employ strategic planning to develop a common purpose for their employees, the results are improved and enhanced communications, organizational culture, and performance. Strategic planning provides a snapshot of currently available opportunities, as well as a way of identifying barriers that impede performance. This information can help organizational leaders make better, more informed decisions.

HRD professionals can benefit from the strategic planning process in several ways. First, participating can help improve HRD's credibility within the organization and will provide opportunities to develop strategic business partnerships (see Chapter 5). Second, HRD professionals benefit by demonstrating a willingness to listen to clients and to help them solve challenging problems. Third, understanding of the organization is improved by working with departments, divisions, and units with whom they previously had no access. Fourth, an attitude of continuous improvement and change within the organization is fostered by implementing ongoing strategic planning activities. Fifth, strategic planning activities enable HRD professionals to develop two critical performance part-nerships—management development (see Chapter 6) and organi-zational development (see Chapter 7). Sixth, strategic planning serves as a mechanism for executing the organizational effective-ness strategy discussed in Chapter 3. Seventh, HRD professionals can help the organization formulate a long-term decision-making plan—one that has the approval and blessing of senior manage-ment—designed to foster change within the organization.

In many ways, strategic planning is a team-building activity be-cause it forces loose confederations of individuals to collectively an-alyze the organization's culture, identify its mission, develop orga-nizational goals and objectives, and select action plans for change. Perhaps the best definition, then, of the strategic planning process is that it helps organizations identify and keep in focus its primary objective, which is continuous organizational improvement.

HOW STRATEGIC PLANNING DIFFERS
FROM NEEDS ASSESSMENT

Strategic planning and needs assessment are quite different proc-esses; however, they use many of the same strategies and tech-niques to identify gaps between current and desired results. The primary difference between the two may be best understood by ex-amining their end products. In the case of needs assessment, the final product is the identification of skills, knowledge, or attitudes that employees are currently deficient in. Consequently, interven-tions are designed to provide these individuals with the necessary skills, knowledge, or attitudes to improve performance. While stra-tegic planning uses an analysis process similar to that of needs as-sessment, its primary product is the identification of gaps in busi-ness results that prevent the organization from operating in an effective manner. Also, strategic planning can be conducted at two different levels. According to Kaufman, Rojas, and Mayer (1992), strategic planning aimed at the micro level is concerned with the quality of an organization's deliverables that are used by internal clients. Therefore, microstrategic planning is designed to improve the internal operations of an organization (organizational perfor-mance). Macrostrategic planning is concerned with the quality of an organization's deliverables to external clients. It is essentially de-signed to improve organizational effectiveness.

While HRD professionals have long been used to identify per-formance needs within an organization, they have seldom been allowed to participate in micro- and macrostrategic planning activities. This is the result of the old philosophy of HRD—that is, training for training's sake. In order to create strategically integrated programs, attention must be focused on strategic planning activities that are designed to improve the internal and external operations of an organization. We do not wish to minimize the importance of needs assessments as it serves a useful function within an organization; however, HRD professionals must understand the differences between needs assessment and strategic planning, then make decisions accordingly.

GENESIS OF STRATEGIC PLANNING

Marketing professionals maintain that all products, services, and ideas have a distinct beginning. This is also the case for strategic planning within organizations. According to Gilley and Boughton (1996), every organization faces four different types of environmental conditions: overconfidence, growth, equilibrium, and crisis.

Overconfidence is a condition where the perceived reality greatly exceeds results. This leads managers and executives to believe they are invincible. In this type of environment, organizational leaders are not receptive to new ideas or ways of improving organizational performance and effectiveness. Equilibrium, on the other hand, is a period in organizational life like that of a calm lake in early morning. Actual and needed results are mirror reflections of each other. During this time, new ideas and innovations are often resisted as unnecessary—after all, why rock the boat? There is a strongly held belief that managers and executives are satisfied with the organization's position and future. Growth is marked by a period in which today's results are not considered adequate to sustain future operations. In other words, a discrepancy exists between desired results and today's reality. During this time, all organizational activities are focused on closing this gap, and most managers and executives are receptive to new and innovative ideas for improving organizational performance and effectiveness. Crisis conditions are marked by organizational results that are significantly below those needed to sustain current levels of operation. This period entails extreme stress and anxiety for all members of the organization. During a crisis, managers and executives desperately seek ways to dramatically improve organizational performance and effectiveness.

During periods of overconfidence and equilibrium, strategic planning activities are not generally accepted with open arms by executives and senior managers, since no need is perceived. Growth and crisis situations force vastly different attitudes on senior managers, urging them to pursue solutions to performance problems and inefficiencies with a vengeance. Strategic planning activities, then, are ideally suited for organizations facing these two conditions. Though some argue that strategic planning is an effective process regardless of the economic conditions challenging an organization, most organizations resist until they are feeling the heat of their indecisiveness.

HRD professionals must develop organizational awareness skills sufficient to identify the economic conditions facing them. In this way, they will be better able to identify opportunities for implementing strategic planning activities. Strategic planning need not be an organization-wide activity. It can also be designed to improve internal organizational performance at the micro level. HRD professionals should resist the temptation to limit strategic planning to an organizational restructuring tactic. By embracing this philosophy, more opportunities to participate in strategic planning will present themselves.

FIVE PHASES OF STRATEGIC PLANNING

As stated previously, the strategic planning process consists of five separate but interrelated phases, which include scoping, analyzing, visualizing, planning, and implementing and evaluating (see Figure 4.1).

Scoping

The strategic planning process begins by identifying the important issues facing an organization. During this phase, HRD professionals try to determine the nature of conditions facing the organization. Since strategic planning can occur at the micro or macro levels, this should be specified and understood in order to accurately focus activities. Gilley and Coffern (1994) approach this phase with the question, "Where is the pain?" They believe the scoping process is designed to ascertain if a real problem exists—not unlike that of a physician determining the exact cause of an ailment by examining the symptoms of a patient.

One of the sources of confusion during the scoping phase is the lack of a generally accepted, useful, and substantive definition of the problem. Simply put, a problem is a gap between a current set

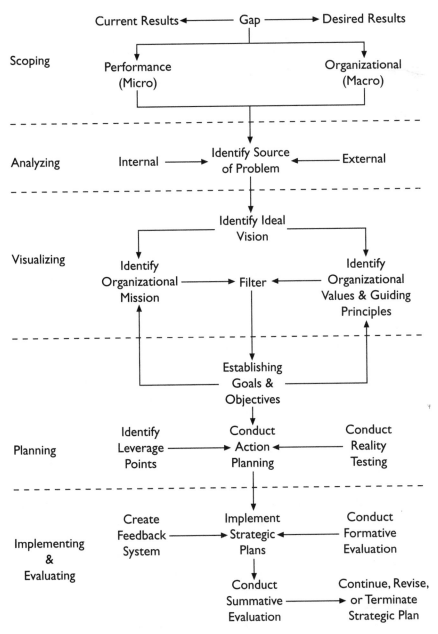

Figure 4.1   Strategic Planning Process

of circumstances and the desired set of circumstances. That is, a problem exists when there is a difference between what is and what should be. This simple but clear definition can be used when examining individual or organizational performance. The scoping phase is complete when a gap has been identified—which serves as justification for the ensuing strategic planning process.

Analyzing

The second phase of the strategic planning process involves conducting an analysis of the internal and external environments of the organization. During this phase, HRD professionals must evaluate the strengths and weaknesses (internal environment) and the opportunities and threats (external environment) facing the organization. Another purpose of the analysis phase is to determine which contingencies will help an organization carry out its mission and which will hinder it. Based on this analysis, HRD professionals can help the organization make adjustments that compensate for weaknesses and threats, while at the same time finding means to help the organization build on strengths and capitalize on opportunities.

Internal Environment

Examination of the internal environment allows for identification of the organization's strengths and weaknesses, which obviously affects execution of its mission. When examining the internal environment, a number of areas must be considered. These include: the organization's financial condition; managerial aptitudes and abilities; current organizational facilities; quality of technology; quantity and quality of material resources; quantity and quality of human resources; departmental and division images; organizational structure; culture; work climate; policies and procedures; managerial practices; organizational mission and strategy; leadership; job and work design; the organization's learning system; its compensation and reward system; the performance appraisal process; and the performance coaching process.

Once these areas have been examined, HRD professionals should describe each relationship in terms of its strengths and weaknesses. It is recommended that several data collection methods be used when conducting such an analysis (i.e., questionnaires, interviews, observations, and focus groups). Combining methodologies ensures a more accurate picture of the internal state of the organization. Gathered data can be used to better allocate material, financial, and human resources in the execution of an organization's goals, objectives, and mission.

Several questions should be asked as a way of determining the strengths and weaknesses of an organization:

1. What is the financial condition of the organization?
2. What are the aptitudes and abilities of managers and employees?

3. What is the current condition of facilities?
4. What is the current state and quality of technology?
5. What is the quantity and quality of material resources?
6. What is the quantity and quality of human resources?
7. What are the current images of various departments and their visions?
8. How is the organization structured?
9. Describe the company's culture.
10. Describe the work climate within the organization.
11. Identify policies and procedures that improve or impede organizational performance and effectiveness.
12. Describe managerial practices within the organization.
13. Describe organizational leadership.
14. Identify the organization's mission and strategy.
15. Describe the job and work design.
16. Describe the learning system.
17. Describe the compensation and reward system.
18. Describe the performance appraisal process.
19. Describe the current usefulness of performance coaching within the organization.

External Environment

External environmental analyses identify the long-term conditions facing the organization and encompass several important variables, including: current economic condition; the legal and political environment; social and cultural values; resource availability; the organization's competitive rank; image in the marketplace; and performance and organizational gaps.

This information reveals the economic health of an organization, its values, political climate, use of technology and resources, competitive rank within its industry, overall image, and areas requiring improvement. Each category provides a wealth of information useful in making decisions regarding the allocation of material, financial, and human resources. Once HRD professionals have identified opportunities and/or constraints challenging the organization, they are armed with information critical to long-term viability. External analysis also provides information regarding the critical financial and human resources available for expansion and growth.

In order to remain viable in the marketplace, many organizations need to maintain aggressive research and development programs. An external environmental analysis helps identify the opportunities and threats facing an organization in a given industry, vis-à-vis the amount, type, and quality of technology needed to remain competitive. With the continued escalation of technology, such an analysis will be extremely important to the long-term competitiveness of most organizations and, ultimately, their long-term success.

The following questions will aid an organization in its examination of the external environment:

1. What are the economic conditions of the nation, region, and local community?
2. What social and cultural values predominate within the industry and its geographic locations?
3. What quantity and quality of technology does the organization employ to ahieve its business results?
4. What external financial, material, and human resources are available?
5. What is the organization's image in the marketplace?
6. What is the company's competitive rank within the industry?
7. What performance gaps exist within the organization?
8. What organizational effectiveness gaps exist?

Visualizing

Visualization helps the organization do three things: identify an ideal organizational vision; create a mission; and develop values and guiding principles.

Identifying Ideal Vision

Senior managers and executives must identify the type of organization to be developed. One way is to create an ideal vision of what the organization should look like in the future. An ideal vision depicts the "perfect" future for the organization. This exercise is designed to look at the best-case scenario rather than practical realities. The ideal vision becomes the target upon which the organization focuses its collective energy. It is a form of commitment to its employees and customers. According to Kaufman, Rojas, and Mayer (1992), without an "ideal," an organization might limit itself to the easily achievable, although not necessarily desirable, future. With an "ideal," organizations will stretch toward a continuously improving future. An ideal vision is not academic but practical (Senge, 1990).

Many organizational leaders are reluctant to identify an ideal vision, believing they will be forced to achieve it. But the process of striving will produce benefits far greater than the failure to establish an aggressive target. An ideal vision will help an organization determine what it will deliver and commit to, which in turn promotes organizational mission, goals, and objectives. By identifying an ideal vision and comparing it with current results, performance and organizational needs can be identified. By comparing these needs with those identified during the scoping phase, similarities and differences are isolated. The more similar needs are, the more focused the strategic planning process will become. Differences may indicate a failure to conduct an appropriate initial analysis.

Creating Organizational Mission

Developing an organizational mission can be a soul-searching, time-consuming process. Each member of the organization has an opportunity to contribute to the creation of the mission as each must ultimately agree with and support it. A well-defined mission gives everyone within the company a sense of purpose, direction, significance, and achievement. According to Kotler (1992), an organizational mission acts as an invisible hand that guides widely scattered employees, working independently yet collectively, toward the organization's goals.

By identifying an organizational mission, HRD professionals give the company a sense of purpose and direction. According to Gilley and Coffern (1994), an organizational mission statement can help organize employees within the organization around a common outcome; serve as a guide to help organizational leaders in decision-making; focus roles and responsibilities; communicate types of changes necessary to improve profitability, competitiveness, and effectiveness; and serve as a guide in developing goals and objectives.

An organizational mission specifies targets achievable within a specific time frame. While vision describes what an organization *would like* to accomplish ideally, a mission statement clearly specifies *what can* be accomplished measurably as an organization moves systematically toward the ideal (Kaufman, Rojas, & Mayer, 1992).

Simerly (1987) provides guidelines for writing a mission statement: (1) a mission statement should never be stated only in financial terms; (2) a mission statement should set a future direction for the organization; (3) a mission statement should be clear and concise in order to appeal to as wide a constituency as possible; (4) a mission statement should have an inspirational quality to it (p. 17).

HRD professionals should use the following questions when helping organizations develop mission statements:

1. Is the mission statement long-term oriented?
2. What role will departments and divisions play in achieving the organization's mission?
3. Has the mission been communicated to all employees?
4. Is the mission clear, concise, and easily understood?
5. Is the mission written for employees as well as customers?
6. Does the mission support the values and guiding principles of the organization?
7. Have organizational members been given the opportunity to participate in the development of the mission?

Developing Organizational Values and Guiding Principles

Identifying organizational values and guiding principles is critical as they directly influence people's behavior. During this phase of the strategic planning process, HRD professionals should help the organization identify the most important feelings, beliefs, and attitudes of employees, managers, and executives. A composite of these values make up organizational culture.

Organizational culture is, perhaps, the most powerful internal force affecting the behavior of an organization. Culture defines expectations about behavior, how work is done, how decisions are made, how social interactions are structured, and how people communicate (Simerly, 1987, p. 16). In order for strategic plans to be effectively implemented, organizational values and guiding principles must be identified. Strategic plans inconsistent with the organization's values and guiding principles stand little chance of success. It is best to consider these as tools that help direct organizational decision-making.

Another component of organizational values and guiding principles is the role leaders play in developing and keeping organizational culture. According to Simerly (1987), one of the chief characteristics of high-performance organizations is that they have strong organizational cultures driven by a central core of values and guiding principles shared by employees. He also believes that successful leaders in high-performance organizations spend considerable time discussing and reinforcing organizational culture. These leaders are successful in monitoring and scanning the organizational environment as a way of demonstrating accountability and responsiveness to their major constituents.

HRD professionals can identify the organization's values and guiding principles by interviewing a cross-section of employees, managers, and executives within the organization. Interviews should include a large number of organizational leaders in order to gain insights about the culture's evolution and its operation in the present environment. While interviewing, it is important to identify the role of organizational leadership as well as outside influences that impact the company's values and guiding principles.

Interviews should begin with a list of common questions asked of each employee, manager, or executive. However, it is just as important to provide these individuals with an opportunity to express their ideas and perspectives regarding those things they believe to be critical to the development of organizational culture. So HRD professionals should provide for open dialogue. This two-phased interviewing approach enables the gathering of as much information as possible regarding values and guiding principles, while maintaining consistency from one person to another. This approach allows individuals to express themselves in greater detail.

The following questions may be used in identifying organizational values and guiding principles:

1. What are the guiding principles of the organization?
2. What behavioral expectations do managers have of their employees?
3. What performance expectations do managers have of their employees?
4. What behavioral expectations do employees have of their managers?
5. Do managers and supervisors provide specific, meaningful, and timely feedback?
6. Do managers and supervisors encourage employee participation in problem-solving and decision-making?
7. Do managers and supervisors have a "desire" to communicate with employees?
8. Is upward communication encouraged within the organization?
9. What role do leaders play in determining or maintaining organizational culture?
10. Do employees and managers feel that their work "makes a difference"?
11. Do employees and managers feel that the organization positively rewards their efforts?
12. Does the organization reward process or task orientations?
13. Does the organization reward long-term solutions?
14. Does the organization reward entrepreneurship?

15. Does the organization reward performance improvement and quality efforts?
16. Does the organization reward teamwork and cooperation?
17. Are employees valued and appreciated by the organization?
18. What is the relationship between employees and managers?
19. How are decisions made within the organization?
20. Does the organization encourage employees' and managers' recommendations regarding performance improvement?

Each of these questions can help HRD professionals identify employees' perceptions concerning the work process, performance improvement criteria, quality issues, and interpersonal interactions—thus, the organization's values and guiding principles.

Planning

As we stated earlier, planning is a very important component as it helps an organization identify where it wants to go. During the planning phase, HRD professionals must help the organization establish its strategic goals and objectives; conduct and establish action planning; identify leverage points where change can be implemented; and conduct reality testing to determine the practicality of the strategic plan.

Goals and Objectives

Once HRD professionals have analyzed the strengths, weaknesses, opportunities, and threats facing the organization, have identified an ideal vision and organizational mission, and have ascertained organizational values and guiding principles, it is time to begin developing strategic goals and objectives. Goals and objectives differ from mission statements in that mission statements suggest from where the organization is coming, while goals and objectives indicate where the organization is going (Gilley & Eggland, 1989).

A strategic goal is a large, generalized statement that indicates an organization's future direction. Generally, a goal statement should be broad enough that it cannot be easily measured in terms of time and space, though also short and easily understandable. Goal statements should be one or two sentences that describe where the organization is headed. An objective, on the other hand, is a subset of a goal. The characteristics of an objective are that it can be: (1) measured in time and space; (2) delegated to someone for implementation; and (3) assigned a deadline for completion (Simerly, 1987). In other words, strategic planning involves establishing goals and then developing specific objectives to achieve each goal.

The strategic goals and objectives of an organization can vary from year to year, depending on the problems and issues facing the company. The purpose of each goal and objective, however, is to carry out the broader mission of the organization while keeping its values and guiding principles. Gilley and Coffern (1994) believe that organizations that do not filter their strategic goals and objectives through their mission, values, and guiding principles will find themselves off course, and will realize they are engaged in activities they were not intended or qualified to do (p. 102). In fact, the most frequently made errors in writing mission statements are: (1) not providing specific and measurable objectives to achieve goals, and (2) not developing feedback mechanisms that regularly monitor people's progress (Simerly, 1987).

Strategic goals help organizations decide where they are headed, whereas objectives identify how the goal is to be implemented. Without specific objectives, goals remain only idealized visions that fail to be realized.

Strategic goals and objectives should be written in a way that helps employees, managers, and executives focus on achieving the overall company mission while creating commitment and agreement on how targets will be met. Effectively written goals and objectives should satisfy five characteristics. They should be specific, measurable, agreed upon, realistic, and timely. In other words, they should be S.M.A.R.T.

S.M.A.R.T. Criteria

Specific: Strategic goals and objectives should be specific, well-defined, and clear, so that anyone with basic knowledge of the organization can read and understand them, and know what they are trying to do.

Measurable: Every strategic goal and objective must be measured. Some recommended standards that can be used in measuring any goal or objective are quantity, quality, time, and cost.

Agreed upon: Members of the organization must agree on the strategic goals and objectives. The more agreement and clarification reached up front, the easier it will be to develop an action plan designed to improve organizational effectiveness. Agreement also makes it easier to respond to changes that may need to occur during implementation of the strategic plan.

Realistic: All too often organizations set goals and objectives that are impossible to achieve given the resources and time available. Unrealistic goals and objectives only set the organization up for frustration and failure. Making goals and objectives realistic may mean adjusting the goal, deadline, or resources.

Timely: All strategic goals and objectives must be tied to a timetable. While this may be difficult when writing the goals, it is an important criteria because at some point the strategic goals must be achieved. It may be more appropriate to identify a general time and date for completion, but, nevertheless, a deadline should be established.

Written: All strategic goals and objectives should be written. This will help organizations better articulate desired outcomes that, in turn, will focus energies during economically difficult, stressful periods. Written goals and objectives communicate commitment to their completion, which encourages organizational members to reciprocate.

The following questions will assist HRD professionals when writing strategic goals and objectives:

- What are the organization's primary, short-term business needs?
- What does the organization wish to accomplish in the next few years?
- Where does the organization want to be in five years, ten years, and beyond?
- What is the HRD program's role and responsibility in helping the organization achieve its strategic business goals and objectives?

Conduct Action Planning

An essential part of strategic planning is the creation of an action plan to be utilized when implementing all strategic goals and objectives. Action plans address two basic issues: (1) What are the possible problem areas in implementing the strategic plan?; (2) How will new strategies be developed if the primary plan falters? Several important points must be considered when developing this phase of the strategic plan. How will the comprehensive plan be implemented? Who will be in charge of its implementation? What is the basic time table for implementation? How will the plan's success be measured (Simerly, 1987)?

An action plan "drives" the strategic planning process and thus is critical to its success (Gilley & Coffern, 1994). In turn, the steps involved in creating an action plan are driven by the strategic goals and objectives.

Identify Leverage Points

There are certain points in the organization where change is more likely to succeed. Change should be introduced at these penetration points and be allowed to spread to the rest of the organization over time. Gilley and Eggland (1989) refer to them as areas of organizational readiness, or leverage points. Either these points are most receptive to change or they possess the ability to influence others to accept change. It is extremely important for HRD professionals to identify these entry points as this is where the organization should focus its attention when implementing change.

Conduct Reality Testing

When creating a strategic plan, HRD professionals may become so future oriented and visionary that they lose touch with everyday reality. In order to prevent the strategic planning process from becoming an academic, theoretical, and unrealistic nightmare, it is important to answer the following question: Are the strategic goals and objectives realistic and attainable given the practical constraints and organizational barriers present today? As HRD professionals answer this question, they are engaging in a process known as reality testing.

During reality testing, the following questions should be kept in mind:

- What financial, material, and human resources does the organization need to accomplish its strategic goals, objectives, and mission?
- If needed resources do not exist, how can they be acquired?
- Who can help acquire necessary resources?
- What barriers will prevent the organization from achieving its strategic goals, objectives, and mission?
- How do organizations overcome these barriers?
- How do organizations deal with conflict during implementation of the strategic plan?

- Does the organization need to rethink or rework the strategic plan?
- Does the organization need to rethink or rework the action plan?

Gilley and Coffern (1994, p. 106) believe that "the reality testing phase is the last opportunity for the organization to modify their strategic goals, objectives, and mission before implementing the strategic plan." Therefore, it is absolutely crucial that HRD professionals conduct reality tests of the strategic plan prior to implementation. Testing will help ensure success.

Implementing and Evaluating

Strategic planning, while undeniably beneficial, remains a difficult process to implement given the many players and constraints involved. The following ten recommendations will assist in successful implementation:

1. Obtain high-level management support for the implementation of the strategic plan.
2. Create organizational readiness for implementing the plan.
3. Create an implementation committee responsible for guiding the process.
4. Allocate an appropriate amount of time for implementing the plan.
5. Monitor implementation.
6. Remain flexible during implementation.
7. Manage high-level conflict when it occurs.
8. Support the total concept of strategic planning.
9. Reward participants.
10. Establish the philosophy that strategic planning is a continuous process.

These guidelines will help HRD professionals in two ways. First, they will help successfully implement the strategic plan. Second, they will serve as a constant reminder that strategic planning is not complete until it has been successfully implemented and change has occurred within the organization. HRD professionals should not take anything for granted—strategic planning can be ordered or abandoned at any point in the process. Implementation is "where the rubber meets the road," and HRD professionals should always guard against the possibility that strategic plans could be compromised.

Feedback System

To improve implementation of the strategic plan, a feedback system should be created. Feedback systems provide information about the success or failure of the plan, which helps in designing future strategic plans that are better suited to realizing desired results.

One means of developing a feedback system is to seek answers to the following questions:

- How will people be rewarded for reaching the organization's strategic goals?
- How will employees celebrate when the organization has achieved its strategic goals?
- How will feedback be reported or measured?
- Can a feedback system be designed to assist in developing strategic plans?
- How will the organization measure progress of strategic plans?
- What alternative plans are available if the original strategic plan fails?

Conduct Formative and Summative Evaluations

At the completion of all strategic planning activities, formative and summative evaluations—which differ in their purpose and intent—provide feedback that is crucial for the successful implementation of the plan. Furthermore, they capture the ultimate outcomes produced by the strategic plan. Evaluation should be a developmental, that is, formative activity. Formative evaluations provide feedback during implementation of the plan and facilitate choosing from among possible modifications. Formative evaluations should be used as a basis for constructively modifying the strategic planning effort and making reccmmendations for future implementations. These evaluations are not simply the basis for keeping the strategic plan alive while alternatively completing the process, but aid HRD professionals in the implementation of the strategic plan. Summative evaluations, on the other hand, are geared to assess the overall outcomes of the strategic planning effort, and to make decisions to either continue, revise, or terminate the activity. This type of evaluation should not be conducted for at least three to six months after the strategic plan has been implemented, otherwise the full impact of the strategic plan will not be known.

Continue, Revise, and/or Terminate

After completion of the strategic planning process, HRD professionals must help the organization proceed in one of three ways. First, the organization can elect to continue the strategic planning process on an ongoing basis. Second, the organization can opt to revise the strategic plan and make modifications deemed appropriate or necessary. Modifications may be made in any of the component areas of the strategic plan, including the company's ideal vision. Third, the organization may decide to terminate the strategic planning process due to failure to accomplish its ultimate aims. Regardless of how the organization elects to proceed, the strategic planning process, to be successful, must help the organization achieve its primary goal: to reduce the discrepancy between current and desired results.

CONCLUSION

Strategic planning helps an organization accomplish desired goals and objectives during a specific period of time. As much a philosophy as it is a plan, strategic planning should not be a one-time event, but, rather, an ongoing activity within the organization. In some organizations, the principal benefit derived from strategic planning is participating in the process itself. Employees, managers, and organizational leaders engage in unique dialogue designed to improve the viability of the organization. Organizational readiness for change is enhanced far greater than by any other type of activity or intervention created by HRD professionals. Consequently, strategic planning is the quintessential organizational effectiveness strategy of choice. HRD professionals would be wise to embrace, encourage, and implement strategic planning within the organization whenever possible.

PART III

Creating Performance Partnerships

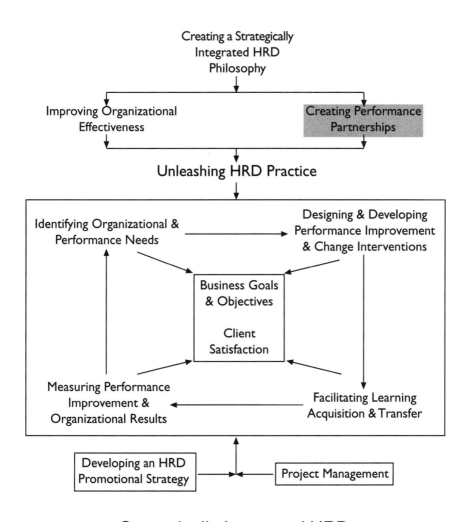

Creating a Strategically
Integrated HRD
Philosophy

Improving Organizational
Effectiveness

Creating Performance
Partnerships

Unleashing HRD Practice

Identifying Organizational &
Performance Needs

Designing & Developing
Performance Improvement
& Change Interventions

Business Goals
& Objectives

Client
Satisfaction

Measuring Performance
Improvement &
Organizational Results

Facilitating Learning
Acquisition & Transfer

Developing an HRD
Promotional Strategy

Project Management

Strategically Integrated HRD

CHAPTER 5

Developing Strategic Business Partnerships

Strategic business partnerships are intraorganizational alliances formed to ensure successful completion of the company's overall strategic plan. As such, members are drawn from any and all departments impacting organizational goals and objectives. Realistically, no division is exempt.

Historically, few HRD professionals succeed in forging strategic alliances within their companies. These professionals lack credibility as they are not viewed as vital, contributing members of the organization. Some HRD programs falter because they are not based on the needs of the organization or are not results oriented. Still others fail because HRD professionals do not properly communicate the value and benefits of their interventions and consulting services to decision-makers within the organization.

While these are all contributing factors, most HRD programs fail because clients' business and performance needs are not satisfied. Consequently, HRD is not perceived as important. When clients do not believe HRD programs can or will help them improve their performance, quality, efficiency, or productivity, these services will not be viewed as essential to accomplishing the strategic goals and objectives of the organization.

What can HRD professionals do to prevent negative perceptions of their programs? One way is to develop strategic business partnerships, which are defined as mutually beneficial relationships created to help the organization better achieve its goals and objectives. Such relationships are synergistic by design. The principal benefit for clients is improved performance, while HRD professionals will enjoy increased credibility within the organization.

Developing strategic business partnerships throughout the organization is a five-step process that affords HRD professionals the opportunity to build long-term alliances that strive to maximize organizational objectives. The steps in developing strategic business partnerships are:

1. create a customer service strategy
2. audit HRD interventions and consulting services in order to identify their values and benefits
3. develop collaborative client relationships
4. help clients make performance improvement and organization development decisions
5. identify demand states facing clients and respond accordingly

Each of these steps enables HRD professionals to move closer to being accepted as equal business partners within the organization—a status long overdue and much deserved.

WHY ARE STRATEGIC BUSINESS PARTNERSHIPS IMPORTANT?

We believe that creating strategic business partnerships is one of the most important activities in which HRD professionals may engage. Alliance building allows HRD professionals to develop mutually beneficial, empathic relationships with their clients, resulting in client satisfaction and achievement of objectives. Strategic business partnerships are long-term and interdependent, allowing HRD professionals to better understand and anticipate their clients' needs. These partnerships help HRD professionals develop the responsive attitude necessary for them to become customer service-oriented.

When HRD professionals become strategic business partners, they begin breaking down the walls between themselves and their clients. Lasting commitments are forged, investments are made in learning, and discoveries made of everything pertinent about clients, clients' customers, and their departments. Consequently, HRD professionals become immersed in their clients' performance problems, needs, concerns, and expectations. Strategic business partnerships encourage them to fully understand their clients' contributions, as well as the values they bring to an interaction. Hopefully, an exchange of values will result.

Strategic business partnerships enable HRD professionals to develop personal relationships that foster trust and honesty. Alliances allow HRD professionals and clients to develop a shared vision of the future through a free exchange of ideas, information, and perceptions. Strategic business partnerships also promote the establishment of working relationships based on shared values, aligned purposes and visions, and mutual support. According to Wilson (1987), strategic business partnerships allow people to develop five basic values:

1. trust—honest exchange devoid of hidden agendas
2. accountability—personal responsibility for the partnership
3. support—commitment to giving and receiving support
4. truth—honest sharing of ideas and feelings
5. effort—commitment to the mission

Creating strategic business partnerships demonstrates HRD professionals' willingness to intimately know those they serve, as well as their ability to learn from clients. Furthermore, partnerships are based upon the business and performance needs of clients, not of the HRD program. Consequently, HRD professionals direct all efforts at satisfying their clients, including designing and developing performance improvement and change interventions in accordance with the client's expressed interests, as well as providing consulting activities that improve the organization and performance management systems.

Another compelling reason to create strategic business partnerships is to help HRD professionals establish credibility within the organization. Improved credibility results from HRD professionals' ability to demonstrate professional expertise as well as their understanding of organizational operations and culture. In this way, HRD professionals are able to provide real value to the organization.

Creating strategic business partnerships enables HRD professionals to address various demand states facing their programs. Demand is a term that describes the number of clients who have the capacity and willingness to exchange their time, effort, and commitment for an intervention or consulting service offered by HRD (Gilley & Eggland, 1992). Over time, demand will change for every intervention and consulting service offered. To be effective, then, HRD professionals must know how to identify ever-changing conditions and how to react. Creating strategic business partnerships improves HRD professionals' responses to client demands by altering their interventions and services.

Better management of limited financial and human resources is another reason for creating strategic alliances. In other words, partnerships help HRD professionals decide which interventions and consulting services provide the highest value and have the greatest impact on the organization. Armed with such information, HRD professionals are in a better position to appropriate resources that will maximize organizational performance and results.

Finally, creating strategic business partnerships produces economic utility, which is measured in terms of increased organizational performance, profitability, revenue, quality, or efficiency. Overall, strategic alliances afford HRD professionals and their clients opportunities to work in harmony for the purpose of improving the economic viability of the organization, and a healthy organization benefits everyone.

FIVE POINTS OF DEVELOPING STRATEGIC BUSINESS PARTNERSHIPS

There are five interdependent activities in which HRD professionals can engage when developing strategic business partnerships. Each will enhance HRD's credibility and acceptance within the organization, while helping clients meet their business and performance needs. Ultimately, the organization benefits via achievement of its strategic business goals and objectives.

Creating a Customer Service Strategy

Creating strategic business partnerships begins by developing a customer service strategy that establishes an HRD philosophy and approach to helping others achieve their objectives. HRD professionals who direct all their efforts at satisfying their clients are practicing good customer service. From this perspective, a customer service strategy is not used to manipulate clients but is focused on identifying and addressing clients' business and performance needs. Consequently, HRD interventions and consulting services are designed in accordance with the client's expressed interests, which helps assure that the HRD program is designed to maximize organizational performance. When interventions and consulting services are based on client needs, the HRD program will be supported and defended by clients during difficult economic periods. It will be viewed as essential to the long-term success of the organization.

Auditing HRD Interventions and Consulting Services

Once a customer service strategy has been developed, HRD professionals can begin auditing interventions and consulting services to determine their values and benefits. The primary purpose of this activity is to identify those interventions and consulting services that bring the greatest value and benefit to the organization. Once identified, HRD professionals are in a better position to determine whether their interventions and consulting services are helping their clients, and thus the organization, achieve their business and performance goals. Then, HRD professionals can create a promotional strategy designed to improve the image and credibility of the HRD program within the organization.

Developing Collaborative Client Relationships

This is the third step in creating strategic business partnerships. Collaborative client relationships are not superficial, but are based on a deep concern for the well-being of clients, and are established through the HRD professional's sincere interest in and acceptance of their clients.

A collaborative client relationship helps HRD professionals develop a positive working environment that enhances communication. Therefore, HRD professionals must be skilled in creating anticipatory communications, establishing positive environments, and overcoming client resistance to change.

HRD professionals also must create client exchanges that encourage open expressions of ideas and feelings, thereby creating an environment that fosters feelings of security. Clients will recognize that the lines of communication are open, increasing their willingness to discuss their business and performance problems with HRD professionals. Finally, a sharing environment is based on trust and honesty, reducing the chances of skepticism and cynicism (Gilley, 1996).

Helping Clients Make Decisions

HRD professionals have the responsibility of helping their clients make positive performance improvement or organizational development decisions. The primary outcome of this responsibility is the selection of HRD interventions and consulting services that help the organization achieve its business goals and objectives, as well as help clients meet their business and performance needs. The decision-making process consists of five steps, which are:

1. recognizing and prioritizing performance problems
2. gathering information
3. evaluating alternatives
4. selecting an alternative
5. evaluating the choice

Identifying Demand States

Clients participate in HRD interventions and use consulting services for a variety of reasons. Some interventions and consulting services are used frequently, while others are never utilized. Such variation in interest, perceptions, and usage is referred to as demand. In order to become strategic business partners, HRD professionals must become knowledgeable about the concept of demand and the various demand states facing their HRD programs. Based on this understanding, formative decisions can be made and appropriate customer service strategies identified and applied that will help HRD professionals become strategic business partners.

CREATING A CUSTOMER SERVICE STRATEGY

Establishing credibility is one of the central elements required when forming strategic business partnerships. Credibility is an HRD professional's lifeblood. If clients do not perceive them as credible, HRD professionals will never be able to earn their trust. As a way of establishing credibility, HRD professionals must have the skills and ability to solve client problems. Most importantly, they must be able to satisfy their clients' business and performance needs. When these attributes are present, HRD professionals can begin creating a customer service strategy.

Forming a customer service strategy involves six steps:

1. establishing a customer service philosophy
2. creating a customer service environment
3. creating customer service opportunities
4. implementing customer service
5. evaluating the utility and shortcomings of customer service

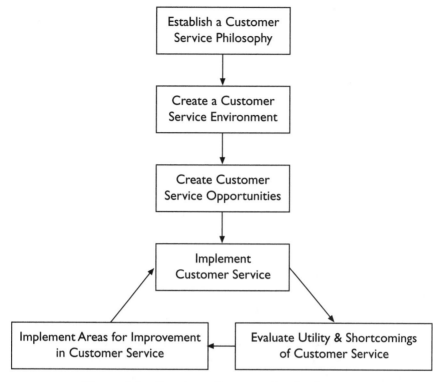

Figure 5.1 Creating a Customer Service Strategy

6. implementing areas for improvement in customer service (Figure 5.2)

Establishing a Customer Service Philosophy

Establishing a customer service philosophy requires HRD professionals to be willing to place the business and professional needs of their clients above their own. Such a philosophy also will require HRD professionals to improve and enhance the performance capacity of the organization. A customer service philosophy encourages HRD professionals to address performance problems and organizational issues in a collaborative and cooperative manner.

When a customer service philosophy has been established, HRD professionals are generally interested in enhancing people by improving their skills, knowledge, or behavior. Moreover, HRD professionals will be designing and developing HRD interventions and consulting services that are viewed by their clients as critical for accomplishing the organization's strategic business goals and objectives.

One of the best ways of establishing a customer service philosophy is for HRD professionals to participate in a personal reflection activity that allows them to be honest regarding their attitudes, beliefs, and feelings toward their clients. HRD professionals should write down why they are currently involved in the HRD profession. Once motives have been identified, they should try to isolate a central theme (e.g., to improve organizational performance, develop a more competitive organization, or ensure organizational profitability). With a central theme identified, HRD professionals are able to create a customer service environment that is designed to accomplish their professional mission.

Creating a Customer Service Environment

In order to develop a positive customer service environment, HRD professionals must become more participatory—a difficult concept to master as it requires the courage to relinquish control over clients. The participatory approach requires a departure from authoritative controls as it encourages client input. In addition to being less threatening, this active involvement on the client's part will yield support for mutual decisions.

The participatory approach requires HRD professionals to understand the importance of having a positive working relationship with their clients. Customers bring a great deal of experience to a situation, and are an invaluable resource to be acknowledged and tapped into. Unfortunately, HRD professionals sometimes fail to understand that clients can contribute a wealth of information that is beneficial in solving problems. Such recognition is indeed difficult but it is essential for developing a positive customer service environment.

Close examination reveals that certain key elements are fundamental in the development of an effective customer service environment. These ingredients—essential to the success of HRD professionals—include understanding and acceptance.

Understanding

Understanding is recognizing and correctly interpreting the feelings, thoughts, and behaviors of clients. Though HRD professionals cannot fully understand their clients, it can be said that understanding clients is essentially a process of sharing.

Acceptance

Acceptance is a basic attitude requiring respect for clients as persons of worth. HRD professionals demonstrate acceptance by allowing clients to differ from one another. This predisposition is based upon the belief that each client is a unique, complex person comprised of different experiences, values, and attitudes (Gilley, 1998).

Creating Customer Service Opportunities

A willingness to care and feel responsible for clients is called involvement. While acceptance and understanding are passive, involvement implies action—mandating active immersion in the clients' problems and needs. Only dynamic, involved HRD professionals will become agents of change. Customer service opportunities are created via face-to-face interaction, the result of unwavering dedication to client satisfaction.

Implementing Customer Service

Customer service requires involvement with clients by establishing rapport and encouraging face-to-face communications. Customer service implementation, a dynamic process, requires that HRD professionals become active participants with clients rather than passive observers. Exceptional customer service embodies ample questioning, listening, and facilitating skills that lead to viable recommendations and solutions.

Customer service is a series of one-to-one exchanges between HRD professionals and their clients. The purpose of each exchange is to solve problems, improve organizational performance, and improve business results (Gilley & Boughton, 1996).

Evaluating Utility and Shortcomings of Customer Service

Any good customer service strategy includes a means for measuring success, which is how clients hold HRD professionals accountable for their actions. In this way, HRD professionals are constantly receiving feedback from clients regarding satisfaction. Feedback is not merely a superficial evaluation but is designed to identify the utility and shortcomings of customer service. It can be solicited in a variety of ways. First, HRD professionals can meet face-to-face with their clients to determine how effectively clients believe their needs are being met. Clients should be asked open-ended questions that allow them to reflect upon the values delivered to the organization by the HRD program. Second, a representative sampling of clients can be identified, assembled in a focus group of no greater than eight, and charged with the responsibility of determining whether or not the HRD program is achieving its desired objectives. Such an analysis may produce a number of suggestions for improvement. As a result, HRD professionals can develop strategies to improve their customer service activities, interventions, and consulting services. Possible changes might include: (1) modified HRD interventions and consulting services to better meet the client's business and performance needs; (2) modified client perceptions of HRD interventions and consulting services; (3) improved responsiveness of HRD professionals and better quality in their deliverables.

Implementing Changes and Improvements in Customer Service

HRD professionals cannot exhibit their capacity to be strategic business partners unless they are willing to implement continuous improvement, such as in customer service. These changes should be made in concert with the evaluation previously conducted. In this way, customer service is always based upon the feedback received from clients. Ultimately, a customer service strategy will become the guiding principle that directs all HRD professionals' decisions and actions.

AUDITING HRD INTERVENTIONS AND CONSULTING SERVICES

One of the best ways of developing strategic business partnerships is to identify and audit the HRD program, its interventions, consulting services, and professionals. An audit is performed to identify the values and benefits of HRD interventions and consulting services, and to determine if these services are helping their clients and, thus, the organization to meet or exceed their goals. An audit should reveal the nature of HRD interventions and consulting services: their purpose, outcomes, and potential impact.

When conducting an audit, HRD professionals should select a representative sample of clients amenable to serving on a task force. The task force should be challenged to assess whether HRD meets the needs of its constituents, which may require interviews of executives, managers, and employees in order to determine the values and benefits of interventions and consulting services.

One of the positive outcomes of conducting an audit is that task force members can serve as internal ambassadors for the HRD program. Advocacy relationships are extremely difficult to cultivate, but once created can be invaluable in helping develop strategic business partnerships within the organization.

Identifying Values and Benefits

A working strategic business partnership involves the exchange of value between parties for interventions or services of equal or greater value. In HRD, interventions and consulting services are offered in exchange for time, energy, and personal commitment. Acceptable and favorable exchange occurs when the intervention or consulting service being offered is equal in value to the time, energy, and commitment returned by clients. If clients fail to perceive value that equals their time, energy, and commitment, they will not engage in the exchange. In other words, HRD professionals can create customer service opportunities by developing exchanges that clients believe exceed what they are giving up. In order for this to occur, HRD professionals must be skilled in planning and managing value exchanges with their customers (Gilley & Eggland, 1992).

During this phase, HRD professionals must identify the values and benefits that clients receive from their interventions and consulting services. Value statements should be developed that describe client rewards as a result of utilizing these interventions and consulting services. Value statements may be as simple as a sentence or two that describe the values and benefits clients glean from the transaction. This exercise helps clearly identify the positive values and benefits of HRD interventions and consulting services, and helps determine which offer the greatest merit within the organization.

Linking Values and Benefits with Strategic Goals

Once values and benefits have been identified, HRD professionals should determine whether their interventions and consulting services truly make a difference. Analysis of the values and benefits of each intervention and consulting service certifies their impact upon the organization's achievement of its strategic business goals. Those that help the organization accomplish its needed results should be promoted, while ineffective offerings should be discarded.

Comparing Values and Benefits with Client Business and Performance Needs

A parallel activity is determining if HRD interventions and consulting services help clients achieve their business and performance needs (which ultimately provides the foundation for organizational success). Again, HRD professionals should assess the values and benefits their interventions and consulting services deliver.

Prioritizing HRD Interventions and Consulting Services

Once beneficial interventions and consulting services have been identified, they must be prioritized in terms of value (impact on the department or organization). Later in this chapter we will explore several prioritization methods. Each of the methods helps HRD professionals create a list of interventions and consulting services that are of the greatest value and benefit to the organization and its clients.

Promoting HRD Interventions and Consulting Services

Many HRD professionals believe that promotion begins and ends with the development of a brochure that describes their programs. Nothing could be further from the truth. The purposes of promoting HRD interventions and consulting services are to inform, persuade, and remind clients of their values and benefits. A properly designed promotional strategy will accomplish these aims, solidify HRD's role as a strategic business partner, and enhance the image, visibility, effectiveness, and credibility of an HRD program (see Chapter 12).

DEVELOPING COLLABORATIVE
CLIENT RELATIONSHIPS

In order to develop strategic business partnerships, collaborative client relationships must be created. Because most HRD professionals are responsible for helping organizational members develop interpersonal communication skills, it is assumed that they have developed superior skills in this area as well. Unfortunately, few have ever been formally trained in interpersonal communications—most of their knowledge having been acquired through trial and error. Regardless, three areas of interpersonal communication are critical in developing strategic business partnerships. They are: (1) developing a participatory communications climate, (2) using interpersonal communication skills, and (3) overcoming client resistance.

Developing a Participatory Communications Climate

Development of a participatory communications climate requires a shift in managerial style for many HRD professionals, resulting in relinquished control over clients, which allows them to participate as equal partners. HRD professionals must recognize that clients bring a great deal of experience to the organization, and are a valuable resource to be acknowledged and tapped.

A participatory communications climate can only be developed when HRD professionals encourage a free exchange of ideas, opinions, and feelings. Clients benefit from this type of environment because they feel more secure, and can speak freely about issues affecting their business and performance needs. Such an environment is considered nonthreatening, comfortable, conducive to sharing, and even nurturing for client growth. A sharing environment goes beyond the superficial, demonstrates a deep concern for the well-being of clients, and is dedicated to the improvement of interpersonal relations (Gilley & Boughton, 1996).

Using Interpersonal Communication Skills

Once a positive communications climate has been established, several interpersonal communication skills are available that enhance client relationships. These skills help HRD professionals gather client information, communicate points of view, share feelings, understand their clients, and provide a moment of silence so that clients can gather their thoughts. These skills serve as a guide in the client relationship process.

Learning to be an effective strategic business partner is a difficult task for many HRD professionals. Our approach simplifies the learning process by focusing on three skill clusters that focus concentration on a set of skills, rather than on a single skill, which promotes more efficient learning. HRD professionals can concentrate on mastering one skill cluster at a time, experience rapid improvement in that area, then move to another cluster. When each of these three skill clusters are mastered, they may be integrated and applied in developing strategic business partnerships. The interpersonal communication clusters include: attending, following, and reflecting skills (Bolton, 1986).

Attending Skills

Used in building participatory communications climates, attending skills help HRD professionals direct their client's focus and attention. Attending skills include acceptance, attentiveness, nonverbal techniques, empathy, genuineness, rapport, and understanding.

Acceptance—is the basic attitude held toward clients and requires respect for clients as persons of worth.

Attentiveness—refers to the efforts made by HRD professionals to hear the messages communicated by clients. Active listening skills enable better understanding of the meanings of client messages and the feelings associated with them.

Nonverbal techniques—is essentially body language, including nods, gestures, eye contact, and shows of approval that encourage clients to communicate.

Empathy—is the ability to recognize, sense, and understand the feelings of clients. It is also the ability to accurately communicate this understanding to customers.

Genuineness—refers to HRD professionals' ability to be themselves in all situations, rather than playing a part or role.

Rapport—is the capability to establish meaningful relationships, to reach accord.

Understanding—acknowledges that HRD professionals never fully comprehend all of a client's issues; however, trying to understand them is one of the essential ingredients in establishing collaborative client relationships.

Following Skills

One of the primary tasks of HRD professionals is to discover the client's perceptions of the organization, their division, and other professional issues. Unfortunately, most HRD professionals interrupt and divert their clients by simply talking too much. So common is excessive speech during client interaction that conversation is monopolized. As a result, many are clueless as to their clients' thoughts or feelings. Following skills allow for refocusing on the client, and include active listening, encouraging, questioning, and silence.

Active listening—is a technique used in gathering client information through verbal and nonverbal cues. HRD professionals concentrate on verbal client messages, their corresponding meanings, and remain alert for nonverbal signals that support or deny what has been articulated. In short, "Shut up and listen."

Encouraging—enables clients to elaborate on their feelings and thoughts. Supportive remarks by HRD professionals such as,

"I understand," "It's OK to feel that way," "That's interesting, tell me more," or "I hear you," are useful when countering feelings of skepticism, doubt, or inadequacy.

Questioning—remains a common yet often misused or underused interpersonal communication technique. Open and closed questions reveal information or direct the conversation in a more constructive and informative manner.

Silence—is a somewhat difficult technique to master as it makes most people uncomfortable. The use of silence enables clients to think through what has transpired during the conversation, which allows them to share additional information or explanations if needed.

Reflective Skills

In order to develop collaborative client relationships, HRD professionals must respond reflectively to what their clients are saying. Reflection yields deeper understanding as HRD professionals attempt to mirror client messages in their own words. There are four basic reflecting skills: paraphrasing, clarifying, interpreting, and summarizing.

Paraphrasing—is used to test one's understanding of the client's basic message by restating it in his or her own words. Another purpose of paraphrasing is to communicate to clients that one is trying to understand their basic message.

Clarifying—is making statements that help one better understand the client's feelings and attitudes.

Interpreting—goes beyond the client's statements to explain cause and effect relationships and specify implications.

Summarizing—is a technique used to identify key points or ideas discussed during the conversation.

Each of these skill clusters can be employed by HRD professionals when helping clients make performance improvement and organizational development decisions. As a result, HRD professionals can gain insights that can help improve their relationships.

Overcoming Client Resistance

To foster development of strategic business partnerships, HRD professionals must learn how to manage clients' resistance to change.

"Resistance is predictable, natural, and a necessary part of the learning process" (Block, 1981, p. 113). Although resistance is common in every organization, many HRD professionals are stunned when it occurs, obviously preferring that it would never happen. Fortunately, resistance provides an opportunity for HRD professionals because it allows them to demonstrate their willingness to become strategic business partners.

When organizational change is proposed, whether encompassing changing of culture or reorganizing a department, people feel uncomfortable. As a result, they may express their discomfort indirectly, saying things like:

"The solution is impractical."
"We've done that before."
"We need more information before we can proceed."
"Your approach is wrong."
"I'm confused."
"The timing is off."
"It's not my fault, it's theirs."
"You're absolutely right."

Conversely, they can remain completely silent (Gilley, 1998). Regardless, sometimes clients do not openly express their real reasons for resisting change.

When change is proposed, clients often fear losing control, power, status, authority, or position. They also fear becoming vulnerable (Brock, 1981), although most are too afraid to admit it. In the face of change, many resist positive improvements because they fear the potential outcomes. The only solution to dealing with resistance is to understand the underlying reasons for it and learn how to address them.

Resistance Resolution Method

Resistance is simply the fear of losing one's current state. The resistance resolution method proves an effective tool for use by HRD professionals in addressing their clients' differing perspectives. This approach should be thought of as a set of skills that help HRD professionals govern conflict (Gilley, 1998). The objective of this method is to surface underlying fears that cause resistance so they may be addressed. The method consists of four steps: (1) acknowledging resistance, (2) clarifying resistance, (3) problem solving, and (4) confirming the answer (Gilley & Eggland, 1992).

Acknowledging Resistance Acknowledging resistance consists of two activities: listening and sharing. First, HRD professionals should listen carefully to clients' messages to determine their meaning. In fact, the very process of listening helps convert tension into words that serve to reduce anxiety, even if the words themselves do not actually reveal the nature of the tension or the reason for it.

The second activity involves sharing of feelings with clients. Sharing is a form of support. When HRD professionals demonstrate their understanding of clients' feelings and are not surprised or upset by negative statements, it illustrates their support, which helps reduce tension. To be successful in this stage, HRD professionals must remain calm and neutral, saying and doing nothing that will increase clients' tensions or fears.

Clarifying Resistance The second step is to clarify clients' thinking so they will be prone to receive new and logical information (Gilley & Eggland, 1992). Few clients are ready or willing to reveal the reasons for their behavior. "They learn to cover up the plausible reasons, explanations, and justifications all designed to prove that they're acting in a well thought out and logical manner" (Gilley & Boughton, 1996, pp. 160–61). There is a word that explains this thinking process: *rationalization* (Gilley, 1998).

The challenge facing HRD professionals is to learn how to make client statements lose force without making the clients lose face. When asked nonthreatening questions, clients are allowed to express their thoughts more freely, which clarifies their resistance. By encouraging clients to give examples and illustrations, HRD professionals are helping them grasp their own meaning more clearly.

Problem Solving Once HRD professionals have clarified client's resistance, they are ready to help clients identify solutions to their problems. A five-step problem-solving process is recommended. This includes identifying the problem, distinguishing solutions to the problem, analyzing the alternative solutions, selecting a viable remedy, and evaluating the solution (see below).

Confirming the Answer When an acceptable solution has been identified, clients must make a commitment—typically some kind of immediate action—that reinforces their willingness to accept the remedy. At this time, client feedback is essential in evaluating the continuing viability of the solution, and of the relationship in general.

HELPING CLIENTS MAKE PERFORMANCE IMPROVEMENT AND ORGANIZATIONAL DEVELOPMENT DECISIONS

Clients are challenged to make decisions every day. Sometimes these decisions are simple and routine, at other times they are difficult and complex. As a way of helping develop strategic business partnerships, HRD professionals must help their clients make effective performance improvement and organizational development decisions. To do so, it is important that HRD professionals understand the five essential steps of the decision-making process.

Step 1—Recognizing and Prioritizing Performance Problems

When clients decide to participate in HRD interventions or to use consulting services, they are doing so in order to solve a perceived business or performance problem. Therefore, the decision-making process begins when a performance problem has been recognized and prioritized.

A performance problem exists when there is a difference between the organization's current and its desired performance, often referred to as an organizational or performance need. A large gap between the two states can impact the productivity and efficiency of the organization. When companies consider possible corrective strategies for closing the gap, they are involved in decision-making.

Business and performance problems differ in the degree of seriousness and urgency. Some demand immediate action, while others require little more than identification. Each problem must be prioritized accordingly, which will help clients determine their involvement during the decision-making process.

Step 2—Gathering Information

Once HRD professionals have helped their clients recognize and prioritize performance problems, they can begin gathering information used in evaluating possible solutions. During this step, some clients are very active seeking information. Several sources may be utilized, such as professional journals, interviews with employees and users, direct inquiry into performance reviews, and personal contacts within the organization. Other clients adopt a more casual approach. A passive client seldom uses more than a few sources of information and will often rely on other organizational members' opinions when selecting appropriate HRD interventions and consulting services.

As clients move to more complex and important decisions, the amount and type of information gathered increases in complexity. When decisions are simple and straightforward, clients gather information randomly and routinely. These information gathering activities are of the simplest type, characterized by low client involvement and commitment. The decision to procure information is made quickly, with little effort or consideration. An example of this includes sending a new employee to an orientation training session to learn more about the organization. The primary responsibility of HRD professionals in this situation is to continually reinforce the value of their decisions by emphasizing their quality and usefulness.

A second type of decision situation is referred to as limited problem solving, which is more complex than random, routine decisions. When clients are faced with selecting an HRD intervention with which they are unfamiliar, they will engage in reasonably extensive information gathering prior to making a decision. Customers are trying to reduce risk by gathering additional information; therefore, HRD professionals must communicate the values and benefits of their services in order to alleviate client fears and concerns.

A third type of decision situation is referred to as extensive problem-solving. Decision-making reaches its greatest complexity when clients are unfamiliar with the impact of HRD's services on the organization. Considerable time and effort is spent searching for information. For example, selecting an organizational development intervention that can help create and enhance the organization's service quality falls into this category. Under these conditions, the intervention is often unknown to clients, so they spend many hours identifying the possible outcomes and impacts of the service. The HRD professional's role in this situation is to educate clients as to the importance, impact, and value of the intervention. In other words, they must reassure the client that the intervention is the best possible solution and will continue to help the organization achieve its business results.

Step 3—Evaluating Alternatives

The process of evaluating an HRD intervention or consulting service consists of five steps. First, possible alternatives, known as the *total set*, are identified. This list, which can be quite extensive, is divided into two categories: the *awareness set*—those interventions and consulting services with which clients are familiar; and the *unawareness set*—those with which they are not familiar. Since HRD professionals possess greater knowledge of their service offerings, they can help clients examine more closely those with which they are unfamiliar. Of the programs they are aware of, clients will want to consider a limited number, which represent the *consideration set*. Remaining services are relegated to an *infeasibility set*. Consideration set programs, subject to additional scrutiny, will generate only a limited number of interesting choices, which will constitute the *choice set*. Remainders are placed in the *non-choice* set. The final step is a careful evaluation of the *choice set*, followed by a selection that is referred to as the *decision* (Kotler, 1992).

Another way of evaluating HRD interventions and consulting services is by considering their different attributes. An attribute is defined as a characteristic or component of an intervention or service that separates it from another. Attributes can be prioritized by HRD professionals in one of three ways. First, each attribute may be assigned different values or weights. This is known as the *ranking method*. Second, via the *rating method*, each attribute may be ranked by using a predetermined scale. Finally, the total set of all attributes can be identified using a 100-point scale, a process known as the *constant sum method* (Gilley & Eggland, 1992).

According to Barry (1986), decision-makers, stakeholders, and influencers have available two models when comparing and evaluating attributes: compensatory and noncompensatory. When using a compensatory model, the weaknesses of one attribute can be compensated for by the strengths of other attributes. When applying the noncompensatory model, the weaknesses of one attribute cannot be offset by the strengths of another. In other words, each attribute must meet a minimum standard to be considered.

Step 4—Selecting an Alternative

For many clients the selection of HRD interventions and consulting services is merely the process of evaluating alternatives. Several factors influence the final selection, including attitudes of others, perceived risk, and anticipated and unanticipated organizational conditions (Kotler, 1992).

Attitudes of Others

If an HRD intervention or consulting service is not supported by members of the organization it will probably not be chosen. Furthermore, the intensity of negative attitudes and the type of client involved may also affect the process. For example, a decision-maker's (executive) opinion will carry more weight than a stakeholder's (user) or influencer's (technical advisor) since he or she possesses more power and authority within the company.

Perceived Risk

Clients face social, political, financial, and psychological risks when selecting HRD programs. In other words, clients are ultimately held accountable for decisions that impact their final choice, even if an intervention or consulting service appears to possess all of the appropriate attributes. Consequently, clients need assistance when considering the amount of risk they are willing to absorb in decision-making situations.

Anticipated and Unanticipated Organizational Factors

Anticipated organizational factors may include a department's budget, type of training provided, or the company's strategic business goals and objectives. Any HRD service chosen must fit into these well-identified constraints. Unanticipated organizational factors include a merger or restructuring that can shift the perceived focus of the company. These unforeseen events greatly impact the selection process.

Consideration as well as anticipation of organizational factors may be illustrated by providing information that will reinforce client decisions. Additionally, HRD professionals may serve as liaisons between various client groups as a means of reducing uncertainty and doubt about the organization's future.

Step 5—Evaluating the Choice

After a decision has been made, customers may have second thoughts leading to a condition known as post-decision dissonance, a tension caused by uncertainty about the rightness of a choice. They may wonder if another alternative would have been the better choice. This doubt may seriously undermine their selection.

Post-decision dissonance is more likely when: (1) HRD interventions and consulting services that were not selected have highly desirable attributes, (2) several desirable services were not chosen, or (3) the selection is irrevocable.

Most clients experience some level of satisfaction or dissatisfaction with their selections. The level of satisfaction is directly related to the client's expectations of the service chosen. If intervention or consulting service outcomes match expectations, the client will be satisfied. If, however, their selection fails to meet expectations, the client will be dissatisfied.

HRD professionals can help improve expectations by making certain that clients' performance outcomes are realistic and attainable. In fact, performance outcomes should be stated conservatively so as not to generate false hopes. As always, follow-up and feedback are important. HRD professionals should develop effective post-communication in order to reinforce client decisions. An abandoned client is a lost client. Finally, client progress and attitudes should be monitored to obtain an accurate picture of their perceptions of HRD interventions and services. To improve client satisfaction, negative feedback should be incorporated when redesigning interventions and consulting services.

IDENTIFYING DEMAND STATES

Client needs manifest themselves in a concept known as demand. In HRD, demand is defined as the degree to which people who have the capacity and willingness to exchange time, energy, and commitment desire an HRD service. Demand can vary for each intervention or consulting service offered.

HRD professionals respond to demand in one of three ways: (1) by accepting the client's requests and taking action, (2) by refusing to address the client's demand state, or (3) by analyzing the situation and determining its importance and seriousness.

Let us provide examples that illustrate each of these responses. An executive vice president of marketing for a property-casualty insurance company requests that customer service training be offered to her employees. What action can an HRD professional take? First, a response may include designing, developing, and implementing a performance improvement intervention that addresses the perceived need. This action demonstrates HRD's responsiveness and willingness to serve the client. However, two conditions must exist for this response to be effective. First, the executive vice president's perception of the performance problem or opportunity must be accurate. A real performance issue (i.e., with customer relations) must negatively impact employee performance and organizational results. Second, a performance improvement intervention must be designed that provides the knowledge and skills necessary to correct the problem. If these two conditions exist, providing training is the correct response. Now what if the executive vice president's perception of the situation is incorrect, or a performance improvement intervention cannot be designed to address the problem? The HRD professional's reactive behavior would merely compound an already bad situation.

Another possible response could involve HRD's refusal to react to the executive vice president's request, if providing a performance improvement intervention does not seem to be the most appropriate reply to the situation. Refusal may be appropriate if the request is not based on empirical evidence or if dedication to customer service would be violated.

Finally, HRD's action may blend components of the two previous options, enabling HRD to remain responsive to the client's needs while basing recommendations on well-documented performance issues. This response illustrates strategic thinking—an approach in which analysis of the situation has been conducted, a real problem has been isolated, and the most effective intervention or consulting service identified prior to taking action.

Several factors determine the complexity of the analysis to be used, including: the time available for analysis, the seriousness of the performance problem or need, the level of management requesting an intervention or consulting service, and the type of service being requested. Once this information has been gathered and assessed, it should be carefully communicated to the person requesting service. Refusing a client's demands is certainly an appropriate response if the evidence does not support the request.

Two critical questions must be answered before preparing a customer service response. First, why does demand differ for HRD interventions and consulting services? Second, what type of customer service response is appropriate for differing demand states? To answer these questions, HRD professionals must understand the characteristics of differing demand states and the appropriate customer service response for each.

Several factors help determine demand states facing clients, including: (1) interest in and need for a specific intervention or consulting service, (2) the credibility of HRD within the organization, (3) the company's financial condition, (4) the organization's culture and climate, (5) managers' and employees' attitudes toward HRD services, and (6) managers' and employees' previous experiences with HRD interventions and consulting services. The critical task, then, is to identify the demand state and select an appropriate response. By doing so, HRD professionals will help the organization achieve its strategic business goals and objectives. Six different demand states have been identified that trigger HRD's customer service response:

Demand	Customer Service Response
1. negative	conventional
2. indifferent	promotional
3. latent	developmental
4. declining	redesigned
5. optimal	consistent
6. surplus	push-back

Negative Demand and Conventional Customer Service

Many HRD programs face a negative demand situation, which is a state where most of the important clients maintain a negative perception of the HRD program, its practitioners, interventions, and consulting services. Some clients may even resent or avoid HRD as a result. When this demand state exists, the image and credibility of all associated with HRD are negative. Moreover, decisionmakers view HRD as an overhead expense that should be eliminated altogether.

Many circumstances contribute to negative demand. First, HRD interventions could be poorly designed, developed, and/or implemented. Second, HRD services may not be based on client business and performance needs. Third, HRD practitioners may lack business competence and credibility within the organization. Fourth, some clients may maintain a negative attitude toward any learning or developmental activities. Fifth, overzealous senior managers may be oversupportive of HRD, causing some middle managers and supervisors to believe they are being forced to support something in which they have little or no say. Sixth, HRD services may not be linked to the strategic business goals and objectives of the organization. Seventh, a comprehensive evaluation strategy, which could provide evidence of the values and benefits of HRD, may not have been developed. Eighth, HRD professionals may lack understanding of company mission and goals, causing clients to view them critically. Ninth, the values and benefits of HRD may not be adequately communicated to existing or potential clients. Tenth, the positive results obtainable through HRD may not be communicated to the organization. Eleventh, HRD professionals may lack the skills necessary to facilitate organizational change and development. Twelfth, HRD may lack understanding of the cultural and political issues that affect the organization. Finally, HRD professionals may not be able to demonstrate how their department helps the organization achieve business results (Gilley & Eggland, 1992).

Any or all of these factors may produce negative demand for HRD services within the organization and, ultimately, contribute to the negative perception of the entire HRD field. Therefore, this situation must be addressed via development of a *conventional* customer service response that reverses negative demand—one of the most challenging tasks any HRD professional will undertake.

The most critical step in establishing conventional customer service is discovering why clients resist HRD services. Resistance can be identified through classic research methods such as questionnaires, interviews, and focus groups. Since focus groups help compare client responses as well as measure their intensity, they are considered an effective method of uncovering clients' negative perceptions. Focus groups are also an excellent way of altering clients' beliefs and attitudes regarding HRD, and help communicate the purpose, intent, and mission of HRD to opinion leaders. By participating in focus groups, clients become better acquainted with HRD professionals and their interventions. Consequently, focus group participants may become ambassadors for the HRD program.

Indifferent Demand and Promotional Customer Service

Many clients are indifferent toward HRD interventions and consulting services because these are perceived as having little value. When an indifferent demand is allowed to continue, the image and credibility of HRD will suffer.

An indifferent demand state may be the result of clients' limited familiarity with HRD—which often occurs when it is assumed that clients are more aware of interventions and consulting services than they really are. Overconfidence may lead HRD professionals to believe that their services are favorably perceived among clients, when in reality, they are not. Consequently, indifferent demand may produce low familiarity or favorability, resulting in bankrupt HRD programs. Some services experience indifferent demand as clients lack knowledge of their purpose and application. Finally, interventions and consulting services are often negatively perceived because they are not linked to the business goals and objectives of the organization and do not help clients meet their business and performance needs.

HRD professionals facing an indifferent demand state must become proactive in their effort to prevent future image slippage. Altering indifferent demand, while difficult, can occur through promotional customer service designed to help clients become aware of their needs.

Promotional customer service consists of four activities. First, HRD professionals should demonstrate how their services can help solve serious performance problems. Second, interventions and consulting services should be linked to the goals and objectives of the organization, and the business and performance needs of clients. Third, HRD's image must be changed by creating managerial development and organizational development partnerships (Chapters 6 and 7). In this way, clients will witness the developmental and results-oriented approach of HRD, rather than the training for training's sake so common in organizations. Fourth, a comprehensive promotional strategy must be designed to communicate the intent and purposes of HRD, as well as the values and benefits of interventions and consulting services. This customer service activity focuses on organizational perceptions of HRD, its practitioners, and offered services (see Chapter 12).

Latent Demand and Developmental Customer Service

When clients have a need for an HRD intervention or consulting service that is not currently available, latent demand exists. Hidden needs for performance improvement or organizational change may prevent the organization from achieving its desired business results. If needs are known, however, interventions or services may be designed, developed, and implemented.

More than any other demand state, latent demand provides a unique opportunity to improve HRD's image and credibility within the organization by creating timely, meaningful, and valuable interventions and consulting services.

Latent demand requires developmental customer service, which includes uncovering existing organizational and performance needs, utilizing traditional needs assessment methods such as questionnaires, interviews, focus groups, nominal group techniques, reports and records, observation, and work samples (see Chapter 8). Developmental customer service fosters design and development of HRD interventions and consulting services aimed at helping clients, and the organization, improve performance and manage change (see Chapter 9).

Declining Demand and Redesigned Customer Service

All HRD services, regardless of their importance or popularity, experience periods of faltering, or declining, demand. This can occur very gradually, and is sometimes not noticed until the situation becomes serious. Reasons for this state can vary from the lack of usefulness of a skill, to introduction of new technology, rapid change, or shifting priorities. Some interventions and consulting services become popular very quickly, but may decline in popularity at an equal rate. These are known as fads (Gilley & Eggland, 1992).

A critical responsibility of HRD professionals is to discover the usefulness of their services and identify new ways for clients to use them. The formal term for this response is redesigned customer service, which may entail the complete overhaul of HRD interventions or expansion to enhance new interests. When this demand state exists, the promotional campaign focuses on the search for new clients within the organization.

Often, existing clients are already familiar with HRD's offerings and their respective values, but have elected to no longer use them. The problem facing HRD during this demand state is the loss of client interest due to the belief that interventions and consulting services no longer address their business and performance needs or are not helping the organization attain its goals and objectives.

Optimal Demand and Consistent Customer Service

Optimal demand is an HRD professional's dream come true, when present demand levels equal HRD's performance capacity. Under this demand state, image and credibility are greatly enhanced. But beware, relaxing and becoming passive is not a good strategy since demand can change rapidly. Conditions such as management changes, reorganizations, internal politics, mergers, changes in economic conditions, and technology require HRD professionals to remain alert and focused.

Maintaining a constant awareness of organizational conditions is reflective of consistent customer service. It requires identification of external and internal forces that threaten to erode or accelerate demand, and development of corrective measures that address ever-changing demand states.

Surplus Demand and Push-Back Customer Service

On occasion, the demand for interventions and consulting services exceeds HRD's ability to adequately deliver, which may result in inferior customer service. Excessive demand can greatly reduce HRD's effectiveness, resulting in damage to their image and credibility within the organization. In other words, growing too fast results in surplus demand, commonly called growing pains.

When surplus demand exists, only one realistic reaction is available: the reduction of demand. Demand must be managed, and somehow client requests for interventions and consulting services must be discouraged. This decision calls for push-back customer service.

Push-back customer service poses a dilemma since programs are established to serve the needs of the organization's clients. Failure to do so may be viewed as indifference, lack of competence, or arrogance, all of which may negatively impact the future effectiveness of HRD. One way of preventing negative reactions to push-back customer service is to conduct direct, frank, and honest conversations with decision-makers, stakeholders, and influencers. Include discussion about the circumstances and potential outcomes anticipated in the absence of additional resources. Discussions such as these are more effective than providing excuses for failure.

Each of the demand states discussed must be analyzed in order to identify the most fitting customer service response. Since more than one demand state can occur simultaneously, multiple customer service responses may be necessary as HRD professionals exercise their role as strategic business partners.

CONCLUSION

Developing strategic business partnerships is absolutely critical to the success of strategically integrated HRD programs. In order to be successful, HRD professionals must create a customer service strategy that helps the organization achieve its goals and objectives while enabling clients to meet their business and professional needs. Interventions and consulting services must be prioritized to guarantee their contribution to the achievement of organizational business results. HRD professionals must develop collaborative client relationships as a way of enhancing their image and credibility within the organization. Additionally, they must help clients make performance and organizational decisions using a five-step decision-making process. Finally, HRD professionals must become knowledgeable about the concept of demand and the various demand states facing their clients. Based on this understanding, informative decisions can be made and appropriate customer service strategies identified and implemented.

CHAPTER 6

Establishing Management Development Partnerships

For years, organizations have attempted to improve their performance and competitiveness through everything from the one-minute manager and situational leadership to implementing reengineering. However, one thing continues to handcuff most organizations: managers are not good at getting results through people. Managers do not know how to communicate with employees, provide feedback, confront employees' poor performance, enhance employee self-esteem or reward their performance. When these behaviors are present managers create a serious problem for the organization that Gilley and Boughton (1996) refer to as *managerial malpractice.*

Managerial malpractice means encouraging and supporting practices that produce unprofessional, unproductive, or incompetent managers. Symptoms of managerial malpractice include: (1) keeping managers who are not good at getting results through people, (2) promoting unqualified people to management, (3) selecting "new" managers because they are the best performers or producers without regard to their people skills, (4) spending valuable time fixing managerial incompetence instead of hiring qualified managers, (5) keeping managers who preach the importance of teamwork but then reward individuals who stand out from the crowd, and (6) allowing managers to say one thing and do another (Gilley & Boughton, 1996).

There are several managerial attitudes, skills, and behaviors that contribute to managerial malpractice.

Attitudes are made up of one's beliefs and feelings toward something or someone. They cannot actually be seen, but the behaviors associated with an attitude can be observed during interpersonal interaction. Attitudes serve as a guide to managers' behaviors.

They are very important because they dictate the way managers interact and treat their employees. Attitudes common to managers guilty of managerial malpractice include:

1. indifference toward employees
2. a sense of superiority
3. favoritism
4. the attitude that employees are easy to replace

Managerial malpractice also occurs when managers lack the skills to build collaborative relationships with their employees. Without these skills, managers will not be able to build the types of relationships needed to foster teamwork, encourage self-direction, build trust, or improve performance. Millions of managers do not possess a fraction of the skills needed to motivate and encourage their employees. Managerial malpractice continues because managers have poor listening, feedback, and/or interpersonal relationship skills.

Behavior is the outward expression of internal thoughts and beliefs. Managers' thoughts become their actions. It is easy to *tell* people that things are important, but managers' actions determine what is truly important. Managerial malpractice is present when there is a significant difference between what is said is important and what is actually done. Common misbehaviors of managers include:

1. failing to conduct performance appraisals
2. failing to provide performance standards
3. failing to delegate work assignments
4. failing to develop their employees
5. lacking patience with employees
6. criticizing employees rather than their performance
7. changing priorities and work requirements
8. creating paranoid working environments

WHAT ARE MANAGEMENT DEVELOPMENT PARTNERSHIPS?

When managerial malpractice is allowed to flourish, the organization's performance, quality, productivity, and effectiveness suffer greatly. One way of overcoming managerial malpractice is for HRD professionals to create management development partnerships throughout the organization. These are joint ventures between

HRD professionals and the organization designed to improve the competencies and skills of managers. Such partnerships are used to improve the quality and professionalism of managers in order to:

1. improve problem-solving
2. improve employee performance and quality
3. achieve better business results

Improve Problem-solving

Management development partnerships help organizations by providing managers with a problem-solving process. This process consists of the following six steps:

- Identifying the conditions and factors that contribute to the problem.
- Identifying the root cause of the problem.
- Identifying the solutions to the problem and analyzing each.
- Selecting the solution that will best resolve the problem.
- Implementing the solution.
- Evaluating the solution to determine if it solved the problem.

Improve Employee Performance and Quality

Improving performance is a three-stage process that begins by identifying performance standards and communicating them to employees. These standards serve as criteria to determine whether a job is being conducted correctly. They also serve as a guide in executing the job or task (Gilley & Boughton, 1996).

The second stage is to measure current performance against established performance standards for the purpose of determining if there is a difference between actual performance and desired performance.

Once deficiencies have been identified managers are ready for the third stage, which is making changes in the way a job is being performed. Changes might include new tasks, procedures, or processes. Actual performance sometimes exceeds established performance standards; however, changes still might be necessary to ensure that long-term productivity continues. When no significant difference between actual performance and desired performance exists, managers should consider possible adjustments to ensure continuous improvement.

Achieve Better Business Results

Usually, organizations are not concerned with how results are obtained, they simply want them achieved. It is the manager's responsibility to get results, including increased revenues, more units of production, improved client service, or increased market share. Results remain crucial. Managers cannot, however, obtain these results by themselves; they must rely on their employees. Managers must get results through people.

By developing management development partnerships, HRD professionals are helping the organization replace traditional roles of planning, directing, organizing, and controlling with performance coaching skills. Such a transformation can be achieved by:

1. selecting better qualified managers
2. training managers to become performance coaches
3. holding managers accountable for getting results through their people

When these three activities have been completed, managers should be able to demonstrate seven performance coaching behaviors, which include:

1. creating positive relationships with their employees
2. training and developing their employees
3. providing career coaching for employees
4. confronting employees' performance when it falls below established performance standards
5. mentoring employees
6. enhancing employees' self-esteem
7. rewarding and recognizing employees' performance

By embracing the transformation to performance coaching, organizations are making a serious commitment to improving the way managers are selected, trained, and evaluated. Such a transformation will have an immediate impact on the organization by helping improve its performance capacity and effectiveness, which will automatically improve the bottom line.

WHY CREATE MANAGEMENT DEVELOPMENT PARTNERSHIPS?

One of the most critical questions that HRD professionals need to address is "Why create management development partnerships?"

There are four reasons for creating such partnerships. First, organizations will never really improve their performance capacity or effectiveness until they improve the quality of managers and their respective practices. This is true because managers are essential to achieving favorable business results. They are the only organizational members who communicate daily with employees and have the opportunity to observe performance. Consequently, performance improvement can really only occur through a daily ritual of observation, feedback, and application. Perfect practice makes perfect performance, which is the primary responsibility of managers.

Second, managers are the lifeblood of the organization. They are the interpreters of the organization's vision and the executors of its strategy. Managers mediate and translate organizational policies and procedures for employees while developing work climates conducive for improving productivity and quality. They help employees to maneuver through the organizational maze and to develop an appreciation and understanding of the organization's culture. In short, managers are the only "leadership" most employees ever interact with during their tenure in an organization.

Third, managers are the gatekeepers of quality and performance improvement because they are the "overlords" of the learning and compensation and rewards system. Consequently, managers are responsible for developing employees' performance capacity, helping them apply new knowledge and skills, delivering performance feedback, appraising performance, and rewarding employees for improving. Consequently, managers hold the keys to maximizing organizational performance.

Fourth, managers are the primary conduit used to improve employee motivation and satisfaction. Managers are the individuals responsible for enhancing employees' self-esteem by involving them in activities and projects that allow a sense of achievement, accomplishment, power, influence, or mastery. Furthermore, managers are truly the only persons in the organization capable of demonstrating appreciation and concern for the well-being of employees.

HOW ARE MANAGEMENT DEVELOPMENT
PARTNERSHIPS IMPLEMENTED?

HRD professionals must create management development partnerships because they cannot possibly improve organizational performance without help from qualified managers. As a way of implementing management development partnerships, HRD professionals can follow a ten-step process. First, HRD profession-als must secure a sponsor or advocate. This person should be a high-ranking and credible executive or senior manager who can help HRD professionals overcome resistance to changes in man-agerial practice, and who can be a spokesperson and ambassador for the partnership. Second, HRD professionals must help man-agers understand the performance coaching philosophy that they will adopt. Third, HRD professionals must determine a manager's performance coaching aptitude. Aptitude can be measured by using a performance coaching inventory, which consists of a self-report and an employee report of managers' competencies. The in-ventory can be used to compare managers' perceptions of their own competencies with those of employees. By doing so, a more accurate identification of managers' performance coaching compe-tencies can be determined in seven areas. These areas include:

1. building relationships
2. training employees
3. career coaching
4. confronting performance
5. mentoring employees
6. enhancing employees' self-esteem
7. rewarding performance

Fourth, the performance coaching inventory can help HRD pro-fessionals identify managers' strengths and weaknesses that can be used as the basis for developing learning acquisition and transfer activities (see Chapter 10). Fifth, HRD professionals should provide feedback and advice that help managers acquire and transfer per-formance coaching skills to the job. Sixth, once managers have had an ample amount of time to integrate and apply performance coaching skills (approximately three to six months) HRD profes-sionals should conduct a comprehensive evaluation of managers' behavioral change, performance impact, and skill development. In order to determine behavioral change and performance impact, HRD professionals should use the critical incident technique, as well as focus groups (see Chapter 8). These evaluation techniques can help determine when managers used performance coaching skills and their corresponding behavioral and performance results. Skill development can be determined by readministering a perfor-mance coaching inventory and comparing differences in each of the seven competency areas. Seventh, HRD professionals should identify the impact that performance coaching skills have had on the organization.

Eighth, managers should be rewarded and recognized for improving their managerial practice. Rewards should be significant enough to encourage continuous improvement. Ninth, HRD professionals should demonstrate how management development partnerships help the organization achieve its strategic business goals. Tenth, HRD professionals should help the organization create policies and procedures for determining the fate of managers who do not develop adequate performance coaching skills. In this way, employees and the organization will no longer be victims of managerial malpractice, which cripples morale, productivity, performance, and quality.

BENEFITS OF MANAGEMENT DEVELOPMENT PARTNERSHIPS

By establishing management development partnerships, organizations benefit in several ways. Benefits include:

1. increasing employee productivity and quality
2. enhancing organizational communication
3. improving employees' understanding of organizational expectations
4. developing organizational commitment to change
5. improving employees' self-esteem
6. creating better employee relations
7. rewarding performance improvement appropriately, which encourages better productivity
8. providing more effective and meaningful training
9. providing specific, measurable, meaningful, and timely feedback to employees regarding their performance, which improves employee performance
10. improving managerial practice
11. enhancing managerial quality
12. providing long-term mentoring opportunities for employees
13. improving employee performance
14. improving organizational effectiveness

WHAT IS PERFORMANCE COACHING?

According to Gilley and Boughton (1996), performance coaching is "person-centered" management that encourages managers to establish rapport with employees. It requires managers to constantly shift from one role to another, and enables them to become active participants with their employees rather than passive observers. Performance coaching relies more on listening and facilitating skills than on managing work and controlling outcomes.

To become an effective performance coach, managers must develop seven separate but integrated competencies. These competencies enable managers to build better relationships with employees, resolve conflicts, solve problems, and improve employee performance. In short, they help managers improve organizational effectiveness and performance. The seven competencies include relationship building, training, career coaching, confronting, mentoring, enhancing employees' self-esteem, and rewarding performance. They combine to create the four interdependent phases of performance coaching, making it almost impossible to move forward unless the previous phase has been successfully completed (see Figure 6.1). The four phases are:

1. developing positive relationships with employees
2. performing the four activities of performance coaching
3. developing self-directed and self-esteemed employees

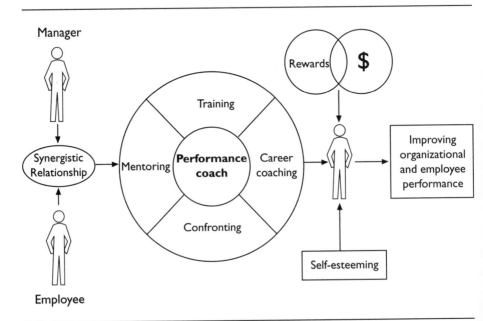

Figure 6.1 The Performance Coaching Process. Reprinted from J. W. Gilley and N. W. Boughton, *Stop Managing, Start Coaching*, McGraw-Hill, 1996.

4. selecting rewards that build commitment and obtain results (Gilley & Boughton, 1996, p. 34)

Phase I: Developing Positive Relations with Employees

This phase can increase employee commitment to improving performance and quality, thereby increasing productivity while implementing change. When successful, organizational performance and effectiveness will improve.

A positive employee relationship is one that benefits managers, employees, and the organization. Each member achieves the specific results desired. However, it is a professional relationship, not a personal one. A positive relationship does not suggest that managers become personally involved with their employees but establishes a professional approach. Increasing employee commitment means encouraging them to make changes in their performance that help their teams, departments, or organization reach their goals. For example, increasing employees' commitment may include establishing performance standards for employees, clarifying the goals of a department or the organization, providing the training necessary so employees can produce adequate performance outputs, or allowing greater employee influence on decisions made regarding their jobs and careers. Employees will often reciprocate by providing higher quality, greater efficiency, and better performance. However, they must be rewarded appropriately for their increasing commitment.

Phase 2: Performing the Four Activities of Performance Coaching

During interactions with employees, managers perform one of four different activities: training, career coaching, confronting, or mentoring. Let's briefly examine each of these activities.

Role 1: Training

In performance coaching, one of the most critical activities is that of training employees. During this activity, the manager serves as a one-to-one facilitator of learning, responsible for the sharing of information that will ultimately impact the growth and development of the employee.

Many believe that managers should not be responsible for training because it is too complex, time consuming, and involved. Managers are perceived as lacking the interpersonal communication, team building, and presentation skills to effectively train employees. Some believe that professional trainers should conduct training and managers should reinforce their efforts. However, the purpose of training is to increase employees' knowledge, skills, and competencies in order for them to improve their performance. In short, getting results through people. The persons responsible for this outcome should be the ones responsible for training. This would be managers because professional trainers are not held accountable for declines in productivity and performance—but managers are.

Role 2: Career Coaching

As a career coach, managers should guide employees through a reasonably in-depth review of their interests, abilities, and beliefs regarding their present and future career paths (Gilley & Boughton, 1996). Managers should help employees consider alternatives and make decisions regarding their careers. Managers should also make the organization aware of their employees' career objectives in order for the organization to plan accordingly.

Because managers have made career decisions similar to those facing their employees, they are in an excellent position to be successful at career coaching. Their experience can provide employees critical insight into the possible outcomes of their own career decisions. Managers can also provide employees with a realistic appraisal of opportunities within the organization. They have access to performance evaluation information on all their employees, which can be used in making realistic suggestions. This information can help managers identify training activities that will help their employees overcome knowledge and skill deficiencies. Finally, managers have established networks that can provide employees greater access to information used in making career decisions.

Using managers as career coaches appeals to many organizations because it allows the individuals most familiar with employees' performance to recommend strategies that help them make career decisions. Using managers can be cheaper to administrate than a separate career counseling staff. Using managers also makes sense because managers are already being held accountable for employee performance and should be motivated to help improve, develop, and promote their employees. Finally, managers are in a unique position to motivate and encourage their employees.

Another purpose of career coaching is to provide organizations with information about their employees' career perspectives so organizations can plan accordingly. Such information helps organizations provide necessary opportunities for employees. To accomplish these purposes, managers must:

- pose hypothetical questions to employees to expand their point of view regarding their careers.
- uncover employees' underlying assumptions regarding their careers.
- examine the seriousness of commitment that employees have toward their career goals.
- present different viewpoints to generate a more in-depth analysis of career options and decisions.
- analyze reasons for current career pursuits.
- review career preferences (Gilley & Boughton, 1996).

Career coaching promotes overall organizational performance through better allocation of human resources. In other words, the career coaching role can help organizations by getting the right person in the right job. Other organizational benefits of career coaching include:

- allowing managers the opportunity to identify the performance deficiencies of their employees
- enabling employees to better understand their career paths
- allowing managers to help their employees understand their career choices
- increasing employee retention
- helping employees gain greater insight into the organization
- encouraging employees to become more self-sufficient and independent

As a career coach, managers can help their employees make better career decisions and help the organization better allocate its human resources. Managers can help employees gain greater insights into the organization, enhance their self-sufficiency, and help employees better understand their feelings regarding their careers. Career coaching can help the organization reduce recruiting and hiring costs, improve performance, enhance teamwork, and improve quality and profitability.

Role 3: Confronting

Many managers have a difficult time confronting employees about performance. They find it difficult to discuss negative information with employees, fearing that employees will become defensive.

Managers make two types of performance improvement efforts. First, employees must improve even when their performance is satisfactory. The second type of performance effort requires managers to move employees from an unsatisfactory to satisfactory level of performance. However, communicating unsatisfactory performance behaviors to employees is quite difficult. Employees often become defensive because they perceive this as a reprimand. Consequently, managers must learn how to communicate performance improvement messages without eliciting negative or defensive reactions from employees.

Confrontation is not necessarily criticism. However, for confrontations to remain positive, managers must: (1) learn to communicate specifically what behaviors or performance employees must improve, (2) focus on the performance problem rather than the person, (3) use confrontation to produce the desired change without causing the employee to become defensive, and (4) maintain a positive relationship with their employees (Gilley & Boughton, 1996, p. 39).

The greatest benefits to the organization can be realized through a manager's execution of the confronting role. Here a manager's entire attention is focused on improving performance and resolving problems. These improvements can help the organization become more competitive in the marketplace, which increases market share and leads to greater profitability.

While assuming this role, managers are responsible for identifying performance shortfalls. In order to accomplish this, managers must identify performance standards and communicate them to their employees, who can then use them to refocus themselves.

Performance standards can be used to help managers create critical performance measures for comparing actual performance with desired performance. When performance falls short of the standard, managers must determine why their employees are failing.

Many managers, however, have difficulty confronting failing employees. Some avoid confrontation—hoping it will somehow work itself out—while others become overly aggressive, making it personal. As a result, emotions explode, accusations are made, feelings are hurt, and everyone feels resentment. Furthermore, performance does not get any better. The outcomes are strained relationships with employees and a loss of credibility on the part of managers. Regardless, it is still the managers' responsibility to make certain that their employees meet or exceed performance standards.

The Confronter Role   Managers must master the art of confronting. To accomplish this, three critical sets of skills must be developed. Each will help managers improve interpersonal relationships with their employees as well as improve performance.

The three sets of skills include:

1. *Assertion skills:* Using these verbal and nonverbal skills will enable managers to maintain respect, satisfy their employees' needs, and defend employees' rights without manipulating, dominating, or controlling them.
2. *Conflict-resolution skills:* These skills enable managers to deal with the emotional turbulence that typically accompanies conflict.
3. *Collaborative problem-solving skills:* These skills include ways of resolving conflicts to everyone's satisfaction.

The Seven Performance Killers   Sometimes the most well-intended and innocent comments can backfire. They can prevent employees from trying new skills, resolving conflicts, and solving problems. They can damage communication, and hurt employees' confidence and self-esteem. We call them the seven performance killers because they can negatively impact or shut down employee performance if used at the wrong time or in the wrong way. They include:

Criticizing: Making negative comments about employees' performance, attitudes, and decisions are all forms of criticism. For many managers criticism is a way of life.

Stereotyping: Some managers label their employees and place them into categories. Most stereotyping has negative overtones. Comments such as, "women are too emotional to be managers," or "all you factory workers are good ol' boys" place employees in boxes that cannot possibly describe their good qualities.

Advising and providing solutions: Giving employees "the solution" to their problems in a way that interferes with their ability to solve it themselves is negative advising. These are often "If I were you . . ." statements. They severely restrict employees' growth and development and force them to become totally dependent upon the manager.

Ordering: Ordering is a process of commanding employees to do what one wants. This approach makes employees resentful and may cause them to sabotage results.

Moralizing: When managers use this performance killer they are telling their employees what they "should do," rather than helping them to decide the best solution. Moralizing is demoralizing. It fosters resentment and anxiety.

Threatening: Trying to control employees' actions by warning of negative consequences or by coercing them is threatening. No one wants to be threatened and it will produce immediate defensive behavior. In addition, "You'll do it or else. . ." rarely works and often backfires.

Reassuring: Many managers try to confront their employees by saying things like, "Don't worry about it," or "It will all work out in the end." While these statements appear to comfort employees, they actually do the opposite. Reassurance is a form of emotional withdrawal because managers can offer it without really getting involved.

Performance improvement begins when employees believe in themselves and their decisions. The seven performance killers prevent this from happening. To become effective confronters, managers should avoid using any or all of these.

Using Assertion Skills to Improve Performance

When confronting employees regarding their performance managers can demonstrate either aggressive, submissive, or assertive behavior.

Aggressive Behavior   Aggressive managers get things done but are often abusive, rude, or sarcastic. They express their feelings, needs, and ideas at the expense of their employees, and almost always win arguments. They may berate employees for poor performance, dominate them, or insist on having the final word on topics of conversation important to them.

Aggressive managers tend to have little interest in what is important to their employees. Such an attitude forces some employees to subvert or undermine coworkers' loyalty and dedication.

Submissive Behavior   Some managers let their employees dictate the level and quality of performance. Submissive managers do not express their honest feelings, needs, values, or concerns. They allow employees to violate them by denying them their managerial rights and ignoring their requests. These managers rarely state their true desires and expectations.

Some submissive managers do express their needs. However, nonverbal behaviors such as shrugging of the shoulders, lack of eye contact, an excessively soft voice, and hesitant speech demonstrate an apologetic approach that prevent managers from being taken seriously. Consequently, their desires and needs are not fulfilled by their employees. At other times, managers think they have communicated clearly but their messages are coded to such an extent employees do not understand.

Assertive Behavior   Assertive managers stand up for their rights and express their needs, values, concerns, and ideas in direct and appropriate ways—without abusing or dominating their employees. While meeting their own needs, they do not violate the needs of their employees. True assertiveness is a way of behaving that confirms managers' personal worth and dignity while simultaneously confirming and maintaining the worth and dignity of their employees.

Role 4: Mentoring

The purpose of mentoring is to help employees advance their careers. The mentoring role allows managers to help employees unlock the mysteries of the organization, while directing them through the perils and pitfalls of organizational life.

Mentors provide insights into the organization's philosophy. They act as a source of information on the organization's mission and goals. Mentors also teach employees how to function within the organization. As mentors, managers must serve as confidants in times of personal and professional trouble.

To be successful mentors, managers must share personal experiences with their employees, deepening their learning and understanding. This type of activity encourages employees and helps build positive rapport. It also demonstrates that managers have had similar experiences and can relate. Because sharing personal experiences, especially failure, can be difficult, the mentoring role is one of the most demanding that a performance coach will perform.

Activities of Mentors   Mentoring activities include encouraging employees to take the risks necessary for professional growth and development, encouraging employees to take actions to attain specific goals, or recommending transfer to another department or division within the organization. As mentors managers must provide feedback on performance that affects the employee's career. Mentors must provide information about the mission, goals, and strategic direction of the organization. They must also help their employees develop political awareness and savvy, and provide insight into the organization. Finally, mentors must provide advancement and growth opportunities for their employees.

Activities of Employees in Mentoring   Employees have several activities they should be responsible for in order for mentoring to be successful. These include:

- willingness to assume responsibility for their own growth and development
- assessing their real potential for success within the organization
- being receptive to positive and negative feedback
- accepting challenging assignments
- willingness to share personal information with their superiors
- willingness to accept suggestions and advice from others
- relinquishing some control over their career path
- willingness to trust the suggestions of others

Phase 3: Developing Self-directed and Self-esteemed Employees

Improving the self-esteem of employees is the primary outcome of the performance coaching process. It benefits managers as much as their employees since it encourages the development of a synergistic relationship.

Every day employees interact with their managers, other employees, and other managers through projects, activities, assignments, meetings, presentations, and proposals. Each of these interactions gives managers an opportunity to enhance or diminish employees' self-esteem. The interactions in which employees engage make up their "private and public world," a world managers can draw from to bolster self-esteem (Bradshaw, 1981). The same world, however, can deplete self-esteem through negative experiences, causing employees to feel depressed, hurt, and angry.

According to Bradshaw (1981), there are four sources of self-esteem that managers can draw upon to help improve their employees' self-concept. These include achievement, accomplishment, and mastery; power, control, and influence; being cared about and valued; and acting on values and beliefs (p. 6).

Employees need opportunities to achieve or accomplish something that is meaningful to them (Gilley & Boughton, 1996). Managing a project, giving a presentation, or writing a proposal are all activities that can help employees enhance their self-esteem. However, to be meaningful, employees must also be granted some control over decisions that affect their activities. Then and only then will personal and professional growth truly occur.

Many employees prefer activities that ensure close personal affiliations, comfortable relationships, and meaningful interpersonal contact as a way of enhancing their self-esteem. This helps employees feel appreciated and valued, which can produce an attitude of unconditional positive regard toward the organization. This attitude can contribute to performance improvement and organizational efficiency.

Another source of self-esteem is enabling employees to act on their values and beliefs. For example, a manager may allow an employee to work flexible hours or fewer days each week in order to maintain a balance between work and family. Such actions enable employees to produce adequate results and to feel good about themselves as they satisfy multiple needs. Thus, organizational performance is improved while employees' attitudes and morale are enhanced.

Self-esteeming Results

When managers provide employees with experiences that enhance their self-esteem, employees feel good about themselves. According to Gilley and Boughton (1996), some of the resulting feelings and behaviors are:

• commitment	• caring	• growth
• risk taking	• openness	• courage
• trust	• cooperation	• candor
• assurance	• uniqueness	• expressiveness
• creativity	• listening	• personal security
• sharing	• realness	• conflict confrontation

When these feelings and behaviors are present employees are motivated to improve their performance, help solve problems, and secure the results needed by the organization.

The reverse is also true. When work experiences produce negative self-esteem, employees' self-concepts ultimately suffer. They begin to find fault with themselves and dislike who they are. When this occurs they exhibit behaviors like:

- low trust
- nonlistening
- anger, rage
- suspicion
- low reactivity

- low risk taking
- low creativity
- fearfulness
- stagnation
- low courage

- conformity
- accommodation
- vulnerability
- manipulation
- sadness

Improved performance and quality cannot be forthcoming from employees who possess these types of behaviors.

Impact of Self-esteeming on Organizations

Organizations, like individuals, are living systems that share many characteristics. Organizations with low self-esteem feel and act in ways strikingly similar to the ways people with low self-esteem behave. That is, organizations with low self-esteem often demonstrate such feelings and behaviors as those listed below:

- easily threatened
- anger, resentment
- autocratic culture
- conflict avoidance

- low creativity
- manipulation
- politicking
- fear

- blaming
- low risk taking
- win/lose postures
- intragroup conflict

These feelings and behaviors inevitably result in poor performance and low self-esteeming for all employees. However, organizations with high self-esteem demonstrate behaviors almost exactly opposite. They perform very well and get the results needed. Moreover, employees acquire positive self-esteem by being part of such an organization.

It is difficult to improve organizations with low self-concepts. But if managers become dedicated to self-esteeming their employees and teams, it will have a positive impact on the entire organization.

Phase 4: Selecting Rewards That Get Results

The purpose of any organization is to get results. For some this includes increasing market share, improving quality, increasing sales, and/or increasing profitability. Regardless, it is the responsibility of performance coaches to get the results the organization needs. But managers cannot do it alone. Managers must get results through people (LeBoeuf, 1985).

There is a straightforward, common sense approach that performance coaches can use to enhance their employees' commitment. Managers should *tell* employees the results or outcomes they want, what level of quality they desire, and when the results are needed.

It would help employees improve their performance if managers simply could provide them with performance standards to guide their efforts.

According to Gilley and Boughton (1996), performance standards offer an easy way for employees to monitor their outputs and evaluate their own performance. Managers should tell employees how their contributions affect the entire project or production. This information helps employees understand the importance of producing outcomes on time and at the proper level of quality.

Employees also need timely and continuous feedback to remain on track. Feedback helps motivate them and provides the information that lets them alter and improve their efforts.

Managers must establish a clear link between producing positive outcomes and having their efforts recognized. Research has shown that the things that get rewarded and reinforced will be repeated (LeBoeuf, 1985). Performance coaches and organizations must install compensation and reward systems that build commitment and improve motivation. In other words, organizations must be rewarding the right things.

Reward Strategies That Enhance Commitment and Get Results

There are four reward strategies that help performance coaches enhance employee commitment and get results. They include: (1) rewarding long-term solutions, (2) rewarding entrepreneurship, (3) rewarding performance improvement and work quality, and (4) rewarding teamwork and cooperation.

Strategy 1: Rewarding Long-term Solutions

Today's organizational leaders are under extreme pressure to produce monthly and quarterly results in order to satisfy stockholders and parent companies. Consequently, short-term achievements are often the only things rewarded. This approach ultimately hurts organizations. In order to improve organizational performance, therefore, managers and executives must begin adopting reward strategies that help accomplish long-term growth and development.

Strategy 2: Rewarding Entrepreneurship

Performance coaches must develop a reward system that encourages risk-taking and decisiveness. This will help employees develop an ownership attitude. Such a strategy will foster an entrepreneurial approach to performance improvement.

*Strategy 3: Rewarding Performance Improvement
and Quality Work*

Improving performance appears to be a mystery to many managers. However, there are several useful actions that help foster the performance managers desire. According to Gilley and Boughton (1996), performance improvement and quality work begin by selecting the right person for the job and giving that person the resources to accomplish the work. By the right person, they mean an employee who has the training and ability to successfully complete the work. On occasion, employees with the aptitude can be trained to complete the work. Regardless, they must be provided with the equipment, data, and time necessary to produce a quality output.

People need to know what is expected of them, the time frame required, and at what level of quality work is to be performed. They also need to know the importance of their personal contributions. Performance coaches should communicate these expectations and establish a clear understanding of how the job contributes to the overall work effort.

Strategy 4: Rewarding Teamwork and Cooperation

Many organizations talk about the importance of teamwork and cooperation. Unfortunately, they continue to reward individual efforts and contributions. If teamwork and cooperation are so important, employees should be rewarded for the efforts of the team rather than their own individual roles. Teams win together, lose together, and should be rewarded together.

Managers must not allow individuals to withdraw and isolate themselves from others. They should encourage communication and avoid setting up win-lose competitions between individuals or groups.

Types of Reward That Enhance Commitment and Get Results

One of the most controversial types of reward is money. LeBoeuf (1985) believes that money does make a difference but managers must understand the different types of compensation strategies that are available and the advantages of each. As performance coaches, managers should understand that not all rewards produce the same results. Therefore, it is important to know which are the most effective. Some of the most effective are recognition, time off, favorite work, advancement, independence, and personal growth opportunities.

CONCLUSION

HRD professionals are at a crossroads. One path leads to business as usual—in other words, training as a way of improving performance outcomes. The other path leads to a radically new approach to performance improvement. It allows managers to become performance coaches responsible for problem-solving, conflict resolution, employee relations, and performance improvement. It enables HRD professionals to become internal performance consultants (see Chapter 9) responsible for organizational development and effectiveness. The path that is selected will help determine the future of many organizations as well as the practice of HRD.

The seven competencies discussed in this chapter: relationship building, training, career coaching, confronting, mentoring, enhancing employees' self-esteem, and rewarding performance equip managers with the skills necessary to improve organizational performance. Therefore, HRD professionals must redefine their roles within the organization. This includes helping managers develop performance coaching skills as well as focusing attention on transfer of learning strategies.

CHAPTER 7

Creating Organizational Development Partnerships

Organizations no longer view HRD as something nice to have. HRD must help organizations improve their overall effectiveness and performance capacity so that they can compete in a global economy. Because of this trend, HRD professionals are no longer simply trainers but must serve the organization in such a way that brings about meaningful organizational change. HRD professionals can do this in two ways: (1) by creating organizational development partnerships (ODP), and (2) by making the transition to organizational development.

In order to create organizational development partnerships, HRD professionals must:

- acquire an understanding of ODP.
- identify the characteristics of ODP.
- identify the goals and objectives of ODP.
- integrate the values of ODP into their practice.

WHAT ARE ORGANIZATIONAL DEVELOPMENT PARTNERSHIPS?

Organizational development partnerships have become important for two reasons. First, employees are demanding better work environments and greater participation in decision-making. Second, economic conditions and market competitiveness have forced organizations to adjust to an ever-changing global marketplace. Both of these are requiring organizations to implement and manage change, rather than simply accepting the status quo. Therefore, substantive and positive changes rest in large part on HRD professionals' awareness of and skill in creating organizational development partnerships.

Organizational development partnerships are aimed at improving organizational performance capacity, growth, and competitiveness. They are long-term processes requiring all members of the organization to get involved. ODP incorporates action research and the scientific method as a way of developing the organization's problem-solving capabilities. According to Gilley and Eggland (1989), ODP are not part of a "fix it" strategy but, rather, a continuous way of managing organizational change that, over time, becomes a way of organizational life. Therefore, it is useful to think of ODP as planned, data-based approaches to change, involving goal setting, action planning, monitoring feedback, and evaluating results. ODP also involve a systems approach that closely links human resources to technology, business processes, and change.

Beer (1983) defined organizational development partnerships as a system-wide process of data collection, diagnosis, action planning, intervention, and evaluation aimed at: (1) enhancing congruence between organizational structure, process, strategy, people, and culture; (2) developing new and creative organizational solutions; and (3) developing the organization's self-renewing capacity. ODP can only occur when organization members work collaboratively with change agents (organizational development consultants) using behavioral science theory, research, and technology. In short, ODP focus upon improving overall organizational effectiveness by developing innovative approaches to problem-solving and by establishing a "survivalistic attitude" in a continuously evolving environment of technological advancement and cultural change. Consequently, organizational development partnerships can be viewed as both a philosophy and a collection of methods for organizational improvement. Both are characterized by an emphasis on collaborative participation in data collection, diagnosis, planning, intervention, and evaluation in order to improve the entire organization.

Organizational development partnerships also rely on learning as a means of bringing about change; however, the focus is upon improving the performance system within the organization rather than on individual employees (see Chapter 3). From this vantage point, ODP can be viewed as part of a "macro perspective" of overall organizational efficiency. In other words, when these partnerships are used the principal benefactor of learning and change is the organization itself, with employees as secondary benefactors.

While organizational learning and change is generally the goal of ODP, it fails to account for the fact that all organizations are made up of a myriad of individuals. Regardless of the intervention employed and changes made by the organization, people are responsible for implementing change. Organizations are made up of people who accept a common set of organizational goals and objectives by which others outside the organization benefit. In return, each employee receives financial compensation as well as other intrinsic rewards. Organizations do not run themselves, individuals release their personal power and control to organizational leaders in order that the organization can be run more efficiently. Without this compliance, organizations could not maintain control or operate efficiently. Consequently, the macro perspective of organizational development partnerships must take into consideration that changes cannot occur, nor can performance improve, without each member of the organization improving respective skills, competencies, knowledge, and attitudes.

In every organization a hierarchy exists within which certain individuals are perceived to be more valuable than others. While this cultural bias exists, it should be understood that the modern organization would grind to a stop within a few months if certain employees such as its secretarial and support staff decided to collectively boycott the organization.

Unfortunately, many organizations operate with a "revolving door" philosophy based upon supply-side economics, where the supply of qualified personnel exceeds the organization's demands (Gilley & Eggland, 1989). Such a philosophy embraces the macro view of ODP rather than enhancing employee performance capacity. The revolving door philosophy also fosters the attitude that employees exist for the organization, and that the organization has control over their career advancement, professional growth, and work assignments. However, many organizations have recognized that this practice is not necessarily the most efficient approach to the management and development of human resources or to the improvement of organizational effectiveness.

CHARACTERISTICS OF ODP

The following characteristics of ODP are among the most often cited:

1. ODP involve a total organizational system.
2. ODP are supported by top management.

3. ODP view organizations from a systems approach.
4. ODP are planned activities directed by third party change agents.
5. ODP use action research, experiential learning, and behavioral science techniques.
6. ODP are ongoing and relatively long-term processes.
7. ODP are intended to increase organizational performance capacity and effectiveness.
8. ODP emphasize the importance of goal setting and action planning through strategic planning.
9. ODP are group and team-oriented.

GOALS AND OBJECTIVES OF ODP

The primary purpose of ODP is to improve organizational effectiveness and performance capacity. In order to accomplish this several goals must be achieved. Some of the most common are improving organizational efficiency, health, and collaboration.

Improving organizational efficiency requires organizations to determine a better way of producing products and services, improving organizational communication, the performance and learning systems, compensation and rewards system, and the overall work design of the organization. One of the more popular interventions used to address organizational efficiency is reengineering. This intervention requires an organization to completely examine its operation in search of incremental improvements as well as improved practices and procedures.

Improving health refers to such subjective aspects of the organization as morale, creativity, and climate. Organizational health is a by-product of the relationship between employees and the organization. Relationship quality can be improved by effectively integrating individual and organizational goals, increasing individual and organizational problem-solving capacities, and developing organizational environments that encourage individual and organizational growth.

Neilsen (1984) sees the primary objective of organizational development partnerships as initiating a collaborative form of organization. Such an organization is characterized by:

- structures and policies that facilitate understanding of and commitment to organizational goals
- reward systems that emphasize group performance while still recognizing individual contributions

- measurement systems that are used as yardsticks of performance improvement and productivity, rather than as rigid performance criteria that become ends in themselves
- participative human resource development procedures that examine individual career aspirations based on the organization's long-term needs, as well as the present and future competencies the individual brings to the organization

The collaborative form of organization may evolve most naturally when organizational leaders believe that employees are valuable resources used in promoting the organization's welfare, and that they are basically committed to the welfare of the organization.

It is important to remember that ODP are not separate or single events but, rather, a series of events interacting over an extended period of time. The intent of organizational development partnerships is not to make decisions for management, but merely to help clarify their choices. In other words, ODP must help organizations generate valid data used in improving the state of the organization relative to its culture, environment, and performance system. ODP must help organizational leaders make strategic choices based on a diagnosis of the current state as well as help them clarify desired outcomes.

VALUE OF ODP

The optimal value of ODP is indeed in improving organizational effectiveness and performance capacity. There are, however, several other values. For example:

1. ODP provide opportunities for employees to function as human beings rather than as resources in the productivity process.
2. ODP provide opportunities for each organization member and the organization itself to develop to their fullest potential.
3. ODP increase an organization's effectiveness by helping it achieve its strategic business goals and objectives.
4. ODP help create an environment where employees can find exciting and challenging work.
5. ODP provide opportunities for employees and managers to influence the way in which they relate to work, the organization, and the work environment.
6. ODP enable every employee to be treated as a human being with a complex set of needs and values, all of which are important in his or her work and life (Gilley & Eggland, 1989).

Some researchers believe that "organizational development partnerships are most likely to succeed . . . with organizations whose members are mature, psychologically healthy adults, who are committed to the organization's welfare and who have important resources to offer, and whose leaders are willing to risk experimentation to enhance individual and organizational health" (Neilsen, 1984, p. 22). Others believe that the ultimate value of ODP is that they allow organization members to become mature, psychologically healthy, and committed to the organization (Burke, 1992). Still others believe that ODP encourage the development of personal skills and competencies that the organization can utilize in its effort to remain competitive and productive. Thus, the principal value of ODP is that they allow the development of people as well as organizations (Gilley & Eggland, 1989).

MAKING THE TRANSITION TO ORGANIZATIONAL DEVELOPMENT CONSULTING

Robinson and Robinson (1995) believe that many HRD professionals have difficulty making the transition from trainer to organizational development consultant because they are not prepared for the complexity, ambiguity, and uncertainty common in the world of consulting. To make the transition HRD professionals must be able to:

- apply the objectives of organizational development consulting.
- adopt the responsibilities of organizational development consulting.
- develop and apply specialized organizational development consulting competencies and skills.
- apply the roles of organizational development consulting to improving organizational effectiveness.
- apply the organizational development process.
- apply the OD roles during the OD process.

Objectives of Organizational Development Consulting

One of the most useful and effective ways of understanding organizational consulting is to consider its objectives. There are six basic objectives arranged hierarchically from lowest to highest amount of influence on organizational change. They are:

1. providing information and solving problems
2. conducting effective diagnosis and making recommendations

3. implementing change
4. building consensus and commitment
5. facilitating client learning
6. improving organizational effectiveness

Objectives one through three are the traditional objectives of organizational development consulting and are most often requested by employees, managers, and executives. Objectives four through six require increased consulting skills and experience in establishing client relationships. These higher level consulting objectives are designed to improve organizational effectiveness and performance capacity.

Providing Information and Solving Problems

The most common reasons for retaining organizational development consultants are to obtain information regarding a performance improvement intervention, performance management system, compensation strategy, organizational needs analysis technique, change intervention, and/or research. Organizations often give organizational development consultants difficult performance, managerial, and/or organizational problems to solve. Such problems vary from organization to organization and from department to department. It is the organizational development consultant's responsibility, however, to make certain that the identified problem is indeed the one that needs to be solved. It can be argued that organizations that can identify the root causes of their problems do not need an organizational development consultant (Gilley & Eggland, 1989). Therefore, the majority of an organizational development consultant's time should be spent helping the client define the correct problem, and then working with the problem in such a way that more useful definitions emerge (Turner, 1983).

Conducting Effective Diagnosis and Providing Recommendations

The second purpose of organizational development consulting is to conduct an effective diagnosis and provide recommendations for the organization. This includes identifying problems, data gathering, data analysis, and making recommendations. Such activities could include examining the economic conditions facing an organization, analyzing the political and technological status of that industry, determining the appropriateness of the organizational structure, measuring managerial abilities and attitudes, or auditing the organizational culture. Because much of this information is confidential many managers are reluctant to share data, fearful that they might be blamed for poor performance or falling productivity. Consequently, the diagnosis and recommendation process can sometimes strain the consultant/client relationship. Regardless, it is critical that managers and executives become involved in this process, which will help ensure they understand their roles and responsibilities. It will also help them develop critical diagnostic skills that may be needed during future analysis.

According to Gilley and Eggland (1989), organizational development consultants must present a consistent, logical action plan designed to solve the problem(s) facing the organization. Such a plan should include suggestions on how clients should implement a solution(s). When making recommendations to organizations, organizational development consultants should carefully consider EEOC requirements, employment conditions, employee attitudes toward change, training required when implementing change, the compensation and rewards system, and performance appraisal procedures. If these considerations are absent, recommendations may end up on the client's bookshelf next to many other expensive and unused reports. A word of caution: written reports and oral presentations that provide recommendations should be clearly written and persuasive.

Implementing Change

Organizational development consultants are often asked to implement their recommendations for change. This is a matter of considerable debate among consultants and managers. Many believe that implementing change is the primary responsibility of managers or executives, because they are familiar with the organization and have the authority to make things happen. On the other hand, implementing change often requires specialized skills or knowledge not present among many managers and executives (see Specialized Skills of Organizational Development Consultants later in this chapter). Implementing change also requires an understanding of how change can potentially impact an organization. This insight can only be gained through firsthand experience that consultants have the opportunity to develop. The most compelling reason for using organizational development consultants to implement change is that a poorly implemented change intervention has a devastating impact on the organization. Such an impact is expensive, hurts employee morale, reduces productivity, and can further complicate an already difficult situation.

Managers and executives also should participate in implementing change because they serve as linkages between important client groups. Without these key linkages change will not occur nor will people be willing to do things differently, regardless of potential positive outcomes.

Building Consensus and Commitment

Positive organizational change requires organization members to work together. It requires employees, managers, and executives to consider the overall good of the organization prior to considering their own personal and professional priorities and goals. For this to occur organizational development consultants must provide sound and convincing recommendations and present them persuasively. Moreover, they must build consensus and commitment regarding the steps required to bring about lasting change. This also requires organizational development consultants to identify essential decision-makers and to decide how to involve them in the change process.

Another way to create consensus and commitment is to monitor the client's readiness and commitment to change. The following questions can serve as a guide:

1. How willing are the members of the organization to implement change?
2. Is upper-level management willing to learn and utilize new management methods and practices?
3. What type of information do members of the organization readily accept or resist?
4. What is the attitude of members toward change?
5. What are the executives' attitudes toward change?
6. To what extent will individual members of the organization regard their contribution to overall organizational effectiveness as a legitimate and desirable objective?

Another way to gauge readiness for change is to determine managers' and executives' enthusiasm for a particular recommendation. This provides an instantaneous measure of interest, resistance, or resentment. Once identified, organizational development consultants can decide whether or not to encourage a specific recommendation.

As a way of developing consensus and commitment, organizational development consultants should build a positive working relationship with each of their clients. This can happen during the interviews and focus group sessions used in gathering information, as well as during the implementation phase. During either of these periods it is important to build trust and a readiness to accept change. According to Turner (1983), an effective relationship becomes a collaborative search for acceptable answers to the client's real needs and concerns. Ideally, this will be a mutually beneficial relationship.

Facilitating Client Learning

When organizational development consultants are facilitating client learning, they are helping clients develop the knowledge and skills needed to adjust to future conditions and to address future problems. One of the best ways of facilitating client learning is allowing clients to participate in the consulting process. This enables clients to gain valuable experience that will help them develop a different organizational perspective. Managers and executives will develop problem identification, diagnostic, and implementation skills. They will also develop an understanding of the importance of consensus and commitment to bringing about change. Another outcome of facilitating client learning is that the organization begins to develop learning culture that fosters additional change. This cycle is essential to an organization's renewing capacity.

Enhancing Organizational Effectiveness

The final objective of the consulting process is referred to as organizational effectiveness, defined as the ability to adapt future strategies and behavior to environmental change and to optimize the contribution of the organization's human resources (Gilley & Eggland, 1989). Organizational effectiveness implies that senior management is dedicated to developing and maintaining the most important systems and linkages needed for improving productivity, efficiency, and profitability. Organizational development consultants must assist in this process so that decision-makers can select the most appropriate change interventions. When consultants are focusing on improving organizational effectiveness, they are concerned with selecting the most appropriate change interventions for an organization, rather than promoting their own biases. Such a focus enables the organization to receive tailor-made recommendations and solutions to its immediate and future problems.

In summary, successful organizational development consultants must be able to:

- demonstrate their knowledge of and skill with organizational design, structure, and culture.

- gather, diagnose, and evaluate data about an organization for the purpose of providing recommendations for change.
- identify the steps needed when implementing change.
- develop linkages within the organization.
- foster employee involvement in bringing about change.

Responsibilities of Organizational Development Consultants

Consultants must accept a variety of responsibilities during organizational development partnerships. Each of these responsibilities is designed to maximize the effectiveness of interventions, improve communications, enhance client relationships, improve organizational performance capacity, enhance the organization's culture, and improve work environments.

First, organizational development consultants must interpret and impart information in order to communicate what changes are needed, to help clients learn how to make needed changes, and to motivate management to accept and adopt change. It is extremely important, therefore, that consultants facilitate the understanding and acceptance of change among employees, managers, and executives. Then and only then will organizations be willing to implement and support change.

Second, organizational development consultants are responsible for supplying information on possible change interventions, helping organizational members to cope with attitudinal shifts, and to handle defensive reactions. Such activities are usually conducted during the implementation phase of the process.

Third, organizational development consultants are responsible for helping organizations acquire new skills, knowledge, insights, awareness, and attitudes needed to implement change. These could include problem-solving skills, giving and receiving performance feedback, listening skills, leadership development, goal setting, resolving conflicts, and diagnosing group interactions. When clients have developed such skills and knowledge, they begin to rely less on consultants and start applying what they have learned.

Organizational Development Consultants' Competencies and Skills

Successful consultants must develop a complex and varied set of competencies and skills. These include:

- interpersonal skills
- conceptual skills
- technical skills
- integrative skills
- analytical skills
- political awareness skills
- conflict resolution skills
- objectivity
- organizational awareness
- specialized knowledge

Interpersonal Skills

Interpersonal skills are at the heart of the consultant/client relationship. Organizational development consultants must be able to foster mutual respect through active listening and interviewing skills. They must also demonstrate respect for the personal boundaries and values of their clients. Interpersonal skills structure the communication process between organizational development consultants and their clients, enabling consultants to develop the acceptance and positive regard of their clients. Finally, interpersonal skills help consultants develop an environment where clients feel safe, so they will be more willing to try out new and unfamiliar behaviors.

Conceptual Skills

Conceptual skills are the resource for managing the content of the organizational development process. Organizational development consultants must have the ability to help clients understand performance problems, change and development opportunities, and new ways of thinking about the organizational system. Every consultant needs a conceptual framework to guide his or her behavior, one that he or she is continuously using to test solutions and recommendations. Such a framework should also be used when conducting organizational analysis, implementing change interventions, and evaluating outcomes.

Technical Skills

Necessary technical skills include the ability to analyze data gathered during diagnosis, to examine solutions, and to evaluate the organizational impact of change interventions. These skills are not only used when analyzing and evaluating change interventions but also when developing new interventions designed to meet the specific needs of a particular client. Technical skills also include good writing and execution skills, and the ability to respond to unforeseen contingencies.

Integrative Skills

When organizational development consultants use interpersonal, conceptual, and technical skills together to manage projects, integrative skills are required. Integrative skills are used to link ideas, concepts, and strategies resulting in dynamic, innovative approaches to problem-solving. Integrative skills require consultants to identify the components of a problem, define their interrelationships, and then fashion interventions that foster performance improvement.

Analytical Skills

It is an organizational development consultant's business to know how to generate information, analyze it, distinguish among problems, symptoms, and causes, identify solutions to problems, and recommend an appropriate solution(s). Such experience is gained by dealing with difficult situations throughout an organization and requires advanced analytical skills.

Political Awareness

Every organization, regardless of its size and complexity, has a political structure and culture that greatly impact its behavior and are necessary to ensure stability and continuity. Employees, managers, and executives must adhere to the organization's structure and culture in order to maintain their individual influence. However, the organization's structure and culture are often a major reason why the organization is experiencing difficulties. To compound this situation, it is often difficult for employees and managers to convince organizational decision-makers that there is something dysfunctional about the organization. It is not, however, impossible for an objective third party to address such sensitive issues. Under these circumstances it would be helpful for organizational development consultants to serve as mouthpieces for employees and managers.

Conflict Resolution Skills

In many organizations conflicting goals, ideas, policies, and practices make it almost impossible to implement meaningful change. However, organizational development consultants who maintain an objective viewpoint may be better able to overcome such resistance to change. They can guide managers and executives through the change process in a way that minimizes resistance because their varied experiences help them to understand why such resistance occurs.

Objectivity

Organizational development consultants must have the ability to remain impartial regardless of personal loyalties, values, or biases, and in spite of an organization's culture, corporate traditions, or vested interests. This perhaps is the greatest single benefit that organizational development consultants can provide.

Objectivity is often impossible for managers and executives because of their perspectives. According to Gilley (1998), it is impossible to effectively address most organizational issues without a high degree of objectivity. Remaining objective enables organizational development consultants to become the social conscience of the organization.

Organizational Awareness

In order to guarantee organizational change, consultants must understand the way organizations operate. Such insight will help them in identifying organizational needs, selecting solutions, implementing interventions, and evaluating the results of change. Organizational development consultants must know where to go for information, insight, recommendations, and coaching in order to avoid the pitfalls common in organizational life. Other benefits of organizational awareness include a better understanding of the political structure and decision-making procedures of the organization, both of which are essential in gaining the support needed to implement meaningful change.

Specialized Knowledge

In order to be useful to an organization, today's organizational development consultant must possess a unique set of skills and specialized knowledge. In fact, too many HRD consultants lack the depth of understanding needed to be successful. The term "consultant" has been used to describe those individuals who design and deliver training programs and workshops rather than those who maintain a unique set of skills and/or specialized knowledge in organizational development. This is having a profoundly negative impact on the credibility of organizational development and on organizational development consultants in particular.

ROLES OF ORGANIZATIONAL DEVELOPMENT CONSULTANTS

A critical set of skills and knowledge needed by organizational development consultants can be grouped into three basic categories: client relationship skills, organizational development skills, and business understanding (Figure 7.1).

Client Relationship Building Skills

Client relationship skills are critical to the success of organizational development consultants, who must develop mutual acceptance and positive regard for their clients by using listening, reflecting, questioning, and summarizing skills. Such skills can help clients develop a sense of security when implementing change for the first time. Consultants must also develop rapport and credibility before

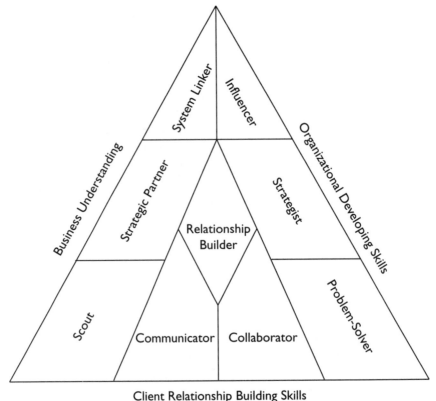

Figure 7.1 Organizational Development Model

clients will be willing to trust their recommendations. There are three roles organizational development consultants assume to build client relationships: relationship builder, collaborator, and communicator.

Relationship Builder

Establishing a positive working relationship with clients is essential for organizational change to be successful. It is the basis of all consulting engagements. Gilley & Coffern (1994) identify several activities that can help organizational development consultants become competent relationship builders. These include turning assertions into questions, giving clients options, making meetings and reports meaningful, helping clients implement solutions and interventions, being accessible, and always, always adding value.

One of the best ways of improving client relationships is helping clients learn. In this way clients develop the knowledge and skills needed for adjusting to future conditions, addressing future problems, and implementing change. Learning will enhance clients' self-esteem, which in turn will help improve the consultant/client relationship. However, client learning must be linked to the organization's strategic business goals and objectives in order to be of lasting value.

As relationship builders, consultants can also facilitate client learning by helping clients develop critical thinking skills. These skills will help clients improve their professional practice, resulting in better approaches to accomplishing work.

Collaborator

As collaborators, organizational development consultants must establish credibility and gain their clients' confidence in order to implement organizational change. Consultants can collaborate with organizational decision-makers in several ways. First, they can tailor their communications to their audience. Second, they can listen and ask appropriate questions designed to demonstrate their understanding of their clients' situation, problems, and difficulties. Third, they can present their ideas clearly and concisely through well-organized written and interpersonal communications. Fourth, they can use informal communication channels as a way of gaining support for change. Fifth, they can identify commonalities among various client groups as a way of determining shared interests. Thus, collaboration is an activity centered on similarities (interests), not overcoming differences through compromise.

Communicator

From the beginning, an effective relationship is a collaborative search for acceptable answers to the client's real needs and concerns (Turner, 1983). Ideally, this will be a mutually beneficial relationship. In order to accomplish this goal, organizational development consultants must become effective communicators to develop trust with their clients. Trust will increase clients' readiness to accept change.

In Chapter 5, we discussed several communication principles and techniques for developing strategic business partnerships within the organization. These same principles and techniques can be used by organizational development consultants in building client relationships.

Organizational Development Skills

As discussed earlier, organizational development can be defined as a system-wide process of collecting and diagnosing data; designing, planning, and implementing interventions; and evaluating interventions. In addition, Gilley and Coffern (1994) believe that organizational development consultants need a set of guiding principles to direct their behavior, and to help anchor them during difficult times. Consequently, consultants must acquire problem-solving, conceptual, research, and analytical skills in order to become effective in managing and implementing organizational change (Gilley, 1998). They must respond to unforeseen contingencies and provide appropriate solutions to complex and sensitive issues as well as conduct a wide variety of activities designed to modify established policies and procedures. All of these situations require organizational development skills. These skills can be found within the following three roles: influencer, strategist, and problem-solver.

Influencer

As an influencer, organizational development consultants are very directive. They attempt to influence their clients' thinking regarding change. When serving as an influencer, consultants must offer specific recommendations addressing difficult organizational problems. Turner (1983) claims that the purpose of an organizational development consulting engagement is fulfilled when the consultant presents a consistent, logical action plan designed to improve the diagnosed problem.

To assure success as an influencer, organizational development consultants must guard against personal biases and overpowering opinions. They must be willing to promote positive change within an organization and demonstrate their openness to new ideas and approaches. They must be able to positively influence others to accept organizational change, as well as to encourage others to take risks in order to achieve organizational goals and objectives.

Influencers must communicate their belief that organizational success depends on the contributions of all members. Such an approach will demonstrate their lack of selfishness and communicate their personal and professional integrity.

Strategist

As strategists, organizational development consultants demonstrate their development skills, knowledge of organizational change, and ability to see the big picture. Consultants must be able to see the entire forest while maneuvering through the trees (Gilley, 1998). They must lead the organization through uncharted territory in the quest for change.

Strategists must be competent in assessing organizational needs using qualitative and quantitative methodologies, in developing and implementing organizational initiatives (i.e., performance management systems), and in evaluating the effectiveness of learning interventions and other initiatives. As strategists, consultants must synthesize the input of others and translate it into action plans, set priorities that are consistent with organizational and departmental goals, direct the organization toward accomplishing its business goals, understand organizational systems, and identify relationships among departments.

Problem-solver

As problem-solvers, organizational development consultants take an active role in the decision-making and change management process. Their primary responsibility is making certain that the perceived problem is indeed the one that is critical to the organization. In other words, consultants must spend the majority of their time determining the accuracy of a problem rather than providing solutions to problems that do not exist (Gilley, 1998). A useful consulting approach involves working with the problem as "defined" by the client in such a way that more useful definitions emerge (Turner, 1983).

Business Understanding

Business understanding is an awareness of how organizations work. Simply stated, it is essential for organizational development consultants to think like their clients. This understanding requires knowledge of how things get done inside an organization as well as how decisions are made there. Business understanding requires consultants to have a knowledge of business fundamentals, systems theory, organizational culture, and politics. By developing business understanding, organizational development consultants will be better able to facilitate change without disrupting the organization's operations.

There are three roles where business understanding can be demonstrated: scout, strategic business partner, and system linker.

Scout

Many organizational development consultants serve in the role of scout, responsible for developing clients' readiness and commitment for organizational change. The following questions can be used as a guide in this process:

1. How willing are the members of the organization to implement change?
2. Is upper-level management willing to learn and utilize new management methods and practices?
3. What types of information do members of the organization readily accept or resist?
4. What are the members' attitudes toward change?
5. What are the executives' attitudes toward change?
6. To what extent will individual members of the organization regard their contribution to overall organizational effectiveness as a legitimate and desirable objective? (Turner, 1983)

Strategic Partner

In order to serve as a strategic partner, organizational development consultants must have a thorough understanding of business fundamentals including core business processes, basic business functions, and operating procedures. They must also understand the critical strategic factors affecting organizational competitiveness. Strategic partners should have the ability to communicate the benefits that change strategies and interventions provide to the organization.

System Linker

Organizations are complex systems made up of many divisions, departments, units, functions, job classifications, levels, and roles. Each is essential to organizational success. One of an organizational development consultant's major roles is to help unify an organization by linking competitive divisions, departments, and units through a common set of guiding principles. These principles help determine the direction, purpose, and focus of an organization.

As system linkers, organizational development consultants are not directly involved in decision-making but help link parts of the organization together. System linkers are able to establish connections between departments by communicating the value and importance of teamwork, thereby allowing fragmented parts of the organization to pull in the same direction to accomplish a common set of outcomes.

Becoming an Organizational Effectiveness Enhancer

The ultimate purpose of the organizational development consulting process is to improve organizational effectiveness. Gilley and Coffern (1994) define organizational effectiveness as "an organization's ability to adapt strategies and behaviors to further environmental change by maximizing contributions of the organization's human resources" (p. 184). Organizational effectiveness assumes that management is dedicated to developing and maintaining the most important systems and linkages to improve the organization's performance capacity.

When improving organizational effectiveness, consultants assist decision-makers by using their client relationship building skills, organizational development skills, and business understanding to identify the best solutions to the organization's problems. Simultaneously, they are helping organizational leaders in overcoming the barriers and obstacles that prevent change. Finally, they must demonstrate their ability to assess organizational dynamics by managing the political environment.

APPLYING THE ORGANIZATIONAL DEVELOPMENT PROCESS

As a way of bringing about organizational improvement and change, organizational development consultants must have a comprehensive approach that they can use over and over. Such an approach will serve as a guide when establishing client relationships, identifying organizational performance problems, identifying clients' resistance to change, conducting diagnosis, providing feedback to clients, selecting appropriate change interventions, implementing change interventions, and evaluating results. This is often referred to as the organizational development process.

Although the number of phases in the organizational development process varies from one theoretical framework to another, there is general agreement that it consists of eight:

1. Establish client relationships.
2. Identify problems.
3. Diagnose problems.
4. Identify the root causes of problems.
5. Provide feedback to clients.
6. Identify, evaluate, and select solutions.
7. Implement interventions.
8. Evaluate results.

Phase 1: Establish Client Relationships

The most critical element in implementing organizational improvement and change is establishing the consultant/client relationship. This is critical for fostering trust and cooperation between consultants and clients. It provides an environment of open and honest communication that can improve understanding and reduce resistance. Also, a positive client relationship helps reduce the impact of hidden agendas so commonly found during organizational change.

During this phase the most important issue to be resolved is that of control. In other words, the balance of power between clients and consultants must be established at the outset, with a clear understanding of who will make what decisions, and how they are to be made.

According to Gilley (1998) and Burke (1992), power can be shared in one of three ways. First, the power to make decisions can reside with the consultants. Second, it can reside with clients. Here they dominate the decision-making process by deciding when and how the consultant's knowledge and skills are to be used. Third is mutually shared power, where clients and organizational development consultants have mutual responsibility for diagnosing needs, generating and selecting solutions, and implementing and evaluating solutions. Except for the client's ultimate veto, neither clients nor organizational development consultants have greater power.

Phase 2: Identify the Problem

The principal responsibility of organizational development consultants is identifying the performance, managerial, cultural, or system problem(s) affecting organizational productivity, performance, quality, or competitiveness. Such problems are often viewed as the difference between "what is" and "what should be." Consequently, most organizations use the organizational development process as a way of narrowing the gap between "what is" and "what should be."

According to Gilley and Eggland (1989), more consulting projects fail when consultants identify the wrong problem than when the wrong solution is selected to solve the right problem. Therefore, it is extremely important to identify the correct problem facing the organization. Furthermore, successful organizational improvement and change efforts begin with rigorous diagnosis of the current organizational state to determine how the organization is presently functioning. This information helps consultants correctly identify whether or not a problem actually exists.

Phase 3: Diagnose Problems

Diagnosing problems involves obtaining, organizing, analyzing, interpreting, and evaluating data. Organizational development consultants may gather data directly or indirectly via interviews, questionnaires, focus groups, records, reports, or observations. In order to develop an effective diagnosis, consultants must make certain that all divisions, departments and units are represented. This will help them make certain they have selected an appropriate diagnostic approach.

Phase 4: Identify the Root Cause of the Problem

All too often, organizational development consultants jump to conclusions and make recommendations before they have uncovered the "real" cause of a problem. If the root cause is not identified, it is possible to waste material, financial, and human resources fixing the wrong problem. Therefore, consultants must examine all possible causes of the problem prior to suggesting solutions.

Phase 5: Provide Feedback to Clients

Once organizational problems have been identified, organizational development consultants must present their preliminary findings to their clients. This will give clients an opportunity to examine the data and provide their reactions and opinions. Providing feedback gives consultants the opportunity to determine the readiness of clients for change. In addition, consultants can make certain that their change strategy is appropriate for the organization prior to implementing a costly and time-consuming intervention that may not help the organization achieve results.

Phase 6: Identify, Evaluate, and Select Solutions

Once the feedback phase has been completed, organizational development consultants must identify the most appropriate change intervention possible. In order to accomplish this outcome, consultants must identify the sources of organizational problems and match appropriate solutions to them. Thus, consultants must be familiar with the variety of intervention strategies available and be able to group them in a meaningful fashion.

Once several appropriate interventions have been identified, consultants, in cooperation with their clients, must evaluate and select the most feasible one using the criteria provided in Chapter 5. When this task has been completed, consultants can make their recommendations.

Phase 7: Implement Interventions

The action taken by an organization to bring about meaningful improvement is generally referred to as an intervention. The success of an intervention is affected by several factors, which include:

- executives' and senior managers' support
- type of organizational resistance
- employees' and managers' readiness for change
- amount and type of employee involvement in the OD process
- payoff and rewards associated with change

Once an intervention has been implemented, organizational development consultants must monitor its progress and determine if adjustments are required. During the implementation phase, it is essential that consultants and clients communicate effectively, because failure to communicate may result in a missed opportunity to bring about meaningful change.

The biggest barrier to implementing meaningful change is employees' beliefs and feelings regarding change. Change can affect the way employees interact and the way they accomplish work. Change can be threatening to employees who see it as something to fear. Organizational development consultants must identify and manage such fears carefully. They must be looking for signs of employee resistance and react accordingly.

Phase 8: Evaluate Results

Two types of evaluation are commonly used during the organizational development process: formative and summative. These are used as the basis for constructively modifying organizational change, not simply as a means for keeping organizational development alive or, alternatively, for completing the organizational development process (Gilley & Eggland, 1989).

Evaluation of a change intervention should be developmental in nature and, consequently, should be formative. Formative evaluation is used in providing feedback for improvement and in making minor modifications in the change intervention. On the other hand, summative evaluations are used in assessing the overall outcomes of the organizational development process and in deciding whether to continue or to terminate the activity. Summative evaluation is usually conducted at the end of a consulting project and is used to determine whether or not organizational goals have been achieved.

APPLYING OD ROLES DURING THE OD PROCESS

Understanding the roles of an organizational development consultant is important but somewhat academic unless HRD professionals know when each role should be used. When HRD professionals are able to integrate these roles their utility becomes apparent.

As HRD professionals (organizational development consultants) apply the organizational development process, they participate in several different roles. Each of these roles is important in the execution of the overall process. Figure 7.2 identifies each of the eight phases of the process and the corresponding roles that are most applicable. Several different roles are used over and over. For example, the communicator role is used in several phases of the

Phases of the OD Process	*OD Roles*
1. Establishing Client Relationships	Relationship Builder
	Communicator
2. Identifying Problems	Communicator
	Problem-Solver
	Scout
3. Diagnosing Problems	Communicator
	Problem-Solver
	Scout
4. Identfiying Root Causes	Communicator
	Collaborator
	Strategist
5. Providing Feedback	Relationship Builder
	Communicator
	Collaborator
	Problem-Solver
6. Identifying, Evaluating, and Selecting Solutions	Collaborator
	Influencer
	Strategist
	System Linker
7. Implementing Interventions	Influencer
	System Linker
	Strategic Partner
8. Evaluating Results	Communicator
	Strategist
	Strategic Partner

Figure 7.2   OD Process and OD Roles Combined

organizational development process such as establishing client relationships, identifying problems, diagnosing problems, identifying root causes of problems, providing client feedback, and evaluating intervention results. Likewise, the problem-solving role is used when identifying and diagnosing problems and providing feedback to clients.

At a more macro level, understanding which combination of roles is used where will help HRD professionals. Figure 7.3 separates the role pyramid into two sections. The bottom half contains *engagement roles,* the top half the *decision-applier* roles.

Engagement roles are used primarily during the first five phases of the organizational development process, when consultants and

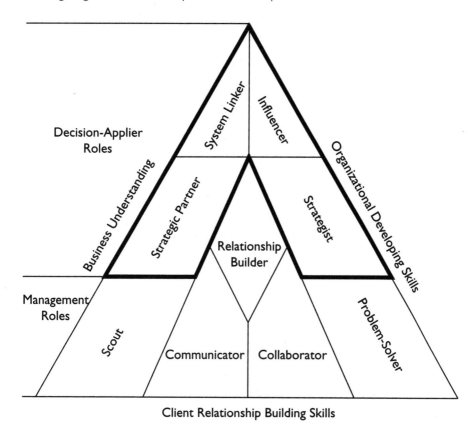

Figure 7.3   Organizational Development Model

their clients are engaged in building positive relationships, uncovering and discovering problems, and reaching agreement on how to proceed. The first five phases form a trial period in which either the consultant or the client can decide to discontinue the activity.

During the last three phases of the organizational development process clients are asked to identify and implement solutions to their problems. Consequently, HRD professionals use more application and partnering oriented roles. For example, consultants are more likely to serve in the roles of strategist, influencer, strategic partner, and system linker.

By understanding and applying these roles to the organizational development process, HRD professionals will be better prepared to address client concerns, focus their efforts, and determine the types of skills needed to successfully complete each phase of the organizational development process.

CONCLUSION

As a way of enhancing organizational effectiveness, HRD professionals must create organizational development partnerships. By doing so, HRD professionals will be able to bring about meaningful and lasting change. Such change can improve the performance capacity of an organization as well as enhance its efficiency, competitiveness, and profitability.

In order to create organizational development partnerships, HRD professionals must make the transition from trainers to organizational development consultants. This transition allows HRD professionals to serve the organization in a strategically integrated way, thereby facilitating client learning and organizational change.

PART IV

Unleashing HRD Practice

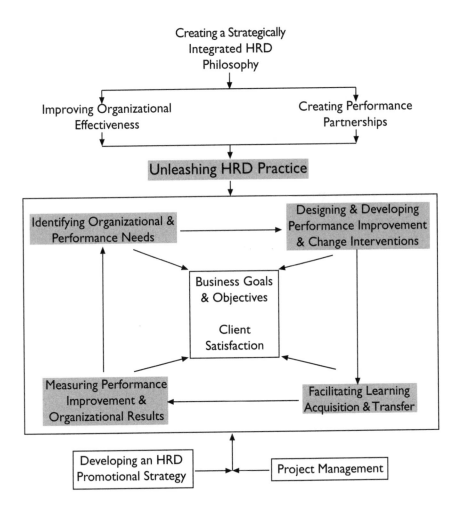

Creating a Strategically
Integrated HRD
Philosophy

Improving Organizational
Effectiveness

Creating Performance
Partnerships

Unleashing HRD Practice

Identifying Organizational &
Performance Needs

Designing & Developing
Performance Improvement
& Change Interventions

Business Goals
& Objectives

Client
Satisfaction

Measuring Performance
Improvement &
Organizational Results

Facilitating Learning
Acquisition & Transfer

Developing an HRD
Promotional Strategy

Project Management

Strategically Integrated HRD

CHAPTER 8

Identifying Organizational and Performance Needs

One of the most important activities an HRD professional can perform is identifying organization and performance needs. Such an activity provides HRD professionals the opportunity to improve organizational effectiveness while building strategic business partnerships, management development partnerships, and organizational development partnerships. By identifying organizational performance needs, HRD professionals can improve their credibility within the organization as well as enhance the image of the HRD program, its interventions, and consulting services.

There is, however, a great deal of confusion surrounding this responsibility. HRD practitioners in vendor-driven programs often view this task as primarily the identification of training needs. Consequently, they engage in a series of analysis projects for the sole purpose of identifying skill, knowledge, and attitudinal deficiencies within the organization—for which they then can provide corrective training interventions. While analysis and training are necessary functions and can fulfill part of HRD's obligation within the organization, identifying organizational and performance needs is a far more complex process than simply isolating training requirements. In this chapter, we will endeavor to explain the four types of analysis that occur within an organization while identifying when each type is appropriate to use.

LEARNING TO THINK STRATEGICALLY

Consider the following situation: While attending a meeting regarding the implementation of a new compensation and benefits program within a large financial institution, an HRD professional (Tom) is approached by the executive vice president of business development (Candice). Candice states in no uncertain terms that she is disappointed with customer service within the firm and considers it one of the reasons that the organization has been unable to increase its market share over the past several years. She continues to explain that she is being pressured by the president and board of directors to increase revenues during the last quarter of the year (so the organization can meet a fairly aggressive goal).

Candice asks Tom if he has any ideas that might be of assistance in her quest to improve revenues. She is convinced that a comprehensive customer service (CS) training program, in which all members of the organization participate, might very well be a means of creating a better CS philosophy within the company. Reluctant to make any premature suggestions, Tom proposes that they sit down early the next morning to discuss the issue in detail. They continue to exchange pleasantries and, finally, arrive at a time to meet the next morning.

At the conclusion of their conversation, Tom immediately goes to his office and begins to examine internal documents that will provide a better understanding of the current financial situation facing the organization. After pouring over several documents, he decides it might be wise to explore another perspective on the situation and so discusses the matter in confidence with another member of the senior management team. During their discussion, the senior manager reveals previously missing information that offers additional insight. Tom solicits advice and recommendations, then quietly reflects upon an appropriate course of action.

During the next few hours Tom is able to gather his thoughts and develops a comprehensive list of questions he will ask Candice the next morning. One of his respected HRD colleagues examines the list of questions and provides a few additional suggestions on sequencing. At this point, Tom feels confident that he will be able to discuss circumstances with Candice in an informed, enlightened manner.

During his morning meeting with Candice, they are able to participate in a dialogue that refocuses her original concerns. They agree that the best way to proceed is to not immediately punish the organization with training, but to examine the situation more closely to determine whether or not a customer service problem exists. They decide to meet later in the week to discuss the parameters of the analysis and to outline their next steps.

We have provided this example to illustrate how an HRD professional can think strategically when asked to provide training interventions that may or may not be appropriate. For many, a request for training from a senior member of the organization is reason enough to immediately take action by providing training for training's sake. Many HRD practitioners would immediately assemble their staffs, set up project parameters, establish timelines, identify available resources, formulate a project schedule, and start the laborious task of identifying the most appropriate training program to deliver within the organization. But is this the correct decision? In many circumstances it is not.

All too often, HRD practitioners react before thinking. In the above example, the HRD professional took time to examine documents, interview an internal confidant, identify a list of questions to be asked during a meeting, and solicit input from another colleague. The ultimate purpose of gathering this type of information is to make informed decisions and recommendations. This HRD professional demonstrated the art of thinking strategically.

Strategic thinking can include a number of things:

1. thinking before reacting
2. listening carefully and selectively to clients' requests
3. filtering suggestions and recommendations through the philosophy of HRD
4. understanding one's role within the organization
5. possessing the courage to say no
6. analyzing all requests *as requests* rather than as commands
7. maintaining consistent guiding principles to ensure credibility (Rossett, 1990)

Simply failing to ask difficult questions can create situations that ultimately produce poor results for HRD professionals and their programs. The solution is to think strategically, continually asking about the organization, its financial and competitive position, strengths and weaknesses, management structure, management capacity, technological state, relationship to competitors, reward and compensation systems used to motivate employees, performance appraisal and review systems, performance management system, and management's attitude toward human resources within the organization (Gilley & Coffern, 1994). Each of these areas of inquiry can help HRD professionals acquire an understanding of the organization and the nature of its business, and demonstrate their understanding of business fundamentals.

During the analysis phase of HRD practice an HRD professional's primary job is to consider what possibilities, circumstances, events, and conditions are causing performance problems or organizational inefficiencies. They have an obligation to determine why an intervention or consulting service is needed. Obviously, providing interventions is sometimes appropriate; however, HRD professionals must make certain of this before recommending and implementing them.

By constantly exploring and asking questions, HRD professionals are not focusing on the status quo, but are continuously looking for new and improved ways of enhancing the organization's effectiveness. Consequently, analysis is as much a state of mind as it is a series of techniques and processes. HRD professionals who are continually examining the state of the organization and comparing it with an ideal vision are constantly in touch with problems and issues facing the firm.

DEVELOPING SUPPORT FOR ORGANIZATIONAL AND PERFORMANCE ANALYSIS

Many organizations fail to see analysis as an important activity. In fact, some even see it as a waste of time, energy, and effort. As a result, there is sometimes very little support for conducting analyses within the organization. Gaining support is critical as it will help condition the organization to use such activities prior to implementing costly interventions. According to Rossett (1990), there are three strategies that can be used to increase support for organizational and performance analysis:

1. Conduct effective analysis, document what has been done and how it has contributed to the bottom line.
2. Make the case for analysis by demonstrating its importance (e.g., what if a physician prescribed treatment without cautious diagnosis?).
3. Avoid using terms such as analysis, needs assessment, or front-end analysis if management does not respond well to these. Instead use terms such as planning, study, or research.

Another way of garnering support for organizational performance analysis is to identify internal sponsors or advocates (see Chapter 5). These individuals should possess credibility within the organization and have the opportunity to encourage and promote analysis within the firm. Well-established networks and important contacts within the organization are vital, as is the ability to articulate ideas in a persuasive manner. In addition, HRD professionals should find ways of participating in high-profile assessment activities—ones that are of great importance to senior managers and executives within the organization, and which impact a large number of decision-makers, stakeholders, and influencers. This analysis will elevate HRD professionals while enhancing their image and credibility.

Overcoming Analysis Paralysis

Ron Walker, executive vice president of professional affairs for William M. Mercer, Inc., shared with us several years ago that organizations sometimes possess a phobia known as analysis paralysis. For example, many new (and some veteran) actors experience stage fright—the fear of performing in public. After all, public performance subjects one to the intense scrutiny (analysis) of critics, fans, and peers. The same is true in organizations, where executives, managers, and employees are being examined by problem-finders and problem-solvers. These individuals resist analysis because they fear incompetencies may be revealed, deficiencies that must eventually be addressed and for which they will be held accountable.

We affectionately refer to analysis paralysis as people's fear of having someone rummage through their underwear drawer. Analysis paralysis can prevent well-intended, well-meaning examination of critical performance problems and organizational deficiencies that lead to poor quality, unacceptable customer service, and negative business results. Analysis paralysis is most common in organizations where HRD professionals do not maintain credibility and are not seen as strategic business partners within the organization. One of the best ways to cure analysis paralysis is to plan examination activities very carefully and to understand the fears of one's clients regarding such events.

HRD professionals must clearly understand the goals of analysis, the kinds of questions that will achieve those goals, the sources of information that must be examined, the cost of material and human resources used during analysis, and potential areas of disagreement. In other words, HRD professionals must know what they are doing in order to effectively, efficiently provide analysis opportunities.

Another effective strategy is to be self-promotional by sharing the findings discovered during analysis (see Chapter 12). In this way, HRD professionals constantly remind organizational leaders and key decision-makers that their analysis activities are making a difference by uncovering information that is critical and useful when making decisions. This strategy also demonstrates an HRD professional's understanding of the utility of organizational performance analysis and encourages the organization's continued use of similar analyses. Confidence breeds confidence and, over time, organizational members will begin to abandon analysis paralysis.

TAILORING ORGANIZATIONAL AND PERFORMANCE ANALYSIS TO FIT THE ORGANIZATION

Vendor-driven HRD programs face a unique barrier when it comes to the practice of organizational performance analysis. Circumstances have been created in which their programs are funded based upon the number of training courses provided and the number of attending participants. Consequently, this philosophy of HRD has two major negative effects. First, no budget exists for analysis. Second, there are few if any incentives for improving organizational development or performance. By embracing a vendor-driven philosophy, HRD professionals are painting themselves into a corner when it comes to the issue of analysis. In fact, the only type of analysis common in these programs is that of needs analysis, which involves identifying skills and knowledge deficiencies used as the foundation for training activity.

According to Rossett (1990), the only solution to this obstacle is to confront it directly. HRD professionals must be proactive and assertive in advocating that organizations could be focusing their attention on the wrong HRD philosophy, rather than on improving performance or organizational development. Organizational and performance analysis will not become a strategic weapon to improve organizational effectiveness until HRD has crossed the line of demarcation from an activity to a results-driven program. By making this transition, HRD programs advocate the importance of incorporating analysis into the organization's everyday activities. Then and only then will organizational and performance analysis become a routine activity within an organization.

FIVE CRITICAL QUESTIONS

HRD professionals engage in organizational and performance analysis as a means of uncovering the diverse needs of the organization. To effectively use the analysis process, they should answer the following five questions:

1. What is the definition of a problem?
2. Where is the pain?
3. What are the four types of analysis?
4. How do HRD professionals proceed?
5. What evidence do HRD professionals have to support their point of view (Gilley & Coffern, 1994)?

The answer to each of these questions will provide a better understanding of what the analysis process is designed to accomplish, in which type of analysis to engage, and why.

What Is the Definition of a Problem?

The organizational and performance analysis process begins with identifying the expectations of executives and managers (i.e., revenue, production, quality, service, return on investment), and comparing them to actual performance. Management's expectations are the desired state, and serve as targets for all operational units, divisions, and departments. Productivity and performance represent today's reality, or current state. A problem represents the gap between the current state and the desired state. Or, as stated in Chapter 4, a problem is the difference between "what is" and "what should be."

HRD professionals are responsible for identifying three types of deficiencies, each of which can contribute to organizational inefficiency if not properly addressed. These deficiencies can be in *proficiencies* (knowledge, skills, and attitudes), *performance,* or *results.* In the case of proficiencies, HRD professionals engage in analysis as a way of identifying training needs, which serve as the foundation for designing and developing performance improvement interventions. Interventions are used to overcome a plethora of skill and knowledge deficiencies, including those of managers and supervisors. By examining performance deficiencies, HRD professionals employ a variety of activities that help them ascertain the impact of the organizational and performance management system on performance outcomes. It is not enough to examine skills, knowledge, and attitudes when one looks at performance. HRD professionals must go beyond such rudimentary analyses to uncover the true causes of performance shortfalls.

Results deficiencies must be examined in light of the entire organizational system rather than just looking at individual employee's skills and abilities. Consequently, analysis focused on results deficiencies are the most complex as they are aimed at the macro level (Kaufman, Rojas, & Mayer, 1992).

Where Is the Pain?

At the heart of the organizational and performance analysis process is the question "Where is the pain?" This question provides direction and focus for HRD professionals as they engage in analysis projects. Locating the pain also helps determine which type of analysis is most appropriate, and when it should be used.

As stated previously, the analysis process begins by identifying the type of gap confronting the organization. According to Gilley and Coffern (1994), four types of gaps challenge HRD professionals:

1. need gaps—deficiencies in skills, knowledge, and attitudes needed by employees to carry out their assignments and duties
2. performance gaps—deficiencies in the way the organization manages performance, designs jobs, or reinforces and rewards performance
3. management gaps—deficiencies in the way employees are managed and motivated within the organization
4. organizational gaps—deficiencies in the way the organization is conceived, designed, and managed

Need Gaps

Need gaps are usually reduced via training activities designed to provide employees with new skills, knowledge, or attitude improvement. When employees adopt these proficiencies they should be able to increase productivity and achieve better results. Need gaps should be examined when it is feared that "training" is the most appropriate solution.

Performance Gaps

Failure to implement well-conceived and designed performance management systems causes performance gaps. In Chapter 3, we discussed in detail the importance of creating such a system. When HRD professionals are asked to examine the performance capacity of an organization, performance gap analysis is in order.

Management Gaps

One of the biggest problems facing organizations today involves the quality of managers. At the center of every organization, managers provide guidance and direction for employees and serve as liaisons between executives and employees, interpreting the organization's vision and ensuring that goals and expectations are met (Gilley & Boughton, 1996). Far too many organizations still accept the notion that managers need not be skilled in the art of managing. Managers are allowed to be indifferent toward their employees, maintain superior attitudes, or consider employees as vessels to be used and abused. Often, managers are allowed to possess poor listening and feedback skills, and are not disciplined when they are unable to build positive, productive relationships with employees. Organizations continue to retain managers who are unable to delegate, develop their personnel, conduct performance appraisals, or establish priorities. In other words, organizations foster managerial malpractice (Gilley & Boughton, 1996, p. 15).

Fortunately, HRD professionals are often asked to determine ways of improving managers' proficiencies and skills. Consequently, the analysis process is used to expose managerial gaps within the organization. Interventions sometimes include performance coaching training (see Chapter 6). More importantly, HRD professionals should cultivate management development partnerships designed to improve overall performance within the organization. By doing so, they create long-term solutions to managerial malpractice. Another appropriate intervention includes the design and development of competency-based selection tools that can be used to recruit and select individuals with the aptitude to become efficient managers capable of securing results through people.

Organizational Gaps

Sometimes HRD professionals are asked to help the organization reinvent itself. Resulting analysis activities are extremely complex, time-consuming, and require the greatest amount of skill among HRD professionals. Nevertheless, organizational gaps need to be examined and interventions designed. The most common types of interventions include organizational development and design activities, and reengineering and change management.

Chapter 7 discussed in detail the importance of creating organizational development partnerships within the firm. These partnerships are key to improving organizational viability and effectiveness, ultimately helping the organization achieve better results.

What Are the Four Types of Analysis?

The four types of gaps confronting organizations are addressed by four corresponding types of analysis:

1. organizational analysis
2. management analysis

3. performance and business analysis
4. needs analysis

Each will be examined in greater detail later in this chapter.

How Do HRD Professionals Proceed?

HRD professionals often struggle with how to best proceed in the analysis phase of HRD practice. One way is to consider three critical principles of change: congruence, pre-disposition, and succession (Bowers & Franklin, 1977). Before enacting any form of analysis these simple but straightforward concepts should be considered.

Vendor-driven HRD professionals often have difficulty with the principle of congruence as they are conditioned to select off-the-shelf approaches to difficult problems. The principle of congruence implies that the analysis process must be selected, designed, and adjusted to fit the structure and function of the organization. Only those HRD professionals who have converted to the results-driven side of HRD (decentralized, strategically driven HRD) embrace the principle of congruence.

In every organization there are certain points at which organizational performance analysis is more likely to succeed. That is, where the organization has a predisposition to change in certain areas. By identifying these "penetration" or "leverage points," analysis is more likely to be successfully adopted and integrated into the organization, allowing the rest of the organization to benefit. HRD professionals must proceed with this concept in mind and continuously search for conditions, circumstances, and situations where analysis will be more readily accepted as well as to identify advocates and sponsors for such activities.

The principle of succession is perhaps the most difficult to comprehend. Succession implies that change does not occur in a direct fashion. That is, some change will only occur after barriers and obstacles are removed from the organizational culture. Because this phenomenon is common in organizations, HRD professionals must devote a great deal of time to identifying and overcoming these barriers and obstacles. Far too many HRD professionals engage in analysis activities prior to preparing the organization for upcoming interventions. Such an overzealous approach can lead to analysis paralysis.

Once HRD professionals have considered these three principles of change they must contemplate how to proceed. In fact, they should account for all three principles simultaneously when developing a strategic approach to organizational, management, and performance analysis. An appropriate strategic approach includes:

1. removing obstacles and barriers that prevent the implementation of organizational performance analysis
2. identifying penetration points where organizational performance analysis is most likely to succeed
3. designing, developing, and implementing an organizational performance analysis that fits the organization

Because of limited resources, analysis activities must be prioritized. While we can all agree that analysis is important, some analysis functions are more important than others. Therefore, it is critical that HRD professionals know the difference between analysis activities that produce limited results (i.e., training needs) versus those that can enhance the overall effectiveness of the organization (i.e., organizational analysis).

The selection of analysis activities must also be balanced with a consideration of those deemed most urgent. Assessing urgency can be difficult, as it is human nature to respond to individuals who create the most noise, have the loudest voices, or are in a position within the organization to command immediate attention (e.g., senior management). Because of limited human and material resources, HRD professionals must identify those analyses that will have the greatest impact on the organization's effectiveness, efficiency, and quality. These become an HRD professional's highest priority.

What Evidence Do HRD Professionals Have to Support Their Point of View?

Prior to embarking on the actual analysis process, HRD professionals must challenge their own point of view. By doing so, they are forced to gather data that either supports or rejects their hypothesis. In this way HRD professionals document the types of evidence needed to make thoughtful, reasonable recommendations that address the organization's problems. There are a number of strategies that may be used to uncover evidence from the various constituencies within the organization. These are referred to, collectively, as methods, and may consist of eight to ten. The seven most useful to HRD professionals will be highlighted here:

1. is/should analysis
2. focus groups

3. critical incident analysis
4. interviews
5. observations
6. questionnaires
7. root cause analysis

It should be noted that each of these methods is designed to identify and solicit the thoughts and ideas of executives, managers, and employees regarding organizational, performance, and training needs. Some are more appropriate than others, and HRD professionals must be able to ascertain under what conditions and circumstances they will use various methods. Since the purpose of utilizing these methods is to solicit information, it is better to rely on several sources as opposed to just one. In this way, HRD professionals can feel more confident about the data collected, particularly when differing methodologies produce identical results.

Is/Should Analysis

The is/should method of data collection provides a simple way to identify problems. It is most useful when users are not familiar with a particular process or performance occurring within the organization. The easiest way to use this method is by developing an is/should chart—a simple list of issues related to a specific problem, reporting the current state in the left column and the desired state in the right column. This is simply a method of organizing information to compare "what is happening" with "what should be happening." Such an analysis does require research in order to discover the current state and to identify standards representative of the desired state.

This method is most useful at the very beginning of the analysis process prior to engaging in a formal assessment activity. The is/should method's primary strengths are that it can be used by groups or individuals, it asks the user to be solution-oriented during problem identification, and it is simple and easy to use.

Two weaknesses are associated with this method. It does not, by design, force the user to prioritize processes or problems. Also, it does not lend itself to the comparison of multiple problems or processes with one chart.

The "Is" side of the chart should be free of bias—constructed from actual observations, interviews, focus groups, or other research. The "Should" side may reflect only a particular group or individual's perspective of what the desired state is, which are often predetermined by industrial or performance standards common in an industry.

The is/should method can be used separately by different individuals to compare perceptions of the is/should criteria. In this way, the method can validate a common issue or confirm opposing viewpoints. In any event, the tool can further discussion that may lead to agreement about performance standards for the desired state. The method itself does not inherently offer reliability or validity, which depends upon its use (see Chapter 11).

Focus Groups

Focus groups are small discussion groups consisting of a few employees led by a facilitator. The purpose is to focus on a topic and take an in-depth look at the group's opinions and points of view regarding the topic. In addition to identifying a problem, focus groups can provide valuable insights as to causes and offer recommendations for interventions.

Ideally, focus groups should be comprised of no more than ten people who represent a cross section of the organization. In selecting participants, a random sample is recommended, placing peer groups together as the probability of honesty, comfort, and disclosure increases with like groups.

When gaining information from a variety of sources, several focus groups may develop organizational recommendations. For example, one group might choose to be represented by management members, volunteers, or valued customers—allowing for a broad range of opinions. HRD professionals will never gain total representation of opinions; however, the more diverse the groups the more accurate overall analysis will be. Generally, focus groups meet for no longer than one-and-one-half hours at a time. If possible, focus groups should be conducted on the organization's time as participants will be more receptive if they are paid.

The focus group methodology can be time-consuming, but it affords HRD professionals an opportunity to gain an in-depth perspective of the group's opinion. The only other method that provides this level of insight is personal interviews, which are even more time consuming. Other feedback mechanisms such as questionnaires and observations answer the "what" but not the "why" provided by focus groups. This is the principal strength of the focus group approach. It also provides an interpersonal method for eliciting information; is a direct, collaborative process; is useful for gathering information necessary in developing questionnaires for quantitative study; and provides easy, fairly reliable access to ideas and attitudes.

Alternatively, the focus group method embodies several weaknesses. First, focus groups rely on qualitative, not quantitative, information that prevents HRD professionals from determining how widespread attitudes or opinions might be throughout the organization. This bias can often cause HRD professionals to focus on minor issues that quantitative methods could eliminate. Second, focus groups often lack a holistic representation of the organization, regardless of how painstakingly they are assembled. Third, focus groups can be quite expensive because they require a great deal of preparation time and entail loss in productivity due to the participation of group members. Fourth, regardless of the facilitator's skill level, some group participants may harbor fears of disclosing and providing honest responses. Fifth, participants may be swayed by the popular, or majority, opinion of the group. Rarely do individual participants stand firm on their opinions and ideas, similar to the sole holdout in the movie, *Twelve Angry Men*. Sixth, focus groups necessitate a lot of work, typically requiring 120 to 150 hours of typing, writing, analyzing, editing, and comprehending the data collected.

What follows are the preplanning and meeting activities of focus groups:

Pre-planning Activities

1. Identify a facilitator to conduct the focus group.
2. Randomly select the participants and representatives.
3. Isolate the problem the focus group is intended to address.
4. Determine the focus group's purpose.
5. Create a general outline of the topic to be explored, along with projected time commitments.
6. Establish an agenda that includes participant roles, purposes, and processes for procedures.

Meeting Activities

1. Randomly select the participants and representatives.
2. Allocate roles for participants (e.g., facilitator, recorder, or participant).
3. Arrange a meeting, in a private room, where the general outline will be introduced and the purpose explained to participants. In addition, explain what will be done with the information gathered.
4. Launch the focus group by introducing each participant and reviewing the agenda (which should include participant roles, purposes of the focus group, process rules, and the anticipated amount of time for meetings).

5. Facilitate the focus group by controlling dialogue and conflict while moving beyond the general to the specific.
6. Close the meeting by reviewing the information gathered, determining whether the group's purposes have been met, explaining next steps and how the information will be used, and thanking participants for their time and contributions.
7. Follow-up by summarizing the outcomes and sending a copy to each participant, along with a "thank you" note expressing appreciation for the group members' time and effort.

Focus groups should be facilitated by a nonpartisan HRD professional capable of asking questions that address the specific needs, concerns, and opinions of the participants. The facilitator may choose to educate group members on a particular topic prior to gathering individual or group responses. He or she may ask participants to problem-solve or brainstorm solutions to specific situations, and to make corresponding recommendations for change. To perform a stronger analysis, the focus group method can be combined with critical incident analysis or individual interviews, depending on the organization's needs and the purpose of the assessment.

Critical Incident Analysis

A critical incident analysis helps HRD professionals make the transition from general problems to specific details of organizational and performance concerns. Critical incident analysis involves interacting with sources to exact specific emotional events by detailing successful and unsuccessful performance. It can be a needs analysis in itself, but is more significant when used as a vibrant part of another method such as an interview or a focus group. A critical incident (sometimes referred to as a significant incident report) records an example of extreme behavior or performance, along with the responses of individuals who observed or were otherwise involved in the event.

Critical incident analysis is extremely useful in identifying details of a problem and its contributing factors. This analysis is also beneficial in determining individuals' feelings and perceptions about a situation. To qualify as a critical incident, the event must involve performance that actually took place on the job, have a clear purpose with identifiable consequences, and it must have first-hand witnesses.

The critical incident method is valuable to use when investigating the effectiveness of on-the-job performance or when examining organizational effectiveness. To be used properly, the critical incident method must address the following questions:

1. What was done that led to effective job performance and/or organizational effectiveness?
2. What was done that detracted from effective job performance and/or organizational effectiveness?
3. What, if done differently, would have been more effective?
4. What attitudes, values, abilities, knowledge, or skills (present or absent) seem to have lead to success or failure?

The critical incident technique is not used to study every job. It is most appropriate for analyzing jobs that are somewhat ambiguous, flexible, or where there are an undefined number of ways to achieve the same outcome. When using this technique, HRD professionals should ask a series of questions that will allow individuals to feel comfortable enough to answer openly and honestly. Seven steps promote the move from general problem-solving to specific details of performance analysis:

1. Direct the individual's attention: "What occurred recently on the job that caused job dissatisfaction?"
2. Focus on specific events: "What part of the job caused the most problems?"
3. Surface underlying feelings or perceptions: "How did this incident make you feel about your job?"
4. Identify causes: "What do you see as the cause of this problem?"
5. Pinpoint solutions: "What could have been done to prevent this from occurring?"
6. Seek recommendations: "What should be done to avoid a repeat of this incident?"
7. Conclude with a confirmation: "Let me summarize what I just heard you say."

When this technique is used to capture critical behaviors of jobs and tasks that allow a high degree of individuality it is an excellent tool. However, when this technique is used to capture elements of a very simple, highly repetitive, and procedurally limited job, results are somewhat disappointing.

Interviews

Another useful technique for gathering information is to conduct one-on-one interviews with employees, managers, and executives. As with any interviewing process, this method allows employees an opportunity to share ideas, clarify misconceptions, and express their opinions, perspectives, and points of view. This technique is most appropriate when examining confidential problems or issues that people may feel uncomfortable discussing in a group. In fact, managers and supervisors often feel more comfortable sharing their opinions in interviews—as opposed to focus groups— even if the group is comprised of their peers. Managers and supervisors usually prefer to voice their opinions about the organization in a more private setting. Furthermore, scheduling a convenient meeting time with one manager is easier than coordinating meetings for a group of managers.

Interviews are a powerful tool, yet they have their own strengths and weaknesses. On the positive side, they reveal more than just information. They also provide HRD professionals an opportunity to observe body language, gestures, and nonverbal behaviors that may be more telling than an individual's verbalized ideas and opinions. For the most part, interviews are flexible; however, they should be developed around a well-designed structure or framework in order to maintain continuity from one individual to the next. Interviewing is an excellent technique when soliciting opinions from subject matter experts who have a great deal to say about a particular organizational or performance problem. Finally, interviewing provides an effective vehicle by which HRD professionals build rapport and relationships with members of the organization—which can only enhance their credibility as well as demonstrate their competence.

The principal weakness of interviews is that they are unpredictable, meaning HRD professionals cannot control the information gathered or the outcomes of meetings. Additionally, interviews can turn sour. They can be viewed by the interviewee as an opportunity to simply vent frustration, anger, or overall resentment concerning the organization. Under these circumstances, interviewers should remain neutral. Interviewing is an extremely difficult technique to master. The challenge to HRD professionals is to develop the skills necessary to discuss difficult issues openly and honestly while maintaining direction and focus, collecting useful and meaningful information, and building rapport with clients.

The following steps should help HRD professionals conduct effective interviews:

1. Preparation for the interview
   a. Identify the interview's purpose.
   b. Review the tasks of the interview.

    c. Develop the interview agenda.

    d. Schedule date(s).

2. Opening the interview

    a. Make the participant feel comfortable.

    b. Explain your role as interviewer.

    c. Explain the participant's role as interviewee.

    d. Discuss the interview's purpose and how information will be used.

3. Conducting the interview.

    a. Ask questions and record answers.

    b. Listen responsively and selectively to interviewees' answers.

    c. Take notes on interviewees' responses.

4. Concluding the interview

    a. Give interviewees an opportunity to ask questions.

    b. Discuss additional information.

    c. Thank interviewees for their time, effort, and opinions.

Observation

When HRD professionals collect data by watching one or more persons performing a series of tasks or exhibiting skills, they are using a technique known as observation. Observation is used when detailed information is necessary and when acquired skills need to be measured for accuracy and effectiveness (Gilley, 1990). Observation can also be used to measure qualitative characteristics like self-control, truthfulness, cooperativeness, or honesty, but only when job activities are observable. It is important to note that the observer and the person under observation should never interact during the activity. An HRD professional needs to be familiar enough with the task to recognize if performance meets existing standards. Whenever possible, the observer should be impartial. Observation is an excellent technique when attempting to establish "best practices," where subject matter experts or exemplary performers can be observed. This technique can also be used as part of the is/should analysis. HRD professionals can use observation when determining the gaps between actual and desired performance, rather than using is/should charts as previously discussed.

Observation can be either structured or unstructured. Structured observations are when the observed performance has been predetermined. When this type of observation is used, HRD professionals utilize structured observation checklists to determine if the activity has been completed correctly. These checklists contain a list of each task along with explanations as to how each is to be performed. The purpose of this activity is to isolate which tasks are performed correctly and which involve errors.

An unstructured observation does not follow a predetermined checklist. Instead, HRD professionals simply write down what they observe (including the steps that the observee used in completing the task), as well as descriptions of what is being observed (such as general information about the performer and performance). Since most of the evidence is based on undocumented, unsubstantiated methods for performing a task, it is critical that information be captured in exactly the form in which it is observed.

Observation is perhaps most useful when setting standards for job tasks. When making observations, HRD professionals must:

- identify the person being watched and their corresponding job function.
- describe the procedures being studied in sufficient detail to allow persons with no knowledge of the activity to follow resulting instructions.
- outline the order in which the task is completed.
- list any forms used to carry out the task.
- identify decision points and construct decision trees showing any alternatives resulting from those decisions.
- pinpoint the circumstances under which the task takes place.
- choose the best time for observation.
- prepare a checklist if one is to be used.
- compare performance with existing standards (Gilley & Coffern, 1994, p. 40).

Questionnaires

One of the most difficult analysis methodologies to be used is that of questionnaires, which are very difficult to write in a clear, concise, uniform manner. Questionnaires are a means of eliciting the thoughts, feelings, beliefs, experiences, and attitudes of employees, managers, and executives. They are a concise, preplanned set of questions designed to yield specific information on a particular topic (Gilley, 1990). Questionnaires are not particularly useful in determining intensity of feelings, even though Likert Scales (ranking scales) are often used. Another disadvantage of questionnaires is that queries are open to interpretation, potentially skewing outcomes. Additionally, a low completion and return rate, sometimes less than twenty percent, makes it difficult to generalize to the population as a whole. In certain instances respondents are unable to read and interpret the questionnaire, which reduces the accuracy of data collected. Finally, questionnaires are linear by design, meaning HRD professionals must know exactly what they are looking for prior to designing the instrument. Questionnaires do not lend themselves to open interpretations and flexibility.

A word of caution: Questionnaires should be used only after all other sources of information have been thoroughly researched, which includes the use of other analysis methodologies. As questionnaires are designed to render exact information, alternative analysis methodologies can be used to gather preliminary data—which will be analyzed for the purpose of constructing a questionnaire.

Questionnaires provide an effective means by which to obtain information from a large group. For example, if the survey is sent to a group of employees within the organization and the response rate is extremely high (fifty percent or more), the amount of feedback received is far greater than can be obtained via interviews, focus groups, or observations. This is one of the reasons questionnaires are a favored form of gathering data. Questionnaires are also viewed by most as confidential, a crucial element when anonymity is desired by respondents.

Questionnaires are often used as a means of sampling individuals who work and live in different locations throughout the country. Because questionnaires can be used to sample large populations in diverse locations, they are very cost effective. Additionally, they are relatively time efficient, typically requiring less than twenty minutes to complete. Furthermore, when properly constructed, analysis is fairly easy.

The major weakness of questionnaires involves obtaining acceptable response rates such that HRD professionals can make inferences relating to the total population. The following suggestions are offered to help improve response rates:

1. Keep the questionnaire as brief as possible.
2. Limit the number of open-ended questions.
3. Use primarily ranking questions (rank from 1 to 10, show the level of agreement using a scale of 1–5, etc.), multiple choice, or closed (yes/no) questions.
4. Keep the survey anonymous.
5. Provide an easy return method (include a return envelope or give instructions to return the questionnaire to an easily accessible location).
6. Obtain a sponsor.
7. Choose the sample group carefully.

According to Gilley and Coffern (1994), effective questionnaires should include the following characteristics:

1. They should deal with a specific topic—one that individuals in the sample recognize as important. The questionnaire's significance should be clearly stated in the accompanying letter or on the questionnaire.
2. They should be attractive in appearance—neatly and logically arranged, and clearly printed.
3. They should contain clear, complete directions and definitions of necessary terms.
4. They should be objective—containing no leading questions that signal the desired response.
5. They should be logical, and flow from general to specific responses.
6. They should be easy to tabulate and interpret.
7. They should include a cover letter explaining the questionnaire's purpose and response deadline.

When constructing a questionnaire, HRD professionals must keep in the mind the following rules:

- Define or qualify terms that may be easily misunderstood or misinterpreted.
- Watch for descriptive adjectives and adverbs that contain no agreed-upon meaning, such as frequently, occasionally, or rarely.
- Beware of double negatives (the respondent must study these carefully to answer properly).
- Underline a word if it should be emphasized.
- Give an example or point of reference when asking for a ranking or rating.
- Avoid unwarranted assumptions.
- Phrase questions so they are appropriate for all respondents.
- Design questions that give complete possibilities for comprehensive responses.
- Provide for a systematic qualification of responses (Gilley, 1990).

Perhaps the key to obtaining a high response rate is writing an effective cover letter. Cover letters should convey to respondents the purpose of the survey, and make a persuasive argument for their cooperation. Cover letters should stress the questionnaire's confidentiality, as well as how the information will be used. High-ranking sponsors such as organizational executives or managers should be identified. Another effective technique involves guaranteeing respondents a copy of the study's results in a timely fashion, thus allowing them to compare their own perspectives with those of others. Similar promises may heighten curiosity and interest. Cover letters should request the immediate return of the questionnaire with a clearly stated deadline. Finally, HRD professionals should express their appreciation, in advance, for respondents' time and cooperation.

Root Cause Analysis

Root cause analysis helps prevent managers and executives from jumping to conclusions. Failure to identify root causes results in wasted financial, material, and human resources while attempting to fix the wrong problem. As a process, root cause analysis establishes a framework to identify the real cause of organizational and performance deficiencies.

The primary strength of this technique is the use of brainstorming to reveal all possible causes. Because of the way the technique is designed to be used, there are no preconceived or predetermined reasons for *why* the problem exists. Hence, on the surface, root cause analysis is bias-free—which can help organizations make significant improvements in their performance and methods via which results are achieved.

The basic steps of root cause analysis are as follows:

1. Identify and agree on the definition(s) of the problem(s). For example, survey results and individual interviews may indicate that employees feel there are no opportunities for promotion.
2. Identify possible causes of the problem. Utilize brainstorming and cause/effect diagrams to surface ideas. Write down all ideas—later the group will discuss and eliminate as appropriate.
3. Verify causes with data. Use existing data or, if needed, identify additional data necessary to help decide which are actual causes of the problem. If more information is needed, identify what it is and who will obtain it.
4. Check conclusions about causes. Do people with knowledge of the issue agree with the conclusions? Do conclusions make sense? Is additional information needed to support the results?

By following these simple steps, HRD professionals can guide members of the organization through a process of determining the real reasons that problems exist within the firm. It is important to remember that root cause analysis is unreliable as a stand-alone tool. Therefore, other analysis techniques should be used to support results.

ORGANIZATIONAL ANALYSIS

The most comprehensive and complex type of analysis, organizational analysis attempts to identify the deficiencies between current and desired organizational results. It consists of eight discrete steps designed to identify *why* there is a discrepancy in organizational results (Figure 8.1). Kaufman, Rojas, and Mayer (1992) refer to organizational analysis as a macroanalysis due to its complexity and disruptive nature. It is a major event—one that all members of the organization are aware of, participate in, and are affected by. Organizational analysis should be the primary responsibility of HRD professionals, offering excellent opportunities for creating and developing organizational development partnerships. HRD professionals are part of the analysis team used to uncover the root causes of organizational deficiencies. They are responsible for each of the eight steps of an organizational analysis, and must possess an understanding of business fundamentals, the nature of business, and the organization. Additionally, they focus organizational analysis at the correct level within the organization. Each of these characteristics will be explained later in this chapter.

Developing Collaborative Client Relationships

This step in the organizational analysis process permits HRD professionals to develop positive working relationships with clients. Doing so initiates client partnerships that will be essential during the analysis process.

HRD professionals must engage in four activities to accomplish this end, including meeting with the client, discussing the client's background, establishing rapport, and developing trust. While these seem very straightforward, common sense actions, they are far more difficult to master than anticipated. There are eight critical components to a healthy, functional relationship, which are:

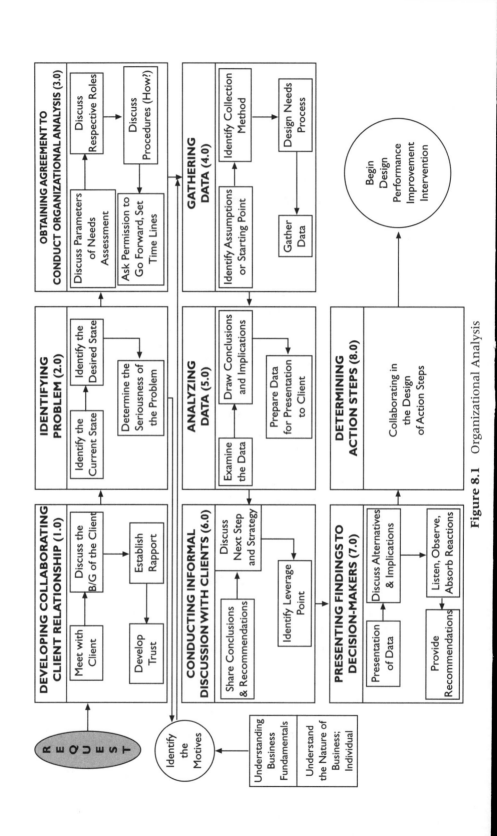

Figure 8.1 Organizational Analysis

1. freedom from fear
2. communication
3. interaction
4. acceptance
5. personal involvement
6. trust
7. honesty
8. self-esteem (Gilley & Boughton, 1996)

Freedom from Fear

Fear kills organizational and individual performance. An environment characterized by reprisals and intimidation will cause frustration, anger, and resentment. Good relationships cannot survive under these conditions.

Fearless relationships allow HRD professionals and their clients to grow, develop, and work collectively. Creativity flourishes when fear is eliminated. Additionally, in a fear-free environment clients are challenged and stimulated to solve complex problems, thus allowing both sides the opportunity to build a positive relationship that ultimately benefits the organization.

Communication

Even in organizations free of fear, communication can break down. Sometimes, HRD professionals allow only one-way communication, from them to their clients. Some are willing to communicate but have poor listening skills, which discourages client communications. Many times messages are misunderstood because HRD professionals and clients possess different frames of reference or use different terms. To overcome this, HRD professionals should encourage two-way communication, making certain to interact on the same level and using the same language as their clients.

Interaction

To have healthy, fear-free, mistake-free communication, personal interaction must be fostered. E-mail, for example, while convenient and efficient, can also present a barrier to interpersonal interaction. HRD professionals must not be afraid of face-to-face contact with clients. Person-to-person exchanges are vital to developing rapport.

Acceptance

Relationships must be nonjudgmental. Acceptance means being ready to listen to and consider what clients have to say. If HRD professionals dismiss client input, the relationship becomes one-way and very weak.

Personal Involvement

HRD professionals must know their clients as human beings, and vice versa. This does not mean that every personal detail of one's life is shared with clients. But it does mean showing concern and interest in clients as persons of worth as well as project participants.

Trust

Trust can only be established if the relationship between HRD professionals and their clients exemplifies truth, confidence, mutual respect, and reliability. Trust assures both sides that all necessary, vital information will be shared, confidentiality will be respected, and proposed solutions will be free of bias. Hence, no hidden agendas. If HRD professionals are perceived as being untrustworthy, clients will refuse to build long-term relationships with them.

Honesty

Collaborative client relationships depend on total honesty in word, deed, and intention. At all times, HRD professionals must adhere to the truth—even if that means presenting the client with information they would rather avoid, such as preliminary results of attitudinal questionnaires. Honesty is in the best interest of all parties.

Self-esteem

When other components of a healthy relationship, such as honesty, trust, personal involvement, and acceptance are in place, the result will be higher self-esteem for both HRD professionals and their clients. At this point, the relationship becomes synergistic—the whole is greater than the sum of its parts. The more HRD professionals respect themselves and others, the more clients will respect themselves and the HRD professional. In other words, reciprocity in the relationship can only enhance the self-esteem of both parties.

Identifying Problems

Throughout this chapter we have discussed steps necessary to identify the problems within an organization. During organizational analysis, the is/should process is put into action, the most important part of which is determining the seriousness of the problem. Is/should analysis, critical incident analysis, and select interviewing are all effective methods helping to determine the size and intensity of a problem.

During organizational analysis, the type of discrepancies being examined relate to overall organizational outcomes or results rather than skill or knowledge deficiencies typically examined during rudimentary needs assessment.

Demonstrating an Understanding of the Organization

Before HRD professionals can proceed in the organizational analysis they must demonstrate a thorough understanding of the organization. Put another way, credibility must be displayed prior to their being allowed to complete the process. For example, understanding may be illustrated via anticipation of work-related activities, which promotes an appreciation of the different types of jobs performed within the organization. In some organizations, this includes working alongside assembly workers, riding in disposal trucks hauling trash, or participating in job exchange programs. Regardless, invaluable insight is gained into the organization's operations and personnel functions. At a higher level, HRD professionals must be able to communicate effectively and efficiently with organizational leaders.

A solid comprehension of business fundamentals enables HRD professionals to understand how organizations operate, how decisions are made, and how business gets done. This builds empathy and ultimately enhances credibility. For some, this may require extensive graduate study in organizational psychology or pursuit of an MBA. Failure to actively improve one's organizational knowledge, and thus credibility, may produce catastrophic effects. In fact, the authors believe that lack of credibility within organizations is the Achilles heel of most HRD professionals. This problem must be solved before HRD will ever be equal to that of other operational divisions within an organization.

Identify the Motives

While this step is not an official element in the organizational analysis process, it must be completed prior to moving forward. HRD professionals should not engage in organizational analysis activities unless they possess a clear understanding of the motives that drive such activities. By identifying the motives of individuals sponsoring or encouraging analysis, future problems and difficulties can be avoided. Again, HRD professionals must guard against simply reacting to the requests of clients. Strategic thinking is essential before moving forward. If individuals' motives cannot be clearly identified, insights and advice should be solicited of more senior members of the organization. In this way, the integrity of the process, the HRD program, and its professionals remains protected.

Obtaining Agreement to Conduct Organizational Analysis

During this step HRD professionals are attempting to gain permission from clients prior to moving forward. While many assume that being asked to participate in or conduct organizational analyses is permission enough to move forward, an ounce of caution is worth a pound of cure. All too often, clients are not fully aware of the consequences when they make requests of HRD professionals.

After identifying organizational discrepancies, a perfect opportunity exists to ask a simple question such as, "Are clients really dedicated to solving problems or are they only interested in confirming that they exist?" Closing the gap between current and desired results may be extremely painful, often requiring that unpleasant decisions be made. Consequently, clients may be reluctant to move forward. Many simply want confirmation that a problem exists, and in some sad way this represents sufficient understanding of the bitter reality facing the organization.

Prior to engaging in a comprehensive, time-consuming, and very costly organizational analysis process, HRD professionals must discover exactly how serious their clients are. In order to do so, four steps are necessary:

1. Discuss the parameters of the organizational analysis process. That is, the scope and depth of analysis must be examined in detail; clients must be made aware of how very intrusive the process can be. While analysis paralysis is not to be encouraged, HRD professionals must be straightforward and honest with their clients.
2. Discuss the respective roles all parties will play during the analysis process, including the client's responsibility to work closely with HRD professionals, and to be prompt and responsive when asked for access to employees, files, and other pertinent information.
3. Discuss the procedures to be used during the organizational analysis process, including gathering and analyzing data, conducting informal discussions with clients, presenting findings to decision-makers, and determining action sequences for the remaining steps in the process.

4. HRD professionals must ask permission of their clients to move forward and establish timelines for the completion of each of the next five steps.

Once these four issues have been properly addressed and clients have granted permission to proceed, the process of gathering data can begin.

Gathering Data

Again, HRD professionals must think strategically during the data gathering process, which includes designing a process that is efficient and effective. HRD professionals must be objective and guard against using favored analysis methods that may not be appropriate. Biases should be addressed in the first part of the data gathering process, the identification of assumptions and starting points. Certain assumptions will serve to focus analysis and offer direction as to how information is to be gathered.

Three steps remain in the analysis process. First, HRD professionals must design the needs gathering framework, which includes isolation of the critical question to be addressed—sometimes referred to as the problem statement. Second, the design process, incorporates relevant information and literature that will provide insight into the situation. Third, the procedures by which questions will be investigated require discussion, including the identification of samples and data collection methods.

Once the analysis design process has been completed, it is necessary to identify the analysis methods that will be used to gather the data. Relevance and appropriateness of each methodology should be discussed in order to ensure that the proper mix is selected. Once an agreed-upon list of analysis methods has been identified, the final step is engaging in the collection of data needed.

Analyzing Data

During this phase of the organizational analysis process, HRD professionals are concerned with examining the data gathered in step four and interpreting it for the purposes of drawing conclusions and identifying implications. This seemingly straightforward process can be quite rigorous as data is seldom obtained in an absolute, clean, and understandable form. If an adequate job has been done of gathering information and selecting analysis

methodologies, analyzing data becomes a much simpler proce-
dure. Once an interpretation has been completed, HRD professionals can prepare the data for presentation to clients.

Conducting Informal Discussions with Clients

It is never a good idea to present findings, conclusions, implications, or recommendations to clients in a formal setting as one
runs the risk of catching clients off guard or sharing information
they perceive to be confidential. Embarrassing interactions such as
this can forever destroy an HRD professional's credibility with
clients. Informal meetings provide a comfortable forum for sharing
findings, conclusions, applications, or recommendations that can
be held in strictest confidence. Information that is perceived to be
too controversial, politically damaging, or in poor taste can be
eliminated from the final report and presentation. Informal meetings allow clients the opportunity to provide reactions before the
findings and recommendations become official. They are also an
excellent opportunity to integrate the insights, perceptions, and
suggestions of clients regarding *how* data or recommendations
should be presented.

Another purpose of informal meetings is to afford clients an opportunity to discuss next steps and strategies with HRD professionals, as well as to identify leverage points where possible intervention and organizational change might best occur (leverage points
were discussed in Chapter 4 and occur in every organization that
has a heightened readiness for change).

Presenting Findings to Decision-makers

Once informal meetings have been conducted, findings, conclusions, implications, and recommendations must be presented formally to the decision-making team responsible for implementing
organizational change. In these meetings, discussions with clients
focus on alternatives and implications that appear to be appropriate given the data collected. At this point, HRD professionals are
challenged to listen, observe, and absorb clients' reactions, making
certain they have been "heard" during the final presentation. Review and reiteration of suggestions during a summary activity provides a powerful conclusion.

Determining Action Steps

Once findings, conclusions, implications, and recommendations
have been thoroughly examined and discussed, attention must be

turned collectively to formulating action steps. This collaborative activity requires, once again, creation of a partnership designed to improve organizational effectiveness. As discussed throughout this book, creating an organizational development partnership is truly the most efficient way of improving organizational effectiveness. Therefore, action steps must be designed to accomplish that end. Then and only then will HRD professionals participate in the ultimate performance partnership.

Action steps can include the identification of organizational development interventions, change management strategies, and performance improvement interventions designed to help the organization achieve its business results. These interventions and strategies also help the organization improve its performance capacity. Regardless of the intervention selected, HRD professionals must help their clients design, develop, implement, transfer, and eventually evaluate interventions (see Chapter 9).

MANAGEMENT ANALYSIS

Another type of analysis process, known as management analysis, is conducted to determine the quality and effectiveness of current managerial practices. HRD professionals provide value to the organization by helping identify the relative strengths of managers vis-à-vis performance coaching skills. To become an effective performance coach, managers must develop seven separate but interrelated competencies. Each enables them to build better relationships with their employees, improve employee performance, help resolve conflict, solve problems, and secure the organization's needed results (see Chapter 6).

PERFORMANCE AND BUSINESS ANALYSIS

Another type of analysis for which HRD professionals are responsible is determination of the performance and business needs of the organization. Critical problems facing the organization can be uncovered with performance management systems and organizational development interventions designed to solve them. Value is added to the organization as performance capacity and effectiveness are improved.

One way of discovering the performance and business needs of an organization is for HRD professionals to analyze the firm's strengths, weaknesses, opportunities, and threats (SWOT). An effective means of obtaining such information involves interviewing critical decision-makers regarding their opinions and perceptions of the organization, its future direction and outlook. These discussions will uncover a variety of areas in which the organization is not achieving needed results.

Another way of discovering performance deficiencies is by examining the firm's annual reports and strategic business plan. Outlined in both are critical business trends and challenges facing the organization. These documents also help identify clients, competitors, and customers.

A performance and business analysis is complete when HRD professionals have identified the types of performance and business needs, concerns, and expectations of their clients. This information will become the criteria used to match interventions and consulting services. Performance and business needs identified during this analysis define the performance deficiencies of an organization, which will help determine future initiatives of its HRD division.

Identifying Key Decision-makers, Stakeholders, Influencers, and Scouts

The performance and business analysis process begins by identifying the individuals who have something to gain or lose as a result of the analysis or recommendations for change. Unfortunately, one of the biggest mistakes HRD professionals make is treating all clients in the same way (Gilley, 1998). Some clients have the power to make decisions and provide the financial and human resources needed to implement and support change. Some can derail an intervention before it gets implemented while others can affect the outcome by altering the perceptions of individuals regarding a situation. Certain clients can provide the technical advice needed to ensure change while others are responsible for implementing interventions or solutions for change. Still others guide the interaction between client groups and provide insight into the implementation of the change intervention.

In any decision-making situation, there are four different types of clients, each of whom has a distinct reason for participating. Organizational roles often affect their behavior, interaction, and decision making. To become effective analyzers of performance and business needs, HRD professionals must understand and address each type of client. The client types include decision-makers, stakeholders, influencers, and scouts.

Decision-makers

Decision-makers are most commonly the senior executives and managers in the organization. They have the authority to give final approval to HRD for change interventions. Decision-makers also have direct access to financial and human resources and can assign them to help implement interventions. Moreover, decision-makers enjoy veto power and can prevent an intervention from being implemented.

A decision-maker's primary focus is the bottom line and the impact an intervention will have on the organization (Gilley, 1998). He or she is most interested in the return on investment that the organization will receive by implementing change. HRD professionals can eliminate decision-makers' concerns by answering their questions and providing evidence that supports their recommendations for change and improvement. The impact of interventions must be clearly communicated. Impact can include increased profitability, enhanced revenue, or improved performance.

Stakeholders

Stakeholders are those individuals who have the most to gain or lose as a result of the implementation of an HRD change intervention. Stakeholders must implement and supervise these interventions; therefore, their impact on departments, divisions, and units within the organization must be evaluated. According to Gilley (1998), stakeholders will have to "live" with the intervention, consequently it becomes a very personal decision for which they will be held accountable.

In order to meet stakeholders' needs and expectations, HRD professionals must reassure them that interventions will indeed help improve organizational performance and effectiveness. HRD professionals should communicate their intent and level of involvement during change interventions. This information will reassure stakeholders that HRD professionals will help them implement complex interventions as well as assist in overcoming employees' resistance to change.

Influencers

Many influencers view their role as someone who screens interventions deemed inappropriate or impractical for the organization. As a result, they serve as gatekeepers by changing the perceptions of decision-makers and stakeholders regarding selected interventions.

In most performance improvement or organizational development situations, influencers do not have the authority to approve the selection of an intervention but can greatly impact the selection process.

Many HRD professionals avoid, discount, or minimize the impact of influencers, which is a serious mistake. One of the best ways of dealing with influencers is by validating them, which is done by soliciting their opinions, ideas, and assistance. Additionally, HRD professionals address the concerns of influencers with quantifiable, measurable evidence or by demonstrating how influencers benefit as a result of the proposed change. Such an approach will help elevate the influencer in the eyes of decision-makers and stakeholders, which is precisely what they desire.

Scouts

In every performance improvement or organizational development situation someone serves as a "point" person, acting as a guide during interactions with HRD professionals, decision-makers, stakeholders, and influencers. They provide and interpret information about the problem, potential causes, types of clients involved, client expectations, and ways to proceed (Gilley, 1998). Point persons may be found throughout the organization, including the HRD department, the stakeholder's department, or other operational units.

Scouts focus on the success of an intervention because they believe the intervention will help improve organizational effectiveness. Consequently, scouts serve as change ambassadors within the firm.

Before HRD professionals solicit the help of scouts, they must make certain that these people have credibility with other decision-makers, stakeholders, influencers, and HRD professionals. Once the scout's credibility has been established, HRD professionals should work closely with them, soliciting and accepting their advice unless it seriously violates professional values or ethics. Credible scouts often have organizational insight and understanding that most HRD professionals lack. They possess an awareness and intuition about what will or will not work within the organization, and are conscious of how each decision-maker, stakeholder, and influencer will benefit from a successful intervention. This insight is invaluable to HRD professionals as they struggle to help the organization change and improve.

Identifying Client Strengths, Weaknesses, Opportunities, and Threats

HRD professionals can gain tremendous insight into their clients' performance and business needs by identifying client strengths, weaknesses, opportunities, and threats (SWOT). SWOT analysis identifies:

1. the client's perspective of the organization
2. the organization's strategic business goals and objectives
3. the business processes used in producing products and services
4. employee performance behaviors

This activity also identifies clients' customers, business trends, competitors, and business challenges. This information can be gathered via structured interviews, questionnaires, observations, and focus groups.

Identifying Clients' Perspectives of the Organization

HRD professionals must understand that their clients often have different perspectives of the organization, which are the result of varying experiences. Based on the quantity and quality of these experiences, clients draw vastly different conclusions. By identifying a client's perspective of the organization, HRD professionals are better able to:

1. understand why clients behave the way they do.
2. identify client's willingness to implement change and performance improvement interventions.
3. identify client's deeply rooted assumptions and beliefs about the organization and its leadership.
4. predict a client's future behaviors and decisions.
5. identify a client's level of support and involvement when implementing HRD and change interventions.
6. identify potential gatekeepers whose main purposes in the organization are to be obstructionists and maintainers of the status quo.

Once identified, this information can provide critical insights regarding clients' performance and business needs.

Identifying the Organization's
Strategic Business Goals and Objectives

To identify an organization's strategic business goals and objectives, HRD professionals should interview decision-makers, stakeholders, and influencers as a way of identifying the organization's strategic direction and financial condition. As discussed earlier in this chapter, organizational reports and internal documents should be analyzed to help determine the livelihood of the organization.

Identifying Business Processes

Business processes consist of multiple steps used in producing a product or service (Rummler & Brache, 1995), and include functions such as manufacturing, marketing, distribution, accounting, and customer service. Each of these business processes consists of sub-processes used in helping the organization achieve its strategic business goals and objectives.

The greatest opportunity for performance improvement occurs by changing or reengineering business processes—the examination of which identifies the weaknesses, duplications, inefficiencies, or irrelevancies of work tasks. In addition, the interface between business processes manifests performance and business needs, because breakdowns can occur where ideas, responsibilities, and information are passed from one business process to another. Rummler and Brache (1995) refer to this as "the white spaces" of the organizational chart, which occur most often in the horizontal view of the organization, where hand-offs are made from department to department. HRD professionals should carefully examine exchanges between business processes and accurately identify problem areas.

Identifying Performance Behaviors

Once business processes have been identified, HRD professionals need to identify the performance behaviors required of employees in order for them to do their jobs. To identify specific performance behaviors, HRD professionals may be asked to interview or observe employees actually performing their jobs. Knowledge of exact performance behaviors allows for isolation of performance breakdowns, thus enabling identification of client performance and business needs. Such an examination is like that of a skills audit or task analysis, where each skill or task is identified and the connections between each are shown. While these activities appear rigorous or mundane, tremendous insight into performance breakdowns can be gleaned.

In the classic work of Mager and Pipe (1984), they identify a series of questions that can be used when conducting performance behavior identifications, which they refer to as performance analysis. The questions are as follows:

1. What is the performance discrepancy?
2. Is the discrepancy important?
3. Is the discrepancy due to lack of skill?
4. Were employees able to perform successfully in the past?
5. Is the needed skill used frequently?
6. Is there a similar way to do the job?
7. Do employees have what it takes to do the job?
8. Is the desired performance inadvertently being punished?
9. Is not doing the job rewarded in some way?
10. Does doing the job really matter?
11. Are there obstacles to performing?
12. What are the limits on possible solutions?

By using these questions, HRD professionals can analyze nearly any performance problem facing their organization.

Identifying Clients' Customers, Business Trends, Competitors, and Challenges

When steps three through six of the Performance and Business Process Model have been completed, organizational strengths and weaknesses have been identified with regard to client perspectives and performance application. Step seven allows HRD professionals to distinguish the opportunities and threats confronting the organization by better understanding their clients' world and the issues that face them.

Developing an understanding of clients' performance and business needs challenges HRD professionals to isolate the opportunities and threats facing them and their organizations. This analysis provides an awareness of the issues, conditions, trends, and struggles confronting clients. Armed with such insight, HRD professionals can demonstrate empathy for their clients and help them select appropriate performance improvement interventions.

To identify the opportunities and threats facing clients, HRD professionals should interview a representative sample of decision-makers, stakeholders, and influencers as a way of identifying clients' perspectives. Areas of inquiry should include identifying client customers, business trends, competitors, and business challenges.

Once each of these four areas has been examined, HRD professionals should have a better understanding of the way clients view their world, which will be helpful when attempting to match HRD interventions, consulting services, and change interventions with client performance and business needs.

Identifying Clients' Performance and Business Needs

The final step of the performance and business analysis process is identification of the client's performance and business needs. While critical, this action is a straightforward, easy activity requiring a simple summary of the information discovered during the previous seven steps. HRD professionals should carefully analyze the information obtained in order to ascertain its meaning, process and redefine the data, and then draw conclusions regarding the client's performance and business needs.

Performance and business needs differ in their degree of seriousness and urgency. Some require immediate attention while others need little more than identification. Due to time constraints and limited resources, HRD professionals can only address a limited number of requests; therefore, performance and business needs must be prioritized and matched with the most appropriate HRD interventions. This activity sequence requires the audit of interventions and consulting services by HRD professionals in order to determine which are of the greatest value and benefit to their clients and the organization (see Chapter 5). Not to be taken lightly, this activity is fundamentally important in developing long-term strategic business partnerships within the organization.

NEEDS ANALYSIS

Needs analysis describes a process that has at least five components: client analysis, identification of areas of demand for performance improvement and change interventions, identification of areas of need, causal analysis, and task analysis (Gilley and Eggland, 1989).

Clientele analysis is the process of comparing the characteristics of participants in an intervention with those of the general population of individuals who could not be served. This will provide the type of descriptive information needed for instructional designers to tailor an intervention for a select audience, thereby ensuring that the intervention is consistent for both groups.

The second component of needs analysis is to identify areas of demand for existing performance improvement and change interventions. This is done in order to offer interventions of significant interest and to encourage participation. Further, this activity provides HRD professionals with information regarding the size of a potential audience and the level of interest in specific types of interventions.

The third task consists of identifying discrepancies between the current and desired state of circumstances, utilizing techniques of identifying and understanding problem areas. Data collection and analysis are included, revealing differences between the current and desired state of circumstances. The magnitude and intensity of differences are also examined.

When this analysis is conducted, HRD professionals should follow six steps that are an integral part of the organizational analysis process previously discussed. The steps are building a collaborative client relationship, identifying problems, gathering data, analyzing data, conducting informal discussions with clients, and determining action steps.

While these steps are similar to those used during organizational analysis, they differ significantly in their scope and intensity. Needs analysis is designed to determine skill, knowledge, and attitudinal deficiencies that impact employees' job performance, thus the focus is on the individual. Organizational analyses are designed to uncover deficiencies in organizational results, which require an examination of the entire organization.

The fourth function of needs analysis is to determine the cause(s) of performance deficiencies. Analysis begins with examination of employees to determine their current levels of knowledge and skill, and to measure their aptitudes. When completed, this information should be compared with the required level—the difference between the two being the basis for future interventions. HRD professionals also should investigate managers and executives to ascertain their effect upon performance efficiencies. Finally, instructional designers should examine the organizational culture, climate, and structure to determine their impact on performance deficiencies.

The final step in needs analysis is to conduct a task analysis based upon the job requirements of the employee. The tasks to be performed by employees are listed, and those for which training is required are selected. These tasks are then analyzed in detail to determine the knowledge, skills, and attitudes required for acceptable performance. Performance improvement and change interventions can then be designed accordingly.

CONCLUSION

Identifying organizational and performance needs is a complex and difficult process requiring HRD professionals to think strategically about their clients' requests, develop support for the analysis process, and overcome analysis paralysis within the organization. Five critical questions must be answered as they prepare to participate in this credibility enhancing activity. Finally, HRD professionals must prepare themselves to conduct organizational, management, performance and business, and needs analysis when appropriate. It is fundamentally important that HRD professionals develop the skills and abilities to expertly and efficiently perform each of these types of analyses, and to determine when each is appropriate.

CHAPTER 9

Designing and Developing Performance Improvement and Change Interventions

HRD professionals concerned with evaluating needs assessments, establishing performance objectives, designing or selecting learning activities, choosing training strategies, and evaluating learning outcomes are engaged in a process known as instructional design (Gilley & Eggland, 1989). At the heart of every performance improvement and change intervention is its design, which serves as a blueprint for all learning and organizational change. Without properly designed interventions learning and organizational change can be inconsistent, which will jeopardize organizational effectiveness and performance.

THE GENESIS OF INSTRUCTIONAL DESIGN

Most HRD programs consist of a number of critical interventions designed to improve performance or bring about organizational change. Most are requested by managers and executives when some symptoms of performance deficiency are recognized. As a way of addressing these, HRD professionals can choose between either an activity strategy or a results strategy. These strategies differ in their focus, how they are measured, and how they are viewed within the organization.

An activity strategy is an approach HRD professionals use to respond to managers' and executives' requests for performance improvement. The focus is on the delivery of training programs on topics desired. It is a numbers game. HRD professionals who embrace this approach are concerned with the number of courses they offer and the number of people attending them. Often this strategy is viewed by organizational decision-makers as "something HRD professionals do."

A results strategy is an approach HRD practitioners use to design and develop interventions that can bring about lasting change in an organization. The focus is on achieving organizational results through learning and skill transfer. HRD professionals who use it are concerned with improving the performance capacity of the organization. It is a way of reducing performance deficiencies. The results strategy is increasing in popularity but, unfortunately, is not the predominate approach. As more and more organizations begin to expect greater results from HRD, however, the results strategy will become the standard of operation.

ROLE OF INSTRUCTIONAL DESIGNERS

Many organizations have turned their attention toward HRD as a way of improving and enhancing organizational performance, which is done in part to remain competitive and profitable. But improved organizational performance does not just happen. Someone must be skilled in the design and development of performance improvement interventions. This person is the instructional designer.

The instructional designer role is born during the customized vendor-driven phase of HRD and is often overlooked in organizations because it is not perceived as critical to improving organizational performance. However, instructional designers are essential to the design and development of interventions that bring about lasting behavioral change and improved organizational effectiveness.

There are five subroles of instructional designers. They are program designer, instructional writer, media specialist, task analyst, and theoretician (Gilley & Eggland, 1989). It is important to remember that several subroles often interact simultaneously.

Program Designer

The lion's share of an instructional designer's responsibility is to design effective, change-oriented interventions. Consequently, the subrole of program designer is essential to an instructional designer.

The program designer's subrole includes identifying performance objectives and selecting learning activities that are needed to accomplish them, then prioritizing them. In most situations, more than one learning activity is required to accomplish a single objective.

Sometimes, experiential learning activities are needed to enhance learning. Because such activities require special facilitation skills and a shift of control to the learners, instructional designers should provide adequate training time for the completion of these activities. Special care must also be given to the design of these activities to minimize adverse effects on learning.

The last responsibility of a program designer is selecting the most appropriate media, materials, and training aids needed for interventions. This is often accomplished as part of the media specialist's subrole.

Instructional Writer

The primary responsibility of this subrole is developing written materials such as binders, modules, training manuals, overheads, handouts, and other supportive materials used during training.

One of the most important activities of an instructional writer is developing written consulting and performance improvement proposals. This is generally done after a needs analysis has been completed—assuming, of course, that the analysis indicated a need for assistance. Such proposals should indicate the need for HRD consulting services or interventions, the objective(s) to be achieved, the expected results, the type of participation required by HRD professionals and interested parties, an outline of the proposed service or intervention, a detailed budget, and the type of deliverables expected.

Media Specialist

The subrole of media specialist includes the identification and selection of the most appropriate audiovisuals and computer-based training simulations needed during an intervention. These types of media are helpful because they encourage learner participation, increase retention, and help organize the presentation of material.

The following criteria can assist in selecting the most appropriate media:

1. group size
2. size and shape of the training facility
3. cost involved

4. personal preference
5. portability
6. content of intervention
7. time availability (Gilley & Eggland, 1989, pp. 156–57)

Task Analyst

Task analysts break down a job into small segments so learners have a step-by-step description of what they are expected to do on the job. In task analysis, instructional designers describe and measure employee performance on each part of a job. As a result, instructional designers are able to focus on what should be taught in an intervention and how it should be measured. Moreover, it helps ensure that what is taught is transferred to the job. Task analysis can also be used in making job modifications. Finally, task analysis provides needed information regarding the measurement criteria of job performance, which can be used to determine whether or not employees meet or exceed performance standards.

According to Michalak and Yager (1979), a comprehensive task analysis should include the following elements:

1. a statement of the task to be performed
2. when and how often the task is to be performed
3. the quality and quantity of the performance required
4. the conditions under which the task is to be performed
5. the importance of each task to the overall goals of the job
6. aptitudes, skills, or knowledge necessary to perform the task
7. the type of learning needed
8. the learning difficulty
9. the equipment, tools, and materials needed
10. where the best place to learn the task is

Each of these provides instructional designers with the information needed to design and develop effective change-oriented interventions.

Theoretician

The final subrole, theoretician, refers to the development of models and theories related to the learning and development process. According to Gilley and Eggland (1989), instructional designers are often asked to conceptualize a "better way" to perform a particular job. This often requires a capacity to visualize abstract concepts and ideas and to determine their relationships. As theoretician, the instructional designer should have a futurist perspective and a willingness to approach problems from unique and different angles. In some circumstances this subrole requires advanced knowledge of adult learning theory and program design. Most critically, it requires a commitment first to the identification of the most efficient way of bringing about change within the individual and the organization, and second to the development of dynamic and evolving interventions.

PHASES OF INSTRUCTIONAL DESIGN

The instructional design process consists of seven interrelated phases. Each phase serves as a foundation for the others, while the activities conducted in each phase are based upon this relationship. The seven phases are:

Phase 1: Philosophy of teaching and learning
Phase 2: Organizational, performance, and needs analysis
Phase 3: Feedback
Phase 4: Program design
Phase 5: Program development
Phase 6: Evaluation
Phase 7: Accountability

Phase 1: Philosophy of Teaching and Learning

The design and development process begins with the instructional designer identifying his or her philosophical orientation to the teaching/learning process. This includes identifying one's personal training style and the learning styles of participants. This self-discovery implies that the training style used will be the most appropriate for a divergent group of learners. Finally, instructional designers must realize that the decisions made during the remaining six phases of the instructional design process will be filtered through their philosophical orientation; that is, their beliefs will influence their decisions. This should provide instructional designers with a framework for decision-making, as well as for materials and methods selection. Such a filter should be used as a guide when designing organizational, performance, and needs assessments, identifying performance objectives and activities, and matching media with activities.

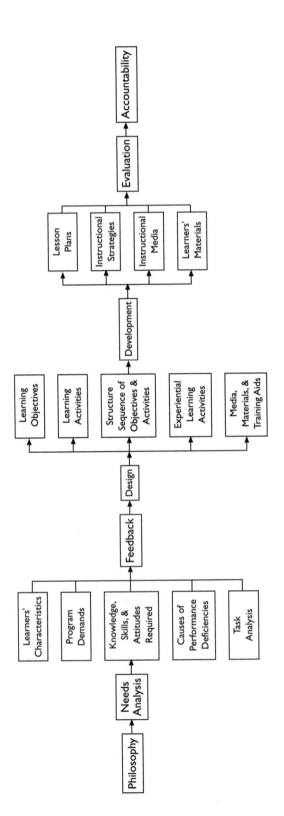

Figure 9.1 Phases of Instructional Design. Adapted from J. W. Gilley and S. A. Eggland, *Principles of HRD*, Addison-Wesley, 1989.

Phase 2: Organizational, Performance, and Needs Analysis

As we saw in Chapter 8, one source of confusion regarding needs analysis is the lack of a generally accepted, useful, and substantive definition of need. It is useful to think of a need as a gap between a current set of circumstances and some changed or desirable set of circumstances (i.e., the difference between "what is" and "what should be").

Various models and techniques can be used to meet the purposes of organizational, performance, and needs analysis. These are addressed in detail in Chapter 8.

Phase 3: The Feedback Process

Once a needs analysis has been conducted it is tempting for the instructional designer to immediately use the information gathered and interpreted to design interventions. Under this approach, however, the instructional designer becomes absolutely responsible for the outcomes of the interventions and limits the effectiveness of HRD. First, by isolating HRD professionals from other organizational members. Second, by preventing managers and executives from sharing in the performance improvement process. Third, by prohibiting managers and executives from addressing the needs of employees once they have been identified. The validation of need, then, at this phase will prevent the design and development of costly, underutilized interventions that would reflect negatively on the image and credibility of the HRD program. Finally, the feedback process helps build essential and powerful alliances and linkages within the organization, improving the utilization of HRD and assuring the future of learning in the organization.

To guarantee that vital decision-makers have the opportunity to share in the design and development of interventions that enhance organizational performance, a four-step process should be followed.

First, instructional designers should present the data collected and respective interpretations to a group of managers and executives who have authority to fund and implement new interventions and consulting activities. Second, an agreement or conclusion regarding the data should be obtained by the group. Third, HRD professionals should seek agreement regarding the implications of their interventions and services. Fourth, the group should decide on actions that should be taken.

The feedback process ensures that interventions will be supported and promoted by others in the organization. People support what they create. It also provides a second validation step prior to the costly design and development phases. Finally, it allows instructional designers to reach agreement with decision-makers concerning the organization of problems and their potential solutions. This is necessary prior to authorizing the use of human and financial resources to design, develop, and implement interventions.

Phase 4: Program Design

Once an agreement has been reached regarding the identification of performance deficiencies within the organization, the instructional designer can begin the task of designing interventions that will improve organizational performance. The design phase is based on the information discovered in the needs analysis phase. This should include trainee characteristics; program demand; knowledge, skill, and attitude requirements; causes of performance deficiencies; and task analysis.

Based on this information instructional designers should develop: (1) performance objectives, (2) learning activities, (3) a structure and sequence for performance objectives and activities, (4) experiential learning activities, and (5) appropriate instructional media, materials, and methods of instruction.

Performance Objectives

Regardless of its type and length, every intervention has a set of desired outcomes. These outcomes are statements of what the learner should be able to know or do as a result of the program. These outcomes are known as performance objectives and serve four primary functions: (1) they define the desired outcomes of the program, (2) they serve as a guide to the selection of strategies and methods of instruction, (3) they serve as criteria for the development and selection of learning activities, and (4) they provide criteria for the evaluation of learning (Gilley & Eggland, 1989).

Performance objectives are statements focused on what should result from instruction, rather than on the methods of instruction used. They serve the facilitator as a standard for which he or she will guide and direct learners. For learners, performance objectives serve as the goals for their effort—a way to monitor their own progress. In addition, performance objectives should be used in the selection of methods of instruction as well as of the different media by which content and information are conveyed. They also provide criteria for constructing tests and performance examinations used in the evaluation of learners.

Writing performance objectives is a very difficult task because so many of the words and phrases we use are open to misinterpretation. For example, to know, to understand, to appreciate, to believe. As with objectives, knowledge, understanding, appreciation, and beliefs are difficult if not impossible to measure. The best way to communicate objectives like these is to describe the desired behavior of the learner in words that are specific enough to preclude individual interpretations. These are called "action words." The example in Figure 9.2 can be used when writing performance objectives.

A well-written learning objective describes or implies the behavior that must be observed as a way of verifying that the intended learning has taken place. In order for this to happen an objective should contain three components. First, the desired performance or learning must be identified. Second, the conditions or circumstances under which the task must be performed, or the learning duplicated, must be identified. Third, the minimal acceptable level of performance or knowledge must be stated. This is often referred to as the standard of performance or knowledge. A standard may relate to speed, accuracy, specifications of performance, or the consequences resulting from inadequate performance or knowledge. Once the performance or knowledge, conditions, and standards have been identified, performance objectives can be written more clearly and precisely.

Learning Activities

During the design phase it is essential that various learning activities be developed that provide the learner an opportunity to acquire the knowledge, skills, and behavior desired. These activities must be based on the identified performance objectives previously discussed, as well as on the information collected and analyzed during the needs analysis phase.

Learning activities may include games, group projects, panel discussions, debates, readings, presentations, reports and papers, and on-the-job observations or performance. Each should be selected based on the unique opportunities they provide the learner. They should maximize the understanding of an idea, truth, skill, or attitude. In short, learning objectives ask the question "where am I going," while learning activities answer the question "how will I get there."

Structuring and Sequencing Performance Objectives

Structuring and sequencing performance objectives provides a logical framework for intervention. By prioritizing performance objectives, participants are given a clear understanding of the focus, direction, and importance of learning and change. Structuring and sequencing performance objectives helps the facilitator

1. Knowledge Level

count	list	recall
define	name	recognize
draw	point	record
identify	quote	repeat
indicate	read	state
tabulate	trace	write

2. Comprehension Level

associate	compare	compute
contrast	describe	differentiate
distinguish	estimate	extrapolate
interpret	classify	compare

3. Application Level

apply	calculate	solve
illustrate	practice	use
utilize	complete	demonstrate
employ	examine	order

4. Analysis Level

group	relate	transform
summarize	construct	detect
analyze	infer	separate
explain	investigate	divide

5. Synthesis Level

arrange	combine	create
design	develop	formulate
generalize	construct	integrate
organize	plan	prepare
prescribe	produce	propose

6. Evaluation Level

appraise	assess	critique
determine	evaluate	grade
judge	measure	rank
recommend	specify	estimate
rate	select	test

Figure 9.2 Performance Objectives by Cognitive Levels. Reprinted from J. W. Gilley and S. A. Eggland, *Principles of HRD*, Addison-Wesley, 1989.

manage various learning activities as a way of meeting the needs of learners and satisfying program demands.

Experiential Learning Activities

Experiential exercises are appropriate for five reasons: (1) they help develop highly complex cognitive skills such as decision-making, evaluating, and synthesizing; (2) they can positively impact learners' values, beliefs, or attitudes; (3) they can induce empathy (understanding); (4) they can sharpen interpersonal skills; and (5) they can help clients unlearn negative attitudes or behaviors (Thiagarajan, 1980, p. 38).

When experiential exercises are appropriate they should be developed to include the following:

1. experiencing (doing the activity)
2. publishing (sharing reactions, observations, and emotions from the activity)
3. processing (discussing the group dynamics that occurred during the activity)
4. generalizing (inferring principles from the activity that relate to the real world)
5. applying (planning more effective behavior for use in the real world) (Dean & Gilley, 1986)

Media, Materials, and Training Aids

The term media refers to any means of conveying a message. Examples include films, print, and audio tapes. The term material refers to printed matter such as texts, tests, and handouts. Transparencies and photographs are also examples of instructional materials. Materials contain messages while media transmit messages. The term training aids refers to both instructional media and materials. Training aids exist to assist the facilitator in the performance improvement process.

The design phase involves the identification of media, materials, and training aids that are most appropriate to accomplish the performance objectives. It is necessary to identify those means that will be used in learning activities and experiential exercises. It is not appropriate, however, to select, develop, or perfect these at this time. During this phase, the task confronting the instructional program designer is simply the identification of media, materials, and training aids. Their development is reserved for the next phase.

Phase 5: Program Development

In the development phase, the designed intervention is translated into actual training materials and strategies. It is important to remember that the inputs for the development phase are the outputs from the design phase. The outputs for the development phase include lesson plans, instructional strategies, instructional media, and learner materials. During this phase the testing and validation of media and materials should also be included.

Lesson Plans

During this part of the development phase, it is essential that the lesson plan be completed. A lesson plan is a document that identifies the audience (who), the topic of content (what), the location (where), the time frame (when), and the objectives (why) (Donaldson & Scannell, 1986). When developing a lesson plan several decisions must be made. These include:

- the content to be covered
- the sequencing of activities
- the selection or design of training media
- the selection and/or development of experiential exercises
- the timing and planning of each activity
- the selection of methods of instruction to be used
- the number and type of evaluation items (Gilley & Eggland, 1989)

These are generally communicated to the facilitator in the form of an instructor's or facilitator's guide.

When selecting the lesson format it is important to determine the frequency of use of the knowledge or skill to be learned, the complexity of the task performed, the time available for the lesson, and the number of people performing the task (Gilley & Eggland, 1989).

Instructional Strategies

Detailed decisions regarding methods of instruction and the ways in which they will be used are known as instructional strategies. These include the choice of methods and media appropriate for each instructional event, and the structure and timing of instructional events within a lesson. There are five distinct instructional events for each lesson. Instructional strategies are required for each. They include the introduction, presentation, application, practice, and review.

During the introduction the facilitator communicates the performance objectives, identifies the rationale for the lesson, and reviews any previous information or learning that is required prior to the introduction of new material and information. The presentation includes the organized presentation of content, information, ideas, materials, and facts. This could also include a question-and-answer session or group discussion. The application is the transfer of knowledge and information into personal action. Practice enables learners to rehearse new information until it becomes internalized. Review includes feedback as well as review of the content previously received.

Each of these instructional events indicates different methods of instruction. The classification of performance objectives is helpful in selecting the most appropriate methods and techniques. For example, demonstrations are necessary for the presentation of skill objectives. A psychomotor skill usually calls for a practical demonstration, whereas a cognitive skill may require a pen and paper demonstration. In addition, the nature of the practice component of a lesson depends in part on the performance objectives. It will also depend on learners' characteristics and available facilities and equipment.

There are several different instructional methods to select from, each with its distinct advantages and disadvantages. The following commonly used methods provide a choice of approaches:

- *Lectures:* one-way communication, a series of facts or information about a particular subject
- *Buzz groups:* a large group discussion allowing questions and feedback
- *Role play:* permits learners to create situations and play a role of one or more individuals
- *Case studies:* an actual presentation, either written or verbal, of an incident that did or could have happened
- *Games:* simulations made competitive
- *Demonstrations:* a show-and-tell technique used to illustrate a point or feature
- *Nominal group techniques:* problem-solving group techniques designed to encourage participation
- *Brainstorming:* designed to elicit as many ideas and responses as possible regarding a problem
- *Question-and-answer sessions:* enable learners to obtain needed and vital information through inquiry
- *Simulations:* a dramatic representation of reality combining case studies and role playing (Gilley & Eggland, 1989)

When instructional designers consider how various instructional events and lessons should be structured, sequenced, and timed, they should consider the following questions:

1. How much time is required to accomplish the performance objectives?
2. How much time is required for instructional presentations, application, practice, and review, respectively?

3. How many objectives can be covered in each instructional period?

4. How many aspects of a topic can be grouped for practice?

The amount of time spent in presentation and practice will depend on the topic and the importance of the learning or change to the organization. Figure 9.3 reveals various possible structures for a lesson.

When planning the timing and lesson structure, designers should consider the attention span of learners and the nature of the performance objectives prior to choosing the methods of instruction and media to be used. Each of these will provide insight into the development of the most appropriate instructional strategy.

Instructional Media

The third output of the development phase is the identification of the appropriate media to be used. In order to be useful, the media should be appropriate to and reinforce the instructional content being presented by the learning specialist.

In selecting the most appropriate media for an instructional event, designers must consider the nature of the task, the learning environment, and the unique characteristics of the learners. Also, instructional designers will need to consider the learning styles of participants, as well as their own training style.

When considering the nature of the task, a very important criterion to examine is the type of performance objectives being addressed by the intervention. For example, some types of media are

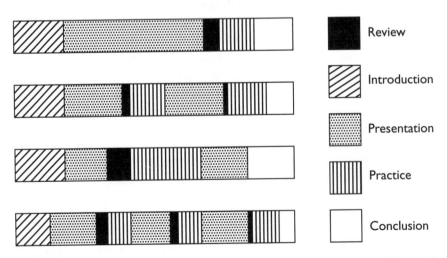

Figure 9.3 Possible Structure of a Lesson. Reprinted from J. W. Gilley and S. A. Eggland, *Principles of HRD,* Addison-Wesley, 1989.

excellent for teaching psychomotor skills but not for cognitive skills. Group size also affects the content of the lesson. An over-head projector is often used during workshops and conferences because it is convenient and considered the proper mode of operation. Other types of media might be more appropriate for a large group such as handouts, computer-based presentations, or films.

The size and shape of the learning environment is a factor. Consider this: many interventions are conducted in hotel and motel meeting rooms that were not designed to accommodate or support learning. As a result, the presentation and placement of visuals can be very troublesome and often ineffective. Meeting rooms with too many windows may prevent the effectiveness of films, VCR presentations, or overhead projectors. Very few HRD programs maintain a large inventory of media to be used. Thus, a single presentation may require a large expenditure for media. Finally, the lack of portability of equipment may prevent the use of certain types of media.

Other characteristics that affect the type of media selected include the experience of the learners—their education, age, and learning styles. The experience of learners affects the selection of media because more experienced participants may need less visual support, such as diagrams and models, than inexperienced learners. All too often an instructional event will include learners with varied levels of experience, making it necessary to decide which groups need which type of support. This, of course, greatly complicates the process of media selection. Education and age will affect the selection of media in much the same way as experience, in that the diversity of learners' educational levels and ages will require different combinations of media. Of course, each instructional event is different, which also complicates the process. Other practical considerations that affect the selection of media are the availability of hardware and software, their respective costs, and the time available for a presentation, its application, and practice.

Learner Materials

The most common type of learner materials are handouts and participant manuals. The purpose of such materials is to provide information pertinent to the learner as well as a quick reference for future study and review.

Handouts and participant manuals include several important types of information that are useful to learners, including performance objectives, exercises, references, outlines, tables and figures, and basic content related to the lesson. Since each lesson is based upon a set of performance objectives, it is important to report these to the learner in order to make clear what is expected and how participants will be measured. Exercises should be included to allow learners to practice necessary skills and deepen personal awareness. References should be included to assist learners in future inquiries. References are also important in order to provide self-directed learning and individualized study. Outlines are used as a way of structuring and prioritizing information that is important. They help in increasing discussion since learners can concentrate on listening, taking notes, and questioning during the instructional event without the need to mentally organize the material at the same time. Also, outlines help facilitators focus on the most important ideas, facts, and concepts and to remain on task instead of discussing minor points or facts. Finally, tables and figures can be used when large amounts of information need to be presented in a concise manner or when a graphic representation is required. Visual learners prefer this type of presentation because it allows them to better understand the information or concept.

Phase 6: Evaluation of Interventions

Successful interventions must meet specific performance objectives. They must measure the effectiveness of facilitators and the competencies of instructional designers. Another purpose of an evaluation is to determine the impact that learning had on individuals and whether or not changes in behavior occurred. Finally, intervention evaluations should measure the overall impact that learning had upon the organization and its employees in order to determine its benefits.

The principal reason for evaluation is to determine if the program accomplished its assigned objectives. In other words, did the intervention help participants develop adequate knowledge, skills, and attitudes used to improve their performance or to implement appropriate organizational changes. Another reason for evaluating interventions is to determine their strengths and weaknesses. Each intervention should be evaluated to determine whether the proper design was employed, the instructional designer developed the intervention correctly, the intervention was implemented correctly, and the appropriate controls were used.

Interventions should be evaluated also to determine the cost to benefit ratio. This is done in order for management to assess the value of a program, and is often referred to as the *justification phase* of evaluation.

The final reason interventions should be evaluated is to establish a data base that can be used to demonstrate the productivity and effectiveness of the HRD program. This is referred to as the *marketing phase* of intervention evaluation, which is important because many HRD programs are not viewed as being responsible for productivity improvements that enhance organizational effectiveness. Thus, it is vital that HRD professionals collect and maintain data regarding their interventions and consulting activities in order to promote their programs.

Phase 7: Accountability

During this phase, instructional designers should utilize the information gathered in the evaluation phase to implement necessary changes. It is also during this phase that the learner, the organization, the manager, the instructional designer, and the facilitator are held responsible for their actions. Unless these individuals are held accountable, newly acquired behaviors will be extinguished. Another problem that arises after training is that behavior improves for a short period of time but begins to decline unless it is reinforced or encouraged by managers and executives.

Learner Accountability

Learners should be held accountable for the information, knowledge, skills, or change process presented during an intervention and should be evaluated after the intervention to assure that these were acquired. Also, they should be evaluated some months later to determine whether or not they have integrated and applied the information on the job. Did the training change their mode of operation? If so, how did it affect organizational performance and effectiveness?

Organizational Accountability

The organization should be held accountable for improved learning and behavioral change because it is the ultimate benefactor. More importantly, the organization has the power to encourage change and to provide the assistance and support needed to bring about improvements. The organization is ultimately responsible for establishing the environment needed for change to occur. The organization should not expect HRD professionals and managers to be totally responsible for learning. The learners, while accountable for improving their own performance and implementing change, cannot be held totally responsible either. The organization has the responsibility to provide leadership, which ensures learning and organizational change, and which brings about organizational transformation.

HRD Professionals' Accountability

HRD professionals should be held accountable for the design and development of interventions that result in organizational change and performance improvement. They are responsible for identifying appropriate organizational, performance and learning needs; establishing performance and change objectives that address those needs; selecting learning activities that enable the performance and change objectives to be accomplished; developing materials; identifying the most appropriate learning methods and media to be used; and developing valid, reliable, and useful evaluation instruments to measure whether performance has improved or change has occurred.

Manager/Facilitator Accountability

Managers, as facilitators, should be held accountable for implementing the intervention in accordance with the design. This includes the proper utilization of media, materials, and methods. They are also responsible for the dissemination of information and the facilitation of learning, which includes establishing a supportive and comfortable learning environment as well as providing interesting learning activities designed to foster improvement. In addition, managers should have mastered the material being presented prior to the beginning of the intervention and be prepared to provide insight as to its application.

CONCLUSION

Instructional design is a process that consists of seven interrelated phases. Each phase is dependent on the others. The process begins with the identification of the instructional designer's philosophy of teaching and learning. The process also provides for the identification of needs, and the design, development, and evaluation of interventions. Each participant in an intervention is accountable for acquiring, integrating, and transferring the information, concepts, ideas, knowledge, skills, or changes to the job.

CHAPTER 10

Facilitating Learning Acquisition and Transfer

One of the best ways organizations can improve employee development and performance is by facilitating learning acquisition and transfer. The learning acquisition and transfer process must produce specific outcomes that organizations can rely on to help them accomplish their strategic goals and objectives. Therefore, learning must help employees achieve organizational results.

LEARNING ACQUISITION AND TRANSFER PROCESS

The learning acquisition and transfer process consists of eight steps that should be mutually designed by managers and employees with the assistance of HRD professionals. These steps should be realistic, attainable, continuous and tied to a timetable. The process consists of:

1. identifying current performance baselines
2. identifying areas of improvement
3. developing learning acquisition plans
4. creating transfer of learning strategies
5. implementing learning acquisition plans
6. implementing learning transfer strategies
7. measuring performance improvement
8. conducting performance appraisals

Identifying Current Performance Baselines

The first step of the learning acquisition and transfer process is identifying current employee performance baselines. In order to do this, managers must compare their employees' current performance to performance standards and requirements in order to determine performance gaps. These become an employee's "performance benchmark" and will determine areas of concentration for performance improvement.

Establishing a performance benchmark should include a realistic look at employees' capabilities as well as their current performance. As a result, an employee's areas of strength should be identified.

Identifying Areas of Improvement

Next, managers must identify the competencies that need improving. This task includes comparing employees' current performance baselines with desired performance. Competency areas that fall below minimum should become part of an employee's learning acquisition plan. However, it is often desirable for an employee to continue to develop competency areas where he or she maintains a high level of proficiency. Therefore, learning acquisition and transfer plans should be created that allow employees to continue to develop their strengths. In this way, employees can acquire and transfer learning that helps them either overcome performance gaps or build on their strengths.

Developing Learning Acquisition Plans

The third step of the learning acquisition and transfer process is creating a learning acquisition plan. Such a plan helps employees develop critical competencies that are used in accomplishing the organization's strategic business goals and objectives.

Developing learning acquisition plans consists of identifying performance objectives, identifying learning resources and strategies, and identifying target dates for completing each learning objective. First, employees must identify what they are going to learn. This activity is used to translate the identified performance need(s) into performance objectives, which are written to describe what an employee will learn, not what an employee will *do* to learn them. Employees should write a specific objective for each identified performance need. Depending on the type of performance objective, appropriate terminology should be used that is meaningful and descriptive (see Chapter 9 for an attached list of terms). Performance objectives may be written to acquire skills, knowledge, attitudes, values, or understanding. The performance objectives identified will provide the focus for the remaining section of the learning acquisition and transfer plan.

A well-written performance objective should be clear and understandable, identify what the employee will learn, describe the observable behavior that will demonstrate that learning occurred, identify the acceptable level of performance for the learned behavior, describe the condition under which the performance will be measured, and be stated in such a way that the degree to which it is accomplished can be estimated or measured.

The following questions can help employees and managers develop well-written performance objectives:

1. What competency areas need improving or which strengths need further development?
2. What would you like to do differently in order to improve your effectiveness?
3. What do you need to learn or be able to do differently in order to achieve your performance goals?
4. At what level would you like to demonstrate your learning (i.e., knowledge, comprehension, application, or evaluation)?
5. Under what conditions will you demonstrate what you have learned (i.e., during a departmental meeting, a performance appraisal, a formal presentation, or actually on the job)?
6. Is the performance objective clear and specific?
7. When you achieve your performance objective can you measure what you have learned or observe a behavioral change? If not, rewrite the performance objective in order to make it measurable and observable.
8. What performance results will occur when you achieve your performance objective?
9. Are the performance results meaningful to the organization? If yes, how so and in what form?

An employee should describe how proposed performance objectives will be accomplished. This includes identifying learning resources and strategies. Human and material resources should be considered as employees identify the most appropriate plan for reaching the selected objectives. Examples of relevant resources include books, journal articles, handouts, newspapers, a list of suggested readings, resource persons, peers, employees, superiors, mentors, professional trainers, videotapes, and cassettes. Strategies are the ways the identified resources will be used, including going to the library or learning resource center; reading book chapters or articles on the identified competency area; making observations; discussing the competency or conducting interviews with experts, employees, or superiors using structured questions; working on inquiry teams (a group responsible for addressing specific questions about a topic or elements of an issue, and which takes full responsibility for discovering the answers or solutions to them). Several resources and strategies may be listed for each identified performance objective.

When developing learning resources and strategies the following questions serve as catalysts for quality improvement:

1. How will you accomplish your performance objective?
2. What resources (human or material) do you need to achieve your performance objective?
3. How will you obtain the necessary resources?
4. What learning support and reinforcement will you need to achieve your objective?
5. Who can you rely on to help you achieve your objective?
6. Are the resources proposed for each performance objective the most authoritative, reliable, and feasible available?
7. Are there other resources—especially human—that should be considered?

When employees select a resource, it should be the most appropriate for the type of performance objective they are trying to accomplish. Each resource has its advantages and disadvantages and should be matched accordingly (see Figure 10.1).

An employee also must identify the date by which each performance objective will be completed. Establishing a date provides employees with planning parameters and forces management to use time more efficiently.

The following questions will help employees and managers determine the target date for completing each performance objective.

1. How much time will it take to complete each learning objective?
2. What factors may influence completion (other projects, reports, vacations, etc.)?
3. When do you think you will complete your learning plan?

Creating Transfer of Learning Strategies

Before learning can be translated into value for the organization, it must be applied to the job. Unfortunately, many employees are left on their own immediately after participating in an intervention.

Type of Objectives	Most Appropriate Resources
Knowledge	Books, articles, lectures, television, debates, dialogue, interviews, symposiums, panels, group interviews, motion pictures, slide films, recordings, book-based discussions, reading, CD-ROMs.
Skills	Skill practice exercises, role playing, in-basket exercises, participative cases, simulations, games, nonverbal exercises, drills, coaching.
Attitudes	Experience sharing discussions, role playing, the critical incident process, case studies, simulation games, participative cases, group discussions.
Values	Value-identification exercises, lectures, debates, symposiums, dramatizations, role playing, the critical incident process, simulation games.
Understanding	Audience participation, demonstrations, dramatizations, Socratic discussions, problem-solving activities, case methods, the critical incident process, simulation games, teaching others.

Figure 10.1   Learning Resource Methods

Management's failure to assist in integrating change, skills, or knowledge on the job causes confusion and frustration on both sides. Consequently, much of the change is lost.

According to Baldwin and Ford (1988), less than ten percent of the expenditures for training result in observable behavior change on the job. One of the primary reasons transfer of learning fails is because organizations know so little about it. To overcome this problem, organizations must come to understand why learning transfer fails to occur, and develop strategies to increase learning acquisition. The critical outcome of such a strategy will be a performance partnership between managers and employees that increases the application and integration of learning. Ultimately, organizational performance will improve (Figure 10.2).

Broad and Newstrom (1992) believe that a properly executed learning transfer strategy enables employees to apply all they have learned during training to their job. Unfortunately, learning fails to be transferred because *no one owns the process.* HRD professionals believe that their primary responsibility is training; managers believe their primary responsibility is producing organizational results; and employees believe their primary responsibility is doing their job. Consequently, no one in the organization sees learning

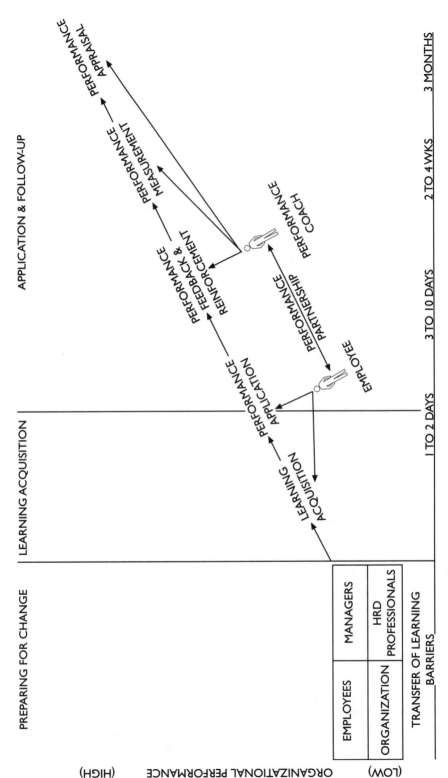

Figure 10.2 Organizational Performance Improvement Model

transfer as a personal major responsibility. Is it any wonder that less than ten percent of learning results in performance change?

Barriers to Learning Transfer

Learning transfer appears to be a straightforward, simple activity. In reality, it is very difficult due to several barriers that prevent it from occurring. These barriers can be clustered into four groups: employees, managers, the organization, and HRD professionals (see Figure 10.2).

Employees are ultimately responsible for improving their performance; however, they are often overlooked as barriers to learning transfer. HRD professionals and managers assume that employees are anxious to use new skills and apply new knowledge. In many organizations, this is a far cry from reality as employees lack the self-discipline to manage themselves and their work environment. In the final analysis, learning fails to be transferred to the job.

Some of the most common reasons employees fail to transfer learning include delayed application, fear of change, and lack of confidence. Delayed application is when employees do not have an opportunity to apply what they have learned in a timely fashion. Consequently, most of the knowledge or skills will be forgotten. All too often training is provided without any immediate opportunity for application, which negatively affects learning transfer. An improvement strategy is a way of overcoming this barrier. It ensures that performance applications are provided during and after training (see Figure 10.3). As a result, employees will have an immediate use for what they have learned. If no immediate application can be found, the performance improvement intervention should be rescheduled closer to the time of application.

Some employees fear change of any kind. They do not want to jeopardize their current productivity and performance even if there is a better way of performing a job. Consequently, many resist new technologies, changes, innovations, methods, techniques, skills, or knowledge. Change can cause employees to feel inferior, inadequate, and insecure. As a way of overcoming these feelings, managers must reassure their employees by displaying confidence in their skills and abilities while providing emotional and technological support.

Another reason employees resist learning transfer is because they lack confidence in their ability to use new skills or apply new knowledge. Employees may not have developed sufficient confidence during training, they may have failed in their first attempts in using the skills or applying the knowledge on the job, or they may fear negative feedback or criticism from managers. Nevertheless fear prevents them from transferring learning.

Many employees need a great deal of support and encouragement when using new skills or applying new knowledge, while others need to "relearn" the skills in a safe environment. Regardless, managers should offer additional training that helps employees gain confidence. Managers should also encourage employees to share how they have incorporated new skills or knowledge on the job, and provide support and feedback during initial application.

Four additional employee barriers prevent learning transfer. These include:

1. *No payoff:* When employees must be given reasons (rewards/recognition) for trying new skills and knowledge.
2. *Value conflicts:* Managers must isolate these concerns and overcome them by providing alternatives.
3. *On-the-job failure:* Managers must encourage employees to take risks by providing work environments that do not punish them for trying to improve.
4. *Peer pressure:* Managers must eliminate negative peer pressure by demonstrating the rewards for improving one's performance.

Many reasons contribute to the lack of learning transfer to the job, but the lack of management support and involvement is the primary cause of learning transfer failure. Managers must identify barriers that prevent learning transfer and implement transfer strategies to overcome them.

Managers prevent learning transfer by failing to coach their employees, and failing to reinforce employees' behaviors. All employees—whether staff, supervisors, middle or senior management—must be made aware of the responsibilities, standards, goals, and objectives of their respective positions. Unfortunately, most managers fail to adequately communicate expectations to their employees—thus, setting the stage for poor performance. To compound this problem, most managers fail to confront performance issues. Either they do not know how or they are uncomfortable doing so (conflict avoidance). Often, the problem becomes nearly insurmountable before being addressed. Sadly, most managers fail to coach their employees to attain needed results.

Gilley and Boughton (1996) believe that managers must use an approach known as the theory of expectation in order to improve learning transfer. First, managers must communicate to their employees exactly what and how they expect them to perform, and how the quantity and quality of their performance will be measured. Second, managers must inspect employee performance in order to determine if they meet or exceed established performance standards. Learning transfer will only take place when managers combine expectation and inspection.

Employees often fail to transfer learning to the job because managers do not provide appropriate reinforcement. Consequently, employees fail to adequately perform new skills or integrate new knowledge, making training a complete waste of time and money. One of management's best reinforcement tools is the performance review. It allows managers the opportunity to measure employee application of new skill and knowledge on the job. Incorporating evaluation of learning into the performance review and appraisal process communicates to employees the value and importance of learning transfer. In other words, if new skills and knowledge are being evaluated, they must be worth obtaining (Gilley, 1998).

Three additional managerial barriers to learning transfer are failing to be a positive role model, failing to provide adequate performance standards, and failing to provide work environments conducive to learning.

It takes a great deal of practice to master new skills and a great deal of discipline to integrate new knowledge. Managers must serve as role models for their employees, demonstrating a thorough understanding of specific knowledge and skills along with their applications. Management proficiency on the job earns employee respect, builds credibility, instills confidence, and highlights the critical essence of learning acquisition and transfer. Managers must also provide performance standards that help employees monitor their own performance and evaluate their own results. If learning transfer is to be successful, managers must understand the importance of developing work environments that are conducive to learning. Such environments are free of barriers, distractions, and interruptions. Finally, managers can foster learning transfer by communicating to employees their understanding of how difficult change can be, and confirming their willingness to help employees develop new skills and knowledge.

It was once said that when "putting a good performer up against a bad system, the system will win every time." Organizational policies, procedures, work environment, management practices, and attitudes toward employees can prevent learning transfer. Unless these barriers are removed, learning transfer will fail.

Typically, managers believe that employees somehow know when they are performing their jobs correctly, perhaps as a result of divine inspiration or the ability to read minds. In reality, most employees do not. In fact, the majority want and need feedback as reassurance that they are performing adequately.

Organizations can follow several guidelines when giving feedback to employees, including:

- being specific so employees know what they did correctly
- being sincere in order for employees to accept feedback without feeling manipulated
- delivering feedback immediately after an employee performs a task correctly
- giving individualized feedback in order to make it special
- giving feedback frequently but randomly so that it strengthens performance behavior
- making feedback clear and concise so that employees understand it (Gilley & Coffern, 1994)

Gilley and Boughton (1996) believe that encouraging and supporting practices that produce unprofessional, unproductive, and incompetent managers are the single greatest reason organizations fail to achieve the results they need. It is also one of the primary reasons why learning transfer fails.

Organizations must realize that they are responsible for developing professional managers, ones who are able to:

- establish positive relationships with employees
- resolve employees' problems and difficulties
- encourage transfer of learning
- provide positive and constructive feedback
- establish priorities
- create a positive work environment
- build the self-esteem of employees
- reward and recognize performance contributions (Gilley, 1998)

Most employees want to be rewarded and recognized for improving their performance. When this does not occur, employees will often avoid transferring new skills or knowledge to the workplace. In other words, when organizations fail to reward performance improvement, learning transfer will not occur and organizations will receive the wrong outcomes from training.

Establishing a connection between performance and organizational rewards is the single greatest factor in improving performance. Rewarding people for improving performance will encourage them to transfer learning. According to LeBoeuf (1985), "The things that get rewarded, get done" (p. 9). Learning transfer, therefore, must be rewarded in order to assure its success.

There are also HRD professional barriers. The most common one is training overload, where too much information is presented to learners in too short a period of time. Overload causes learners to become confused, overwhelmed, and bewildered, inhibiting their ability to use or apply skills. Consequently, employee performance fails to improve.

As a way of overcoming training overload, HRD professionals must get away from the traditional training approach and adopt a more effective method, such as the concept-unit (C-U) approach, which allows learners to absorb and apply new skills and knowledge (Gilley, 1998). Under the C-U approach interventions are broken down into smaller units around a single concept or group of concepts. Each unit is approximately two to three hours long and the entire program is spread out over several weeks. The same amount of information is covered but the amount of time allowed for integration is expanded.

Learners benefit under the C-U approach by:

- staying focused on the topic because they do not have to worry about what they are missing while at training
- absorbing and applying small bits of information rather than complex and lengthy ones
- practicing and applying skills immediately on the job
- reporting their progress at the beginning of the next intervention session
- obtaining feedback from the facilitator or other participants immediately, rather than trying to figure it out on their own

Other barriers commonly created by HRD professionals are:

- failing to realize that the performance improvement process is the responsibility of everyone in the organization
- failing to involve stakeholders in the performance improvement process
- failing to relinquish training to managers and supervisors
- failing to link performance improvement and change interventions to the strategic business goals and objectives of the organization

Each of these barriers can be overcome by forging a performance partnership with managers and employees (see Figure 10.2). The process includes four important activities: training managers to become trainers, designing and developing performance improvement and change interventions that bring about real change, partnering with managers in specialized learning, and linking performance improvement and change interventions to real performance problems.

So, employees, managers, the organization, and HRD professionals all provide barriers to the learning transfer process. Consequently, performance partnerships cannot exist until each of these groups becomes an active participant dedicated to the application, integration, and facilitation of learning.

The following questions can help HRD professionals, managers, and employees improve learning transfer:

- How are skills, knowledge, and attitudes being used on the job?
- What barriers prevent learning from being transferred?
- What role do managers and supervisors play in transferring and reinforcing learning on the job?
- What should be done before, during, and after implementing a performance improvement learning plan to enhance learning transfer?
- What role do employees play in learning transfer?
- What role does the organization play in learning transfer?
- What activities should be used to improve learning transfer?
- What can be done to increase learning effectiveness and efficiency?

Implementing Learning Acquisition Plans

Once a learning acquisition plan has been developed, it must be implemented. Implementation includes obtaining the learning resources that will be used during the learning plan; gathering information from peers, employees, and superiors about how to improve one's performance; participating in formal learning or training activities, workshops, or seminars; and participating in on-the-job learning activities.

The following questions will help managers and employees implement learning acquisition plans:

- When will you begin your learning plan?
- What help or support will you need to implement it?

- How will you track your progress?
- How will you integrate your learning plan into your daily work routine?
- How will you apply what you have learned on the job?
- When will you know that you need help in achieving your performance objectives?
- When will you know that you have achieved your learning objectives?

Implementing Learning Transfer Strategies

Implementing learning transfer strategies is everyone's responsibility, including employees, their managers, HRD professionals, and senior management. One way of improving learning transfer is to make certain that learning is performance focused—allowing time for practice and application, and enough content to foster performance improvement. During training, employees should have the opportunity to participate in job-related exercises that replicate real-life situations and conditions, thus providing a forum in which employees integrate and apply learning. After training, employees should continue to participate in performance applications in order to enhance learning transfer (see Figure 10.2).

Managers can do several things before training to promote learning transfer. Namely, identifying performance standards, communicating their support of training, communicating the importance of training, identifying rewards, and developing performance coaching skills (Gilley & Coffern, 1994).

During training, managers must provide a positive learning environment, encourage participation, utilize practical learning exercises, provide positive feedback, bestow rewards and recognition, and develop participants' readiness to learn (Gilley & Coffern, 1994). Each of these activities will encourage learners' involvement and foster performance applications during training.

One of the most effective ways of improving learning transfer is to develop performance improvement plans for each employee. Normally, such plans are developed at the beginning of a performance improvement opportunity. Figure 10.3 provides a sample of a performance improvement plan using the learning acquisition and transfer process. The plan consists of ten components, which include:

1. job responsibility
2. behavior/skills to be changed
3. performance objectives

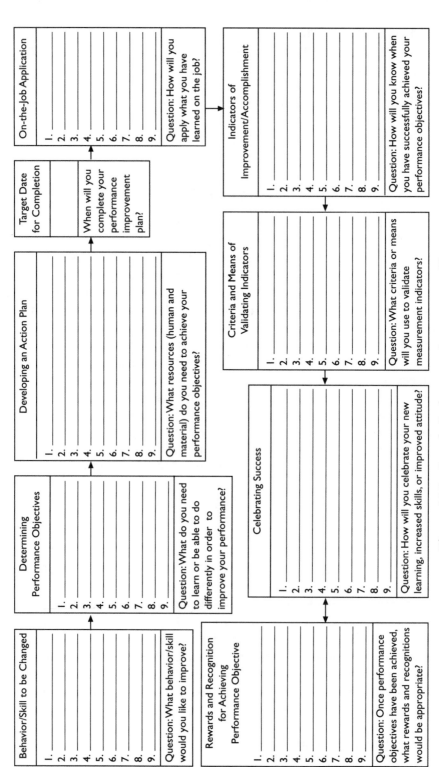

Figure 10.3 Sample Performance Improvement Plan

4. learning resources and strategies
5. target date
6. learning transfer strategy
7. indicators of accomplishment
8. criteria and means of validating indicators
9. ways of reporting results
10. possible rewards and recognition for accomplishment

Such a plan can be used along with scheduled training activities or as an independent and self-directed learning exercise. Regardless, learning transfer can be greatly improved when a performance improvement plan is used (Galbraith, 1991).

Whenever possible, it is helpful to integrate performance-based feedback during the execution of the performance improvement plan, as frequent measurement of progress and impact is needed in assuring learning transfer. Another valuable strategy is using job-performance aids. Also, support groups can be established as a way of helping employees integrate and transfer learning.

Making adjustments in performance based on feedback received from managers and peers is the next part of implementing learning transfer. Some adjustments will be minor while others may require employees to participate in additional professional development activities.

According to Gilley and Coffern (1994), there are several types of professional development activities that managers can provide after training to enhance learning transfer. These include developing refresher courses, providing job aids, providing follow-up activities, developing mentoring activities, and using daily logs and journals to track improvement. In addition, managers can provide positive reinforcement and public recognition to encourage learning transfer.

Measuring Performance Improvement

The primary objective of a learning acquisition and transfer plan is to improve organizational performance. Therefore, learning must be measured to ensure that employees achieve their performance objectives, change their performance behavior, and enhance organizational effectiveness (see Figure 10.2). In order to measure performance improvement, employees must identify indicators of accomplishment, identify the criteria and means of validating indicators, gather performance improvement data, compare performance improvement data with performance standards, compare performance improvement data with performance baselines, and determine the amount and degree of improvement.

First, employees must identify the type of indicators they will collect to demonstrate the degree to which they have achieved each performance objective. The kind of evidence presented will depend on the type of performance objective stated. Indicators range from demonstrating improved skills to writing a paper outlining the principles or methods learned, judging the quality of a performance, obtaining peer and employee observations concerning improvement, breaking down a performance competency into its component parts, applying a new skill or method, translating material from one form to another, interpreting material, and so forth.

The following questions will help managers and employees identify indicators of accomplishment:

1. How will you know when you have successfully achieved your performance objectives?
2. Who will you rely on in order to determine that you have successfully completed your performance objectives?
3. What evidence will you use to judge that you have successfully completed your performance objectives?
4. How will you measure what you have learned or are able to do differently?
5. How will you measure the results produced by your new knowledge, skills, or attitude?

Following are examples of indicators for different types of performance objectives:

Type of Objective	Examples of Indicators
Knowledge	Reports of knowledge acquired, as in journals, essays, examinations, oral presentations, audiovisual presentations.
Skills	Results from performance exercises, videotaped role plays critiqued by observers, peer critiques of actual performance, employees' observations, superiors' observations, formal assessment activities.
Attitudes	Attitudinal rating scales, performance in real situations, role playing, simulation games, critical incident cases with feedback from participants and/or observers.

Type of Objective	Examples of Indicators
Values	Value rating scales, performance in value identification groups, critical incident cases, simulation exercises with feedback for participants and/or observers.
Understanding	Examples of utilization of knowledge in solving problems, projects, decision-making activities, and feedback and coaching opportunities (Galbraith, 1991).

After employees have identified indicators of accomplishment for each performance objective, they must identify the criteria used to validate each indicator. According to Galbraith (1991), the criteria will vary according to the type of performance objective. For example, appropriate criteria for knowledge objectives might include comprehensiveness, depth, precision, clarity, usefulness, accuracy, etc. For skill objectives appropriate criteria may be speed, poise, quality, accuracy, or flexibility. For attitude objectives appropriate criteria might include consistency, appropriateness, and commonality. After employees have specified the criteria, they should indicate the means by which the indicator will be judged. Common means of evaluating the indicators include the use of rating scales, descriptive commentaries, observation and feedback, and evaluative reports. Evaluators may include peers, employees, superiors, experts, trainers, or others who are qualified to judge the evidence of performance improvement.

The last four steps of this part of a learning acquisition plan are fairly easy and straightforward. They include gathering performance improvement data that demonstrates growth and development, comparing it to performance standards, comparing it with an employee's performance baseline, and determining the amount and degree of improvement. This analysis should help employees determine whether or not their performance objectives have been achieved.

Conducting Performance Appraisals

Once evidence has been gathered that shows performance improvement has been achieved, it is critical to identify ways of reporting it within the organization. A common way of reporting is through formal performance appraisals and reviews that permanently record accomplishments to which rewards and recognition can be linked (Figure 10.2). Another popular means is to discuss one's success with employees or peers—either informally (e.g., over coffee) or formally (e.g., in weekly meetings)—so that they are aware of recent achievements. Such conversations can also occur with superiors. Finally, employees should simply report the good news.

When employees engage in a learning plan that improves their knowledge, skills, attitudes, values, or understanding, they should be rewarded and recognized for their achievements. Therefore, a learning acquisition and transfer plan is not complete until rewards and recognition are identified for improving performance. Once appropriate rewards and recognition have been identified, they should be presented to employees in order to encourage continued growth and development through learning acquisition.

The following questions will help managers and employees celebrate their successes:

- After receiving your performance objectives, how will you report what you have learned, what you are able to do differently, and the results you have achieved?
- How will you be rewarded for achieving your learning objectives?
- How will you celebrate your new learning, increased skills, and improved attitude?

CONCLUSION

Learning acquisition and transfer does not simply happen. It must be engineered through a carefully crafted set of steps and activities. Anywhere during the process, learning can be derailed and lost. Consequently, HRD professionals and managers must devote a majority of their development time to making certain that learning acquisition is encouraged and enhanced, and that transfer is guaranteed.

CHAPTER 11

Measuring Performance Improvement and Organizational Results

One of the most important and powerful components of HRD practice is that of evaluation. Evaluation is a process, not an event, that involves all key decision-makers, stakeholders, and influencers, and should be influenced by a clear understanding of the organization's performance and business needs, as well as its strategic goals and objectives. As a process, evaluation is used to measure every aspect of strategically integrated HRD. To this end, it should measure the strategically integrated HRD philosophy and practice, as well as the impact and utility of strategic business, management development, and organizational development partnerships.

Every aspect of the organization affecting strategy should be included in the measurement process to determine whether or not they are operating at peak efficiency. Evaluations can be used to determine the effectiveness of organizational communications, the operational efficiency of the organization, the effectiveness of critical interventions such as strategic planning and organizational development interventions and projects, their impact on the organization, and the benefits derived from them.

Evaluation should be a daily practice presiding over each component of HRD practice, including organizational and needs analysis, the design and development process, and the learning acquisition and transfer process. As an operational approach: evaluate, evaluate, evaluate. When uncertain of usefulness, effectiveness, or credibility: evaluate. Then and only then will HRD professionals be able to determine the viability and utility of their activities, initiatives, interventions, and processes.

During the evolution of HRD, evaluation displays the distinctive characteristics of each phase. During the vendor-driven HRD phase, the majority of evaluation occurs at the completion of the training program when participants' reactions are solicited. This process is consistent throughout the first four phases of the evolution of HRD, including the vendor-customized phase.

As HRD programs cross over the line of demarcation from an activity to a results orientation, the evaluation process changes dramatically. During the decentralized and strategically integrated HRD phases, evaluation becomes a tool for measuring performance improvement and the impact of various interventions throughout the organization. In the strategically integrated phase, evaluation is as normal and commonplace as breathing, and is used to measure every aspect of the life of an HRD professional. Consequently, evaluation captures the scope, depth, and degree of impact HRD professionals and their interventions have on the organization.

EVALUATING STRATEGICALLY INTEGRATED HRD PHILOSOPHY AND PRACTICE

As stated above, evaluation is an everyday process for strategically integrated HRD professionals. As a result, *everything* is evaluated. Evaluation is seen as a feedback and improvement process designed to enhance customer service and quality. Since strategically integrated HRD professionals are blended into the fabric of the organization, evaluation becomes less of a formal event than during previous HRD phases.

Strategically integrated HRD professionals understand that traditional evaluation processes, such as return on investment and cost-benefit analysis, are historically used to "prove" the value and benefit of HRD interventions within the organization. Due to the increased demand for such data, many HRD professionals have adopted similar strategies in order to demonstrate their credibility within the organization. Strategically integrated HRD professionals, however, reject the notion of demonstrating their own credibility and importance since they realize that organizational decision-makers are interested in enhanced productivity, efficiency, and effectiveness (which can only be brought about through building strategic business partnerships, management development partnerships, and organizational development partnerships—not through better evaluations or documentation). Improvements in efficiency or productivity can only be realized through the proper use of an organizational effectiveness strategy designed to improve all aspects of organizational performance and HRD practice. Strategically integrated HRD professionals realize that their true value to the organization is their ability to help the organization achieve its desired business results. Therefore, projects must be evaluated to determine whether or not the desired outcomes have been achieved. Strategically integrated HRD professionals also understand that evaluations conducted at the conclusion of a series of interventions to determine their return on investment merely constitute a Band-Aid approach. They also realize that after-the-fact evaluation methods are not a viable long-term strategy for improving HRD, and can oftentimes create an adversarial relationship between HRD professionals and their clients.

The Evaluation Process

Regardless of the type of evaluation conducted, the evaluation process consists of six steps, each of which is essential and based upon the previous steps. In simplest terms, the evaluation process compares results with objectives. The six steps include:

1. collecting data
2. analyzing data
3. interpreting and drawing conclusions from the data
4. comparing conclusions to stated objectives
5. documenting results
6. communicating results to key decision-makers, stakeholders, and influencers

During the evaluation process, a variety of data collection techniques are available for use (see Chapter 8). The most common are questionnaires, interviews, focus groups, organizational reports and records, pretests and posttests, and management's perception of change. Each of these techniques can be used to collect the data necessary to draw conclusions and make recommendations to clients.

The evaluation process is not unlike that of the organizational performance and needs assessment process discussed in Chapter 8. The primary difference, of course, is that an evaluation is conducted at the conclusion of an intervention, while organizational performance and needs analyses are conducted to determine if such an intervention is necessary.

To expedite the evaluation process, HRD professionals should use an intervention analysis worksheet. This is a simple, straightforward tool designed to capture more salient information regarding the impact of interventions and change strategies. Figure 11.1 illustrates a simple worksheet useful in capturing critical information that will help identify the utility of interventions.

This tool captures a great deal of information in a short period of time and can serve as the foundation for individual interviews and

What is the intervention?	
What organizational change, performance skills, knowledge, or business result changed or improved as a result of the intervention?	
What on-the-job performance behaviors changed as a result of the intervention?	
What were the organizational benefits received as a result of the intervention?	

Figure 11.1 Intervention Outcome Analysis

focus group activities. When tools like this are employed, they help HRD professionals capture information that can be used to improve interventions and their implementation, and to solicit recommendations for changes. The ultimate benefit of the intervention outcome analysis tool is that it affords HRD professionals the opportunity to discuss their interventions with key decision-makers, stakeholders, and influencers in such a way as to borrow their perceptions and points of view, which ultimately fosters client relationships and cements strategic business partnerships. This engagement can only help improve the image and credibility of HRD professionals within the organization.

EVALUATING THE ORGANIZATIONAL EFFECTIVENESS STRATEGY

One of the distinguishing characteristics of a strategically integrated HRD program is the presence of an organizational effectiveness strategy. As discussed in Chapter 3, an organizational effectiveness strategy consists of two blended parts: (1) an organizational system, and (2) a performance management system; both of which work to improve organizational performance capacity and effectiveness. Since the organizational effectiveness strategy is so critical to the success of strategically integrated HRD programs, it must be carefully evaluated to determine if it is achieving desired results. While this may appear to be a logical conclusion, it should not be taken for granted.

Evaluating each of the fifteen functions within the organizational effectiveness strategy is of critical importance, as it will glean a great deal of information regarding the overall approach used by HRD professionals. Evaluation results impact the philosophy of HRD, mutual performance partnerships, HRD practice, and ultimately improve on the organizational effectiveness strategy.

Organizational Systems

When evaluating the organizational system, HRD professionals must be cognizant of the fact that this system's seven functions are the most stable within the organization. In other words, they tend not to be altered by minor events or activities within the organization. Consequently, HRD professionals can use previous evaluations as a baseline to determine if the organizational system has changed dramatically since previous evaluations. Any changes that may have occurred in the leadership, structure, work climate, organizational culture, mission and strategy, managerial practice, or policies and procedures should be documented and examined carefully. Any strategic planning activities or organizational development change interventions that were designed to alter any of these components within the organizational system should be examined as well.

Since the organizational system tends not to change dramatically from one point in time to another, it is important for HRD professionals to capture any gradual, evolutionary changes that might be occurring. It may be appropriate, therefore, to go back several years to examine previous evaluations and compare them with current realities. Only then will the gradual shifts that may be occurring within the organizational system become evident. Then adjustments can be made in customer service activities, practices, procedures, or interventions.

Performance Management System

Perhaps one of the most important evaluation actions in which HRD professionals may participate is the "macro" evaluation of the performance management system. One of the best ways of evaluating such a system is to assess the overall performance improvement activities that have occurred from one specific point in time to another. By looking at the aggregate of such activities, HRD professionals determine which interventions have been successful and which have not. They can also determine whether or not a breakdown has occurred between any of the eight functions within the performance management system.

Macro evaluation should be viewed as a type of circuit analysis designed to make certain that the performance management system is working to its designed specifications (not unlike that of a home electrical system, which requires periodical checks to make certain there are no shorts that could shut down the system, or, worse, initiate a catastrophic event that could ultimately destroy the home). This process helps guarantee that the performance management system is viable, functional, and working to produce desired results. Consequently, evaluating performance management systems is best achieved via careful examination of the system's eight functions to determine their adequacy, efficiency, and effectiveness (Figure 11.2).

Human and Material Resources

HRD professionals must continually measure the adequacy of human and material resources within the organization. Since these are inputs used to produce desired results, they must exist in the right quantity and quality to achieve organizational effectiveness. This requires consideration of their placement, accessibility, and interchangeability. Each of these criteria will help determine whether or not these resources are being utilized efficiently.

Since human and material resources are at the center of the performance management system, the linkages between these and each of the other components are absolutely critical. A "circuit" test of all aspects of human and material resources within the performance management system provides an effective evaluation method.

Learning Systems

When evaluating the learning system, HRD professionals must examine the organizational, performance, and needs analysis processes, the program design and development process, and the learning acquisition and transfer process. Each of these critical HRD practice areas offers information regarding the effectiveness and quality of HRD interventions. While these three areas are tra-

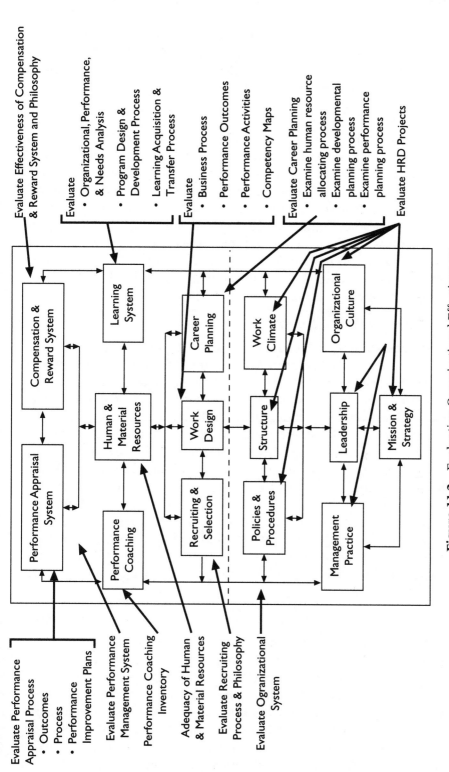

Figure 11.2 Evaluating Organizational Effectiveness

ditionally the most common areas of evaluation, they still have a tremendous impact on the image and credibility of HRD programs and professionals. Thus, it is extremely important that evaluations in these areas be conducted with the utmost care and efficiency.

Evaluating Work Design

Evaluation of work design focuses attention on the four areas of competency maps, performance activities, performance outcomes, and business processes. Use of these four criteria allows HRD professionals to construct a work design audit for any job within the organization. These four activities are circular in nature, beginning with competency maps and ending with business processes. That is, the outputs of one action are the inputs of another. As a result, analysis may commence at the end (business processes) to determine whether or not each of the previous steps has been successfully completed.

Evaluating the Selection and Recruiting Process

When evaluating this process, HRD professionals are concerned with the skill of managers in recruiting employees. They should evaluate the selection and interviewing process to ascertain whether managers possess the skills necessary to conduct interviews that isolate the most ideal candidate *and* whether they are adequately using competency maps. The organization's recruiting process also comes under investigation, to determine whether or not it is the most effective method possible. Additionally, HRD professionals should help the organization determine if it has an adequate recruiting and selection philosophy that is consistent with its organizational mission and strategy. This evaluation should be conducted in light of the work design and performance coaching processes. Finally, there should be a direct connection between selection and recruiting processes and the adequacy of human and material resources.

Evaluating Performance Coaching

The performance coaching model outlined in Chapter 6 is an effective evaluation tool for judging how well managers have improved their performance coaching skills over time. Though observations and interviews, HRD professionals can compare and contrast managers' perceptions with those of employees, revealing the degree to which managers have improved their competencies and skills. Another way of evaluating the performance coaching process is to use the critical incident technique outlined in Chapter 8. This technique indicates how well managers demonstrate performance coaching skills and their impact on employee performance.

Evaluating the Performance Appraisal Process

Outcomes are the focus when evaluating the performance appraisal process. These include the decisions made by managers and employees regarding performance improvement strategies; the design, development, and implementation of employee improvement plans used to help employees acquire and transfer learning to the job; and the recommendations for compensation and rewards based on employee performance. HRD professionals should also examine congruence between managers' development and feedback philosophies and their actual execution. Finally, performance appraisal activities such as data gathering, feedback discussions, conflict resolution, and reaching agreement on next steps must be conducted in an effective manner.

Evaluating Compensation and Reward Systems

Compensation and reward systems provide the primary motivating force for most employees, therefore HRD professionals must be concerned with their effectiveness and impact on long-term performance improvement. Are the compensation and reward system's intent and philosophy being maintained? In other words, is the organization rewarding entrepreneurial activities, long-term results, and those performance behaviors that realize needed business results? By examining these issues, HRD professionals make certain that the compensation and reward system indeed helps the organization achieve its strategic business goals and objectives.

Evaluating Career Planning

When evaluating career planning, HRD professionals should conduct a four-part examination. First, they should determine how work design and the learning system impact the career planning process. Second, HRD professionals should examine the human allocation process to ascertain whether employees are being matched properly with job assignments. This analysis includes comparing employees' knowledge and skills with job descriptions and task analyses to gauge the match, then determining whether the correct number of employees are assigned to each job classification within the organization. Third, evaluation of the developmental planning process, focuses on a realistic analysis of future career options and opportunities, and the creation of activities that will prepare employees for future job and career decisions

(Gilley & Eggland, 1989). This examination establishes whether employees are being given opportunities to obtain the type of experience necessary for future job assignments and career advancement. Evaluating the developmental planning process may require the study of performance improvement plans being created by employees (during the performance appraisal process), which reveal the nature of development plans, their rigor, and quality. Fourth, HRD professionals should examine the performance planning process, which centers on the identification of specific job demands, goals, priorities, and reward expectations associated with current job assignments (Gilley & Eggland, 1989). Specific learning acquisition and transfer plans, performance activities, performance priorities, and financial compensation all are linked to successful completion of stated goals and objectives. Ultimately, HRD professionals are responsible for determining the organizational impact of these performance planning activities.

Evaluating Organizational Communications and Operations

HRD professionals can use the organizational effectiveness framework to evaluate organizational communications, taking into account applicable organizational and performance management functions (e.g., the performance appraisal process, performance coaching, human and material resources, work design, structure, work climate, organizational culture, leadership, and managerial practice). Consequently, the appropriate functions can be used to determine the organization's appetite for and ability to produce effective organizational communications. HRD professionals can also use the corresponding functions to determine how well organizations communicate interpersonally and intrapersonally within the firm. Finally, they can ascertain the impact of technology and organizational structure on organizational communications and determine which strategies are most appropriate for overcoming areas of deficiency.

When examining organizational operations, five organizational and performance management functions should be considered in creating a strategy for evaluating their efficiency and effectiveness. They are human and material resources, work design, structure, policies and procedures, and mission and strategy. A comprehensive review of the organization begins by blending the organization and performance management systems to determine the appropriateness, efficiency, and quality of overall organizational operations. Such an analysis provides considerable insight into ways for improving each of the functions, as well as into methods for improving overall organizational operations.

Evaluating Strategic Planning Activities

Evaluating strategic planning activities consists of both formative and summative evaluation processes. The formative process gives feedback to HRD professionals regarding how well the implementation process is progressing. Summative evaluation provides comprehensive evaluation data as to the effects and impact of the strategic plan on the organization. HRD professionals can greatly improve the strategic planning process by carefully examining each of its four components (scoping, analyzing, visualizing, and planning), and determining whether or not these meet the standards and expectations derived at the outset. A three-way process exists to evaluate strategic plans. It includes an ongoing feedback loop that provides feedback as to the implementation of strategic plans, a comprehensive review of the impacts and effects of the strategic plan, and an internal audit of the strategic planning process.

EVALUATING THE EFFECTIVENESS OF STRATEGIC BUSINESS, MANAGEMENT DEVELOPMENT, AND ORGANIZATIONAL DEVELOPMENT PARTNERSHIPS

HRD professionals have an obligation to evaluate the three types of partnerships formed within the organization. Each of these partnerships is designed to produce different outcomes and results, and should be carefully analyzed to determine their usefulness in improving the image and credibility of HRD, as well as in helping the organization achieve its business goals and objectives.

Examination of strategic business partnerships involves five steps. HRD professionals should:

1. evaluate their customer service strategy.
2. analyze the procedures employed to audit HRD interventions and consulting services.
3. measure the effectiveness of their client relationships.
4. analyze how effective they are in helping clients make performance improvement and organizational development decisions.
5. ascertain whether or not customer service responses match client demand states.

When all of these evaluations, analyses, and audits are complete, HRD professionals will better understand their effectiveness in creating strategic business partnerships.

Evaluation of management development partnerships begins by identifying the current performance behaviors of managers and supervisors in order to establish a managerial malpractice baseline against which to compare future results. Second, managers' current performance coaching competencies must be measured to determine their present level of proficiency and to focus performance improvement interventions on overcoming weaknesses and building upon strengths. This information can be uncovered by administering a performance coaching inventory, which includes a manager's self-report and employee report, as discussed in Chapter 6. Third, employee development plans for each manager should be constructed using the criteria outlined in Chapter 10.

Once learning acquisition and transfer have occurred and managers have had an opportunity to practice their skills, HRD professionals should readminister performance coaching inventories (both a manager's self-report and employee report) in order to isolate areas of improvement. This cycle continues until managers reach a mastery level of competency in performance coaching.

Organizational development partnerships should be evaluated from two perspectives. First, organizational development intervention quality and effectiveness require examination to determine what changes have occurred. Second, HRD professionals must investigate the degree to which their colleagues have successfully made the transition from the traditional role of trainer and instructional designer to that of organizational development consultant. By doing so, HRD professionals will be able to determine strengths and weakness among colleagues, and isolate opportunities or threats that either encourage or discourage the transition. The transformation from trainer to organizational consultant is critical to the success of the strategically integrated HRD approach and must be the central focus of HRD professionals during the evaluation process.

EVALUATING HRD PRACTICE

HRD professionals engage in three types of analysis when examining HRD practice. First, they audit the organizational, management, performance, and needs analysis processes to determine their effectiveness in uncovering appropriate organizational and performance needs (see Chapter 8). Second, HRD professionals evaluate the design and development process to discover areas of improvement and efficiency (see Chapter 9). Third, they examine the learning acquisition and transfer process to assess its impact on organizational performance and effectiveness. Each of the eight steps in the process require careful inspection to determine whether employee development plans are being designed properly. When deficiencies are found, corrective action must be taken immediately (see Chapter 10).

Evaluating Organizational, Performance, and Needs Analysis Processes

HRD professionals should consider several areas of inquiry when evaluating the organizational, performance, or needs analysis processes. The manner in which they accept and react to requests for HRD interventions should be carefully examined. In this way, they will be able to determine whether or not they are thinking strategically or simply reacting to clients' requests for training. Five critical questions drive the analysis process (see Chapter 8). The manner and timeliness in which HRD professionals respond to each of these questions should be carefully assessed to determine if they are being handled correctly.

HRD professionals also must critically analyze each of the different types of analysis processes in order to determine if they have adequately followed the steps appropriate to each. The best time to conduct this evaluation is at the conclusion of each of the assessment processes. This allows HRD professionals to measure the outcomes of the processes, and how well they were able to conduct each of the critical steps.

Evaluating the Program Design and Development Process

The principal question to be addressed when evaluating the program design and development process should be, "Were the performance objectives and purposes of the intervention accomplished?" To answer this question, attention must be turned to the outline created at the beginning of the intervention, and to measurement of program design against it. During this evaluative step, it is important to measure the utility of the intervention's content. In Chapter 9 we outlined in great detail how HRD professionals should go about evaluating their interventions.

Another important component of the program design and development process is evaluating the facilitator to determine how well he or she met the performance objectives of the intervention. When evaluating the facilitator, participants' perceptions are essential. It is sometimes helpful to use critical observers as evaluators during the intervention to determine how well facilitators perform.

Facilitators should be evaluated based upon their ability to:

- hold the learner's interest
- assist learners during difficult periods of learning acquisition
- summarize clearly
- identify clear performance objectives
- communicate ideas, facts, and concepts
- organize the learning environment
- relate to the learner
- establish a comfortable and supportive learning environment
- select appropriate methods of instruction
- select appropriate learning activities
- know the materials being presented (Gilley & Eggland, 1989)

While each of these is critical when measuring facilitators' abilities, HRD professionals are often the persons responsible for the identification and selection of many of these activities. It is therefore vital that facilitators be held accountable for only those activities for which they are directly responsible.

Evaluating the Learning Acquisition and Transfer Process

The primary objective of all interventions is to improve organizational performance and effectiveness. The learning acquisition and transfer process exemplifies this important aim. In Chapter 10 we carefully outlined the eight steps of this process and identified their interdependencies. The final step in the process is conducting a performance appraisal, which is used to determine how well an employee is performing against a set of established standards. It is also used to determine the degree to which employees have acquired new knowledge and skills and transferred them to the job.

HRD professionals must be able to guarantee that the learning acquisition and transfer process has been conducted adequately, which requires a comprehensive analysis of each of the eight steps in the process. On the surface, this may appear to be an overwhelming undertaking, though in reality it is not. Built-in evaluation points guarantee that each step of the process is being conducted in an efficient, effective manner (see Chapter 10).

EVALUATING HRD TOOLS AND TECHNIQUES

HRD professionals must evaluate the tools and techniques used to improve the image and credibility of their programs and the interventions they produce. This evaluation includes scrutiny of the promotional strategies being used to enhance the image and credibility of HRD (see Chapter 12), and the projects designed, developed, and managed by HRD professionals (see Chapter 13).

Evaluating HRD Promotional Strategy

Evaluating the promotional strategy of HRD begins with auditing the image of its programs and practitioners, which can be accomplished by uncovering organizational members' familiarity with and perceptions of HRD. Determining the credibility of HRD professionals within the organization is another critical component of this process. Interviews, focus groups, and questionnaires reveal the opinions, ideas, and perceptions of decision-makers, stakeholders, and influencers regarding HRD and its practitioners.

Evaluating HRD Projects

One of the major components of the project management process involves evaluating the outcomes and impacts of the project on the organization as well as determining how effectively they were managed. HRD professionals have a ready list of recommendations for improving project management practices within the organization. Project management techniques and relationship building actions that are an integral part of project management can be evaluated at project's end.

VALIDITY, RELIABILITY, AND UTILITY

The evaluation in which HRD professionals participate must be accurate. Therefore, the three criteria of validity, reliability, and utility should be used to measure the effectiveness of an evaluation. Each will be examined separately.

Validity

Validity is concerned with the extent to which an evaluation measures what it is supposed to measure. Evaluations that are developed with this in mind will be more objective as they attempt to isolate and control independent variables capable of skewing the evaluation's accuracy. Three types of validity relevant to HRD evaluations are *content, predictive,* and *concurrent* validity.

Content Validity

Content validity aims to ensure that evaluations represent specific competencies, performances, and skills that reflect actual practice. When constructing an evaluation, HRD professionals must guarantee that the questions used to assess employee performance or level of competence accurately measure real-life events. Content validity ensures that evaluations test real-life practices under circumstances and conditions similar to those encountered on the job. Making certain that evaluations are accurate along these lines allows for the creation of evaluations that are meaningful as well as useful.

Predictive Validity

Predictive validity refers to an HRD professional's ability to predict future performance. It confirms that the evaluations used accurately reflect what an employee accomplishes on the job. Two types of data are involved: (1) the results of an evaluation, and (2) individual performance on the job. If an employee scores high on an evaluation and performs at a high level on the job, the evaluation has high predictive validity. Evaluations exhibiting this type of validity serve as the foundation for predictions of future performance and organizational outcomes. This becomes valuable information for supporting the utility of HRD interventions and is useful in improving the image and credibility of HRD, its programs, and professionals.

Concurrent Validity

Concurrent validity is concerned with whether or not evaluation results provide an accurate estimate of present performance. As with predictive validity, concurrent validity involves the relationship between the evaluation and some other measure. For example, comparing the results of a written test with that of performance observations enables HRD professionals to test the accuracy of each evaluation technique. A strong correlation in results allows for use of the most cost-efficient evaluation technique, since either one can predict on-the-job performance accurately.

Reliability

Consistency and stability of an evaluation indicate its reliability. In other words, an evaluation is reliable if results are consistent and scores do not change significantly over time. This is also referred to as test/retest reliability (Gilley & Eggland, 1989). Evaluations are also considered reliable if scores do not change a great deal when different variations of the same evaluation are used. For example, if the order of questions used during a focus group or an interview varies from evaluation to evaluation, but the evaluation includes the exact same questions and the results are similar, the evaluation is considered reliable. This is referred to as equivalent form reliability (Gilley & Eggland, 1989).

Utility

In addition to being valid and reliable, the evaluation methodology must also be easy to use (Michalak & Yager, 1979). HRD professionals must consider ease of scoring, administering, and interpreting various evaluations prior to selecting the most appropriate form. Additional factors influencing utility include evaluation subjectivity, comparability of scores and performances, and cost (in terms of time needed to administer evaluations, and the number of HRD professionals needed to adequately conduct the evaluation).

CONCLUSION

Simply stated, HRD professionals should evaluate, evaluate, evaluate. Evaluation is a state of mind, not a technique, and should guide everyday practice and activities, thereby providing invaluable information that can only help improve the image and credibility of HRD within the organization.

Evaluation is the key to reflective insight and continuous improvement. Without evaluation, HRD professionals will never truly know how well they are performing or how they are perceived within the organization. Failure to evaluate is equivalent to HRD malpractice and deception.

PART V

Applying Tools and Techniques to Improve HRD and Organizations

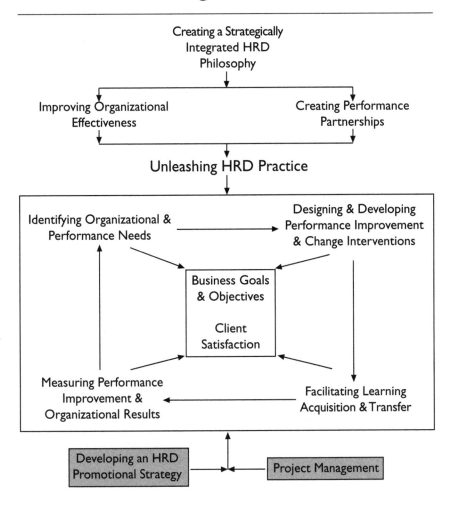

Creating a Strategically
Integrated HRD
Philosophy

Improving Organizational
Effectiveness

Creating Performance
Partnerships

Unleashing HRD Practice

Identifying Organizational &
Performance Needs

Designing & Developing
Performance Improvement
& Change Interventions

Business Goals
& Objectives

Client
Satisfaction

Measuring Performance
Improvement &
Organizational Results

Facilitating Learning
Acquisition & Transfer

Developing an HRD
Promotional Strategy

Project Management

Strategically Integrated HRD

CHAPTER 12

Developing a Promotional Strategy That Enhances the Image and Credibility of HRD

For the past several decades, the field of HRD and its practitioners have been perceived as nonessential support services to organizations. As a result, senior management's attitude toward HRD is one of support during good economic periods, but one of reduction during bad periods. This roller coaster approach has severely weakened the image and credibility of HRD within organizations.

DEVELOPING A PROMOTIONAL STRATEGY FOR HRD

HRD professionals have several alternatives from which they can choose in order to overcome their image and credibility problems. First, they may adopt the strategically integrated HRD approach (Chapter 1). Second, they may establish strategic business partnerships and alliances (Chapter 5). Third, they can make the transition to organizational development consulting and focus on organizational performance rather than training for training's sake (Chapter 9). Fourth, they can enhance their credibility by improving learning transfer and application (Chapter 10). Fifth they can adopt and implement a promotional strategy designed to enhance their perceived image (Figure 12.1).

Fundamental Laws of Promotion

In order for HRD professionals to improve the image and credibility of their HRD programs, they must adhere to two fundamental

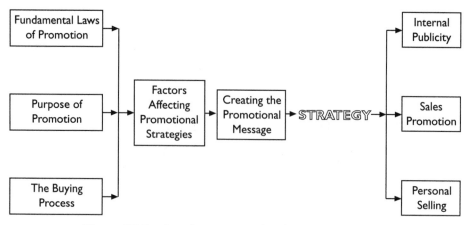

Figure 12.1 Creating a Promotional Strategy for HRD

laws of promotion: the marketing concept and the exchange process.

The Marketing Concept

The first law of marketing is the marketing concept. According to Gilley and Eggland (1992), it can be defined as the directing of all an HRD professional's efforts at satisfying clients' needs and expectations for the purpose of improving organizational performance and achieving the organization's strategic business goals and objectives. From this perspective, marketing is not used to manipulate clients but is focused on identifying and addressing the performance problems facing an organization. Consequently, performance and change interventions are designed and developed in accordance with clients' expressed interests, guaranteeing that HRD programs are focusing on real client problems and needs. But the marketing concept cannot be applied unless HRD professionals adopt a service-oriented attitude—which reflects the needs of their clients—prior to developing interventions.

The Exchange Process

The second law of marketing, the exchange process, can be defined as the offering of value to another party in return for something of value (Gilley & Eggland, 1989). HRD interventions must be viewed by clients as at least equal in value to the time, energy, effort, and personal commitment exchanged for them. If the value received from an intervention is viewed as greater than or equal to the time, energy, effort, or personal commitment required from clients, an exchange will take place (Gilley & Eggland, 1992). If the value gained is less than the value given, an exchange will not transpire. Consequently, the more positive exchanges that HRD professionals can engage in, the better the HRD program will be perceived.

In order to improve the image and credibility of HRD, its professionals must become skilled at understanding, planning, and managing exchanges. In this way, they will be focusing on the interests of their clients and continuously providing interventions that are of value.

Purposes of Promotion

Each of the three promotional activities maintains a common set of purposes: to inform, persuade, or remind clients of the advantages and benefits of interventions.

To Inform

Information is often closely guarded, secreted away, and shared only on a need-to-know basis. The failure of many HRD professionals is relying on inadequate or insufficient means for disseminating information. A successful promotional strategy greatly enhances HRD's perceived value and position within the organization. Therefore, promotions should highlight interventions, consulting services, and special projects.

As stated earlier, promotion is communication. HRD professionals must communicate the message they want clients to hear, which is often as simple as communicating the purpose of one's consulting services or making clients aware of interventions that are available.

To Persuade

Another purpose of promotion is to persuade clients to take action, such as participating in interventions. This may be as simple as recommending a particular training activity that will help improve employee performance. Whatever the promotional activity is, it must be persuasive, appealing to one or more of the clients' developmental needs or performance problems.

To Remind

When an intervention has been available for a long period of time, it is often forgotten by clients. Therefore, one purpose of promotional activities is to remind clients of intervention availability. In addition, some clients may avoid new interventions when they are first introduced. Because of this, they should be reminded of their availability later.

The Buying Process

All promotional activities have the same objective: to inspire clients to participate in or use interventions or services. Clients arrive at purchase decisions via the buying process, which consists of four activities: gaining clients' attention, arousing their interest, creating a desire for interventions or services, and encouraging clients to take action.

Promotional activities must first be designed to gain clients' attention. Once clients are aware of the interventions that are available, promotional activities must then arouse their interest. This can be accomplished best by communicating the advantages and benefits of interventions. Promotional activities must reveal how a particular intervention or service can solve clients' problems or meet their needs. If successful, the promotional activity should produce a desire to participate in interventions. HRD clients will then take action based upon a desire to solve their performance deficiencies or satisfy developmental needs. Using the buying process as a guide, promotional activities can be developed that gain attention, arouse interest, create desire, and prompt action.

Factors Affecting a Promotional Strategy

Several factors will affect the selection of the particular promotional activity used by HRD professionals. The most important ones are the nature of interventions offered, the promotional objectives of the HRD function, the competitive position of the HRD function, and the financial condition of the organization.

The Nature of HRD Interventions

Many HRD professionals rely on program announcements and brochures to promote their offerings, hoping these activities will encourage potential clients to attend their interventions or use their consulting services. This approach may work, but in most situations it only wastes time and money. Why? The reason is simple. Most HRD interventions are too complex to be explained effectively through program announcements and brochures. They require more creativity and personalized promotional efforts to be successful.

It follows that the nature of an intervention will have a great effect on the kinds of promotional activities selected. For example, a complex intervention such as project management requires a different promotional activity than a simple, straightforward one. In this situation the most appropriate promotion activity would be personal selling, because it allows a performance consultant to discuss the details of the program and answer questions regarding its application and benefits.

The Promotional Objectives of HRD

Before a promotional strategy is developed, the promotional objectives of the HRD program must be considered. If the primary objective is to enhance the program's image, then publicity and sales promotions would be most effective. If, however, the objective is to increase participation in specific interventions, then personal selling would be more effective. When the objective is to improve client awareness of upcoming interventions, then program announcements and brochures (a specific form of sales promotion) would be most appropriate. Remember, the promotion activity selected should be directly related to the promotional objectives identified.

Competitive Position of the HRD Program

HRD professionals must consider their competitive position prior to selecting promotional activities. If the HRD program is small, it might be more appropriate to concentrate on a smaller segment of the organization rather than adopting a comprehensive approach. In some situations, HRD programs can develop a small number of specialized interventions that are designed to overcome specific organizational issues. This is often referred to as a marketing niche strategy.

Some HRD programs maintain an organization-wide focus. As a result, they must embrace a more comprehensive promotional strategy that includes internal publicity, personal selling, and sales promotion in order to reach their clients.

Financial Condition of the Organization

The financial condition of the organization will affect the promotional activities selected. Some activities are much more expensive than others. For example, sales promotions and personal selling are both very expensive promotional activities, while internal publicity is free. The promotional activities selected must, therefore, be within the HRD's budget.

Creating the Promotional Message

The success of a promotional strategy depends on the message that is communicated to potential clients. Emphasis is not on how the message is delivered but rather on the content of the message itself.

Critical Factors Affecting Promotional Messages

Five critical factors should be addressed before creating a promotional message. First, HRD professionals must identify the unique and distinctive characteristics of their interventions. Second, the key benefits that clients will receive as a result of attending interventions or using consulting services must be isolated. Third, HRD professionals must identify the image they want to project through promotion. Fourth, the competitive niche on which to focus must be identified. Fifth, the promotional message should be based upon HRD's strengths.

Simerly (1989), in the *Handbook for Marketing Continuing Education,* identified several questions that can help evaluate the HRD program's promotional message. They include the following:

- Does the message make a meaningful promise to clients?
- Is the message single-minded, simple, and specific?
- Is the message distinctive and interesting enough to stand out?
- Does the message have staying power and durability?
- Is the message believable?
- Does the message successfully position the intervention within the organization?
- Is the message directed at the right target audience?
- Is the message tasteful and appropriate, enhancing rather than undermining the desired program's image?
- Is the message conveyed in the same language used by the client?
- Is the message persuasive enough to stimulate the desired action?
- Does the message support the established promotional objectives?
- Does the message fit strategically into the overall goals of the HRD program?

Identifying the Benefits of HRD Interventions

The promotional message should be based on the client's needs, interests, and expectations. Since the primary purpose of promotion is to secure participation in interventions or the use of consulting services, the promotional message should be written so that the benefits of these interventions and consulting services are clearly understood by clients. The message should also demonstrate how clients can achieve the results they want.

Clients are interested in knowing how a specific intervention or consulting service will improve their employees' performance, satisfy their developmental needs, improve productivity, and/or increase profitability. HRD professionals must inform clients what the specific results of an intervention will be. For example, a manager may have poor supervisory skills, resulting in performance deficiencies. If so, he or she may be interested in a performance coaching intervention. A program could be designed to produce the following outcomes:

1. The program will help participants develop better employee relationships.
2. The program will help participants develop performance confronting skills.
3. The program will help participants delegate effectively.
4. The program will improve participants' feedback skills.
5. The program will help participants link rewards to employee performance.

This list tells the client what improvements to expect as a result of participating in the intervention.

Writing Promotional Messages Using Eight Guiding Principles

The most effective promotional messages incorporate eight guiding principles. Each one is designed to help facilitate a positive response toward interventions or services. The principles are as follows:

1. Clearly define the target audience before writing.
2. Know the needs of the target audience and write with the purpose of helping them fulfill these needs.
3. Emphasize benefits.
4. Catch the reader's attention within the first three to four seconds.
5. Engage the reader with a compelling story.
6. Use action words and powerful messages that have a sense of urgency, and encourage action on the part of the reader.
7. Arrange the promotional message so that it leads the reader to take the action desired.
8. Test and retest the promotional message to determine if it accomplishes its intentions (Simerly, 1989).

Selecting a Promotional Strategy

HRD promotional strategies involve communication between HRD professionals and their clients. Promotion is done to improve image and credibility as well as to increase participation in interventions.

An HRD promotional strategy includes three marketing communication activities. Each is used to inform, persuade, or remind clients of the importance and value of HRD interventions. They are:

1. *Internal publicity:* The exchange of goodwill through news stories transmitted through a mass medium (the organization's newsletter, reports, brochures, organizational newspapers, or industry magazines and journals) at no charge.
2. *Sales promotion:* An activity designed to directly induce clients to accept interventions (flyers, brochures, HRD open houses, contests, etc.).
3. *Personal selling:* A process of informing, persuading, and reminding clients to purchase or select interventions using personal communications.

Internal Publicity

Internal publicity is primarily a communication tool to advance one's marketing objectives. It also seeks to influence clients' attitudes and beliefs toward the HRD program by altering negative perceptions. Positive internal publicity makes it easier for clients to participate in interventions and to use consulting services.

Because internal publicity is often in the form of a news story, it may appear more objective, and therefore may have greater credibility among clients. However, these communications are usually low-key and do not provide an opportunity for repetition. The most common types of internal publicity include service announcements, editorials, feature articles, or news stories.

The effective use of internal publicity begins with the identification of the objectives to be accomplished. The principal objectives of internal publicity are to obtain a favorable image of the HRD program and its professionals, humanize the HRD program, counteract any rumors or negative publicity, and develop client respect for the HRD program and its professionals.

Each of these objectives can best be accomplished if HRD professionals deliver internal publicity that is newsworthy, credible, and personable. It must be directed at the needs and interests of the target audience, and must be written in such a way that readers can identify with the situation or context. Clients should believe the message being communicated and trust that the information is true.

Internal publicity tends to be the least used of the promotional activities, although it has great potential for improving the image of HRD programs and its professionals. It should be used to enhance clients' awareness and appreciation of interventions and services offered by the HRD program.

The following are three steps HRD professionals can take to improve the effective use of publicity:

1. Identify the objectives of internal publicity.
2. Select the internal publicity message.
3. Implement and evaluate the results of internal publicity (Gilley, 1996).

There are several types of publicity appropriate for HRD professionals. The most common is a news release about a new or improved training program, intervention, or consulting service, as well as stories about members of the HRD program. These news stories generally are less than three hundred words. A second type of publicity is a captioned photograph with a brief description that explains the picture's content. An example is a picture of a new employee who is joining the department or an employee recently promoted.

Selecting the specific types of publicity to be used depends on a variety of factors including the type of information to be presented, the characteristics of the target audience, the importance of the information, the receptivity of media personnel, the importance of the news to other organizations, the amount of information to be presented, and the relationship that HRD professionals have with the media.

Getting published is an overlooked and underestimated form of publicity. Every month thousands of articles are published in trade and professional journals. Publishing an article in a professional journal can enhance the image of the author as well as that of the organization and HRD program. Getting published, however, is more difficult than writing an article and submitting it for publication. Most journals maintain an acceptance rate below thirty percent. Therefore, HRD professionals should develop a ten-step strategic approach to getting published:

1. Establish a long-term strategy. Have a "real" purpose for writing the article.
2. Target the manuscript, select the journal carefully, determine the article's focus, and tailor the article for the journal's readers.
3. Discuss the article with colleagues, then incorporate their suggestions.
4. Call the editor and discuss ideas. Identify the editor's interests and use his or her suggestions.
5. Be willing to change the article to comply with editorial considerations and style.

6. Research the journal's style, intent, and purpose—focus the article accordingly.
7. Obtain feedback from editors, then rewrite and resubmit the article based upon the feedback received.
8. Contact the editor during the review process. Demonstrate a willingness to make the manuscript better.
9. Prepare a well-written and professional-looking cover letter. Demonstrate a professional approach.
10. Develop a professional and attractive manuscript. Remember that the product is one's signature, it reflects the image of the author and his or her organization (Gilley, 1996).

If the article is rejected, obtain a copy of the reviewer's comments in order to improve it. Remember, getting published is a learning process: Rejection is not a personal insult. The most important consideration is to learn the process and become good at it.

Once objectives have been identified, HRD professionals must determine whether there are any interesting stories to tell about their interventions, partnerships within the organization, or colleagues. A search along these lines will uncover many stories worth sharing. If the number of acceptable stories is insufficient, create newsworthy events. This requires HRD professionals to discover interesting facts about everyday activities. While this may appear to be a difficult task, remember that people love to read about those they know who are involved in interesting and challenging situations. Clients also enjoy reading about their service providers' accomplishments.

HRD professionals should be able to write an effective news release—one that meets the standards of various media editors. A well-written news release must contain five journalistic components: the who, what, why, when, and how of a story. In other words, the message must provide the reader with essential information about training participants, the HRD program and its professionals, and the interventions offered. In addition, the name of the organization, its address and telephone number, as well as the name of someone to write or call regarding the story should be provided. Include the deadline with each release. Many large organizations have internal media departments, often called "corporate communications" or "marketing communications," willing to assist in the development and distribution of promotional items, including internal publicity.

To obtain the maximum benefit from publicity, HRD professionals should create and maintain a systematic and continuous publicity program. If possible, an HRD member should be assigned the responsibility of managing the program on a permanent basis. This person must then establish an effective relationship with media personnel.

HRD professionals need some way to measure the effectiveness of their internal publicity efforts. Internal publicity could be measured in terms of the amount of exposure achieved or the changes in awareness or attitude of the target audience toward the program. Ultimately, the increased usage of services by clients is the true measurement of the success of internal publicity.

Internal publicity is often underutilized in relationship to other promotional activities. Yet, in many cases, it creates the kind of memorable impact on clients that other activities, such as sales promotion and personal selling, cannot. Furthermore, internal publicity often possesses more credibility as news than other forms of promotion.

Sales Promotion

Sales promotion is critical because HRD is an intangible product. Hence, clients are interested in receiving materials that help them visualize what they are participating in or implementing. In addition, most adults are visual learners, and sales promotional materials help facilitate their understanding of interventions. Sales promotion is important because it is a means of speaking to many existing and potential clients.

Sales promotion is one of the few avenues HRD professionals have available to reach thousands of clients at the same time. Sales promotions convince clients to take the desired action. It is a form of mass selling that leads the client through the buying process just as a salesperson does in personal selling. Therefore, sales promotion must attract the client's attention, develop an interest in the intervention or service promoted, create desire for the benefits of the intervention or service, and convince the client to take some action.

HRD professionals should consider whether the purpose of sales promotions is to inform, to persuade, or to remind clients about their interventions. This type of analysis will give a sales promotion program direction and purpose. HRD professionals must also identify what they want to accomplish through a sales promotion campaign. Therefore, it is necessary that they identify clear, precise, and measurable objectives. One of the primary objectives is to persuade clients to participate in interventions. Sales promotion also help clients confirm their decisions, aids personal selling efforts, and helps create a positive image of HRD. Sales promotions are best when used along with other parts of the promotional strategy. They serve to inform and remind clients of interventions they should participate in and services they should use.

Sales promotion can aid personal selling in two ways. It can pre-sell certain clients prior to meeting with them. For example, a brochure might grab a client's attention, develop interest, and create desire for a consulting service even before an HRD professional calls. In this way, sales promotions can propel a client through the action stage of the buying process. Sales promotion is also important in overcoming clients' resistance. It can, therefore, help HRD professionals get appointments to see prospective clients, which makes this part of the personal selling process easier. Consequently, when HRD professionals call, the client already has some knowledge of available services. If the client believes these services have benefits, HRD professionals will find it easier to secure an appointment. In this manner, effective sales promotion paves the way for the sales call.

The type of sales promotion creates an image in the mind of the client. If most of the sales promotion is directed at emphasizing the HRD program's role in improving performance through performance management systems, the client will think of that business as performance consulting rather than as a training house. This is critical in developing the type of image desired.

Of course, sales promotion alone cannot create image. HRD professionals must determine what type of image to portray and then make certain that all promotional activities aid in the establishment of this image. Sales promotion is just one promotional activity. It must be supported by all other promotional activities in order to create the image HRD professionals want to convey.

Some other objectives of sales promotion include the following:

1. To introduce a new performance improvement intervention or service.
2. To encourage greater participation in interventions or greater usage of services.
3. To educate clients about improvements or enhancements in interventions and services.
4. To stabilize a fluctuating demand state.
5. To increase reselling opportunities.
6. To increase the total number of clients participating in interventions or services.

Sale promotions are quite appropriate for HRD programs that participate in organizational meetings and conferences. However, the decision to develop promotional material can be difficult, and should be based on meeting size and the type of clientele who attend. Other factors are cost of point-of-purchase materials, rental expenses for equipment (video recorders, computers and monitors), promotional expenses for giveaways (plastic handbags, calculators, buttons, pens), and salary expenses for employees who are to serve as liaisons during meetings and conferences.

Even after all expense factors have been considered, HRD professionals may have difficulty determining if participating in such events is worthwhile and cost effective. Research indicates that there are five important criteria that should be considered when making a decision regarding the use of sales promotional materials at organizational meetings or conferences. They include:

1. proportion of decision-makers among attendees
2. proportion of attendees from the most critical departments, units, or divisions of the organization
3. total number of attendees that are potential clients and/or stockholders
4. type of location and traffic patterns of attendees
5. amount of compelling promotional material at meetings and conferences

Sales promotion techniques that are appropriate for HRD professionals include video demonstrations, point-of-purchase materials, banners and buttons, catalogs, newsletters, program announcements, and brochures.

Videos are excellent attention getters and are often used to encourage client participation. This technique provides an opportunity to preview the content that will be presented during a performance improvement intervention or explore the benefits received from using a consulting service. While such activities can appear a bit dramatic and costly, they enhance client involvement and participation while bringing attention to HRD programs.

Point-of-purchase materials include display racks and counter pieces used for tangible products such as books, films, training videos, and training materials. Point-of-purchase materials are designed to attract attention to interventions and services, to inform clients about the HRD program, and to encourage further examination. The best materials are those that blend into the environment, allowing the interventions and services to be featured.

One of the most common sales promotion techniques is to use simple but effective items such as buttons, pens, and banners. These items are inexpensive to develop and produce, yet draw attention to the HRD program while communicating a clear message to clients. Banners can be used to convey a critical message or theme. They should be displayed in strategic locations or high traffic areas in order to maximize their effectiveness.

Catalogs are a popular sales promotion technique used by HRD programs. A catalog lists available interventions or services and should include complete descriptions of each. The primary purpose of a catalog is to inform and remind clients of future training activities and consulting services, but also serves as a way of communicating the depth and breadth of those services. In addition, a catalog provides HRD professionals with an opportunity to promote several interventions at one time. It is, therefore, one of the most cost-effective promotional activities.

Many HRD professionals communicate with their clients via newsletters. The purpose of this promotional technique is to inform clients about interventions and consulting services. For instance, newsletters can include information about a recent training session and who attended the event, or they can announce other upcoming activities. Changes in training time or locations as well as other important information can also be provided. In addition, newsletters can be used as a vehicle for introducing new management techniques or skills that can be used in improving performance and efficiency.

Some HRD programs publish their newsletter as a report, including important training and research information that is meaningful to their clients. In this way, the newsletter is not viewed as a promotional piece but as a learning tool that can enhance organizational effectiveness.

A program announcement is another promotional technique used by HRD professionals. These are short—usually one page or less—reminders of upcoming events. Because they are inexpensive, they should be used to bridge the gap between issues of the newsletter or catalog. Program announcements are strictly promotional pieces, while newsletters and catalogs are viewed more as educational mediums.

The favored form of sales promotion is the brochure, which communicates in detail the advantages and benefits of interventions. Brochures come in every shape and size. They are designed to provoke clients to take action—that is, to participate in interventions and consulting services. Brochures, however, should be developed in the same manner as other persuasive mediums. Six steps should be followed when designing brochures. They include:

1. identifying developmental needs or performance problems
2. suggesting that the interventions being promoted are the best way to satisfy the identified needs or to solve performance problems
3. identifying the advantages and benefits of interventions
4. identifying why interventions are best for the client
5. substantiating claims and advantages
6. asking the client to take action (Gilley & Eggland, 1992, p. 170)

A word of caution: brochures are often overused as a promotional technique. They have limited impact and will not be effective in all situations. Therefore, other promotional activities and techniques should be incorporated into the promotional strategy.

Personal Selling

Robert Louis Stevenson once said, "Everybody lives by selling something." This includes HRD professionals responsible for interventions. However, many HRD professionals are not willing to admit their responsibility for this activity. Perhaps the reason for such resistance is the negative connotations of the term selling, or the image salespersons manifest.

Regardless, personal selling remains a critical component of any successful promotional strategy. It also serves as an essential communications vehicle for advocating the advantages and benefits of interventions. HRD professionals must master the art of selling if they ever hope to achieve success. It is a promotional activity that cannot be overlooked or ignored.

Personal selling is the only promotional activity that brings HRD professionals and their clients together. As a result, HRD professionals have the opportunity to communicate persuasively and personally with clients. Personal selling is important because nothing happens in HRD unless the intervention or service is sold. In most cases, it takes personal selling to accomplish this.

Personal selling has been defined as personal, persuasive communications that help clients to participate in interventions or use consulting services that will fulfill their needs or solve their problems. Several parts of this definition need explanation. First, selling is personal, which means that a person-to-person discussion occurs between HRD professionals and their clients. During this process, they have the opportunity to present information about the intervention or consulting service to the client, answer the client's questions, and explain how the intervention or consulting service will provide benefits. Remember that personal selling not only persuades, it also communicates. Communication is a two-way process requiring listening and articulation skills on the part of both parties. To determine their clients' needs, HRD professionals must listen carefully and foster open, honest communication.

The process of selling focuses on satisfying the needs and expectations of clients. It enhances client relationships and ensures that all of the recommendations made by HRD professionals are focused on closing the gap between expectations and actual performance.

The selling process consists of nine interrelated steps, which include:

1. developing rapport with clients
2. discovering performance problems and developmental needs
3. identifying and analyzing solutions
4. selecting a solution
5. presenting solutions to clients
6. implementing the solution
7. supporting the decisions and conclusions of clients
8. evaluating the solution
9. following-up with clients

Step 1: developing rapport with clients. Many times, HRD professionals enter into a selling situation with little or no previous involvement with clients. Naturally, clients are often skeptical of the consultants' motives and even distrusting of the recommendations they make. This barrier must be overcome before an open and honest discussion can take place about the developmental needs and performance problems facing an organization.

HRD professionals must create an environment that encourages the free exchange of ideas and feelings. The benefit of this type of environment is that clients feel secure, and will recognize that the lines of communication are open. In addition, a sharing environment goes beyond the superficial to demonstrate a deep concern for the well-being of clients and the problems they face.

Step 2: discovering performance problems and developmental needs. Many clients are indifferent to sales pitches, possessing the belief that they do not need interventions. This attitude can be brought about by a failure to examine the clients' individual situation before recommending a solution. As a result, clients are insulted by an apparent lack of respect and do not view HRD professionals or their recommendations as credible. HRD professionals must, therefore, analyze their clients' situations thoroughly before making recommendations.

The discovery phase of the selling process helps HRD professionals obtain information that will be used to determine clients' levels of interest, their decision-making authority, tenure with the organization, past behavior, and so forth. There are four objectives of the discovery phase:

1. gathering additional qualifying information
2. developing a strategy as to how to approach the client
3. gathering information that can be used to develop a better presentation, thus avoiding making serious errors
4. enhancing the client's confidence in the HRD professional's abilities (Gilley, 1996, p. 12)

The discovery phase allows HRD professionals to explore in detail the problems with which clients are struggling. There are three approaches HRD professionals can use to accomplish this purpose: the questioning approach, the significant-fact approach, and the service approach.

The questioning approach is used to isolate specific problems affecting a participation or purchase decision. For example, HRD professionals could ask prospective clients how well their managers conduct employee reviews. If they answer, "not very well or poorly," managers may need to be trained in effective performance appraisal techniques, which can be provided by HRD. However, if they respond, "the best in the company," then suggesting such a program would be foolish. Using the questioning approach to uncover needs and problems will help HRD professionals avoid making unnecessary suggestions or recommendations.

HRD professionals should be prepared to ask several types of questions to uncover areas of need, concern, or interest. The most common types to ask are situation and problem questions.

Situation questions are designed to discover the current state of the client. They establish a baseline, revealing what the client is thinking and experiencing. They are also very safe, nonthreatening, easy to answer, and help the discussion flow. Situation questions are critical during the early stages of a relationship, when rapport is fragile. Moving too quickly can jeopardize the new relationship. Examples of situation questions might include: "What are your current sales revenue goals?" "How often are employees required to complete performance audits?" or "How many employees will be affected by the reorganization plan?"

Problem questions reveal the client's desired state. HRD professionals ask clients which performance problems they would like to have solved or which developmental needs, if improved, would help enhance quality or efficiency. HRD professionals may want to ask clients what difficulties they are experiencing or with what they are dissatisfied. Problem questions allow clients to indirectly describe their desired state. Examples of problem questions include: "Describe the ideal working environment for your department?" "When things are functioning smoothly, how do your employees communicate with each other?" or "If your employees improve their time management skills, what do you think the results would be?"

The second approach is known as the significant-fact technique. When using this technique, HRD professionals approach clients with a statement of fact that has meaning for them. For example, HRD professionals state to a divisional manager, "I understand that the president's performance enhancement team has identified employee performance improvement as their number one priority for the next two years, and he is very concerned about how managers confront employees' performance problems." This approach is an indirect way of asking the divisional manager what he or she thinks about the quality of employees' performance and how managers approach employees who have performance problems. The division manager's response will reveal a great deal about his or her interest or concern about this topic, which focuses the conversation and drives potential recommendations.

The third technique is referred to as the service approach, which attempts to determine if there are any services that HRD professionals can perform for the client. The service approach is often an open-ended discussion allowing a number of concerns to surface. It is an effective approach for HRD professionals comfortable with spontaneous and unstructured discussions. Such an approach requires HRD professionals to quickly determine whether they are qualified to address the concerns or requests of the client. For example, HRD professionals use this approach when describing a service, conducting performance analysis used to determine current performance deficiencies, and asking clients whether they are interested in participating.

Step 3: identifying and analyzing solutions. During this phase, HRD professionals help clients identify proper actions required to close the gap between expectations and actual performance. HRD professionals should brainstorm with their clients to generate potential solutions, without evaluating or examining the viability of each idea. The goal of brainstorming is to generate as many activities and solutions as possible.

Once all possible solutions have been identified, each one can be analyzed based upon established criteria that serve as a standard by which to filter each idea. Ideas that meet most of the criteria are grouped together for further analysis. Ideas that do not meet the established criteria should be filed for future consideration.

Step 4: selecting a solution. The purpose of this step is to select the best possible solution and decide whether it is practical and reasonable to implement. This includes identifying the cost and potential results of each solution.

Another critical part of this phase is to identify possible obstacles or barriers that may prevent applying a solution. As these barriers are isolated they should be analyzed to determine the possible effects they may have on various solutions. Actions should be identified to overcome each obstacle or barrier, examining financial, human, and emotional cost. This information will help HRD professionals decide the best solution.

Identifying the best alternative(s) should be the outcome of this phase of the problem-solving process. Now clients will have an approach to follow in their quest to solve performance problems.

Step 5: presenting solutions to clients. Clients are often skeptical of the solutions HRD professionals may recommend. This occurs when recommendations are not based on the identified performance problems and developmental needs discovered during the second phase of the selling process, or when clients do not believe the solution recommended is capable of improving performance as promised. Therefore, suggestions must be specifically related to identified needs.

This phase of the selling process consists of two parts: the presentation and the handling of objections. The presentation should be based on the needs, interests, and expectations of the clients. Its primary purpose is to secure participation in interventions or the use of consulting services. In order to accomplish this, HRD professionals should communicate the benefits of interventions when making a presentation.

HRD professionals can use two approaches when making a presentation to clients. When the sales presentation is very complex and detailed, use the prepared approach, beginning with a prepared presentation that allows clients to ask questions or express concerns. The prepared approach relies on a structured, memorized statement and is often used in response to clients' requests for a proposal, wherein they have identified their needs, interests, and expectations, and have asked HRD to provide recommendations to satisfy them. Unfortunately, this type of an approach forces HRD professionals to do most of the talking, which can be a disadvantage.

The second approach, known as the needs-satisfaction approach, is quite different and involves developing an understanding of the client's needs before making any suggestions or recommendations. This approach adopts the problem-solving process identified earlier, utilizing questioning techniques to identify the most critical problems facing the client. When using this approach, the client does most of the talking, revealing information while HRD professionals listen for concerns and needs. The presentation of solutions occurs after discovery of the client's problems or needs.

Each of these approaches must be based on recommendations that are perceived by the client as being of value and meeting their needs. This will reduce the number of objections. Most likely, objections will be raised, and when they are, HRD professionals should not become defensive. Objections are simply questions that clients have about the intervention being recommended, and should be viewed as opportunities to provide more information, uncover additional needs, or clarify objectives and benefits.

HRD professionals should not argue with clients when they voice an objection. At the same time, HRD professionals should not allow clients to answer their own objections because they may not answer them correctly. The following is a five-step process for handling objections:

1. Let customers express themselves completely.
2. Repeat the objective and get agreement as to its accuracy.
3. Ask them to elaborate on their objections.
4. Answer their objections.
5. Confirm answers and get agreement that the objections were eliminated.

Step 6: implementing the solution. HRD professionals must help their clients carry out the best solutions to their problems. During this phase, HRD professionals test solutions to determine results by choosing a department, division, or unit where the solutions have an opportunity for success. This allows HRD professionals to test solutions under the best possible conditions before applying them to the entire organization.

Implementing solutions should be a slow and deliberate process, allowing for ample time to assess real outcomes. It is often a good idea to implement a solution in several parts of an organization before introducing it to the entire organization, refining and redesigning the solution as needed.

Step 7: supporting clients' decisions and conclusions. HRD professionals must understand that clients participate in interventions and use consulting services in order to solve performance problems and satisfy development needs. Therefore, dissatisfaction with a solution will create bad feelings toward the HRD program and its professionals. As a result, HRD professionals must be supportive and responsive to the decisions and conclusions of their clients.

HRD professionals face another dilemma. They must close the sale. Unfortunately, many HRD consultants fear being rejected by their clients. As a result, they avoid closing the sale by becoming excellent at uncovering needs and presenting solutions, hoping the strength of their presentation will compel potential clients to enlist their services. Closing is simply asking clients to make decisions that will help improve their organizations' performance capacity and effectiveness. If HRD professionals have prepared adequately and thoroughly—uncovering and addressing their clients' needs and objections—then asking for and securing the sale will be the natural conclusion reached by clients desirous of improving their organizations.

One of the best ways HRD professionals can balance these two problems is to assume that their solution is the best possible action the client can take, and that any reasonable person would want to follow this course. In other words, assume the sale and move forward.

Step 8: evaluating the solution. Once the solution has been tested in several settings, results are gathered and compared. If the solution helps close the gap between expectations and actual performance, it can be considered a success. If, however, the gap remains the same, HRD professionals may need to consider alternative solutions.

Regardless of the success or failure of a solution, the information and knowledge gained is valuable. Findings should be communicated to others within the organization so they can benefit from the experience.

HRD professionals should document the outcomes of every intervention tried and keep a record of the dates and locations of each one. This information will be an invaluable resource for future problem-solving efforts.

Step 9: following-up with clients. The selling process should not end with the close of the sale but should continue with follow-up. During this phase, HRD professionals contact their clients to determine satisfaction with the solution. Positive and negative feedback should then be used to improve interventions. Feedback should also serve as a learning opportunity for HRD professionals regarding their selling skills and abilities. Only after several hundred selling opportunities will HRD professionals begin to develop the type of selling skills that will help improve the image and credibility of HRD within the organization.

CONCLUSION

The image and credibility of an HRD program and its professionals can be improved by delivering excellent, timely, and value-added interventions. Creating a strategically integrated HRD program also enhances its image and credibility. Developing a promotional strategy designed to improve the acceptance of HRD within organizations is essential. Without such a strategy much of the "good work" provided by HRD professionals will go largely unnoticed.

CHAPTER 13

Designing, Managing, Implementing, and Evaluating Performance Improvement and Organizational Development Projects

Every HRD professional is a project manager, although many lack the practical approach and techniques for completing a project efficiently. Few know how to plan and manage a project, even though every performance improvement and organizational development intervention is a project that must be managed, implemented, and evaluated. Thus, HRD professionals must become competent at managing projects in order to evolve to the strategically integrated HRD level.

WHAT IS PROJECT MANAGEMENT?

Project management is a method and set of techniques based on the accepted management principles of planning, organizing, directing, and controlling. Each of these principles is used in combination to reach a desired end result, on time, within budget, and according to established specifications. Project management is also a way of thinking that keeps desired results in focus. As project managers, HRD professionals achieve specific objectives using proven tools and techniques such as critical paths (charts), scheduling technologies (Gantt charts), goal and risk analysis, stakeholder analysis, controlling techniques, and project diagrams. Personnel are organized and their efforts directed toward achievement of desired results. Finally, project management requires evaluation of project objectives against measurable criteria.

Project management involves planning objectives and activities for successful results, organizing people to get things done, directing people to keep them focused on achieving desired results, and measuring progress to provide useful feedback.

Planning

Planning involves identifying clear, specific goals and objectives that must be attained on time, within budget, and at a desired level of quality. Work activities to be carried out by members of the project team must be specified, including individual tasks and expected results. Furthermore, specific dates, times, and individuals responsible for producing the desired results must be identified.

In order to control the outcomes of a project, HRD practitioners must develop comprehensive plans—no plan means no control. Alternatives must be assessed and more than one way of accomplishing the desired result must be distinguished. This is an effective means for guarding against unforeseen changes, which can alter the outcome of the project. For example, HRD professionals must be able to adjust to unexpected contingencies, such as having the funds allocated for completing a project drastically reduced or eliminated. This unforeseen contingency can dramatically affect the quality and timeliness of project outcomes. In fact, it would be nearly impossible to produce the same desired results absent the budget or human resources allocated to accomplish it. Obviously, project quality will suffer greatly, as will one's ability to deliver desired results on time. To alleviate the impact of unanticipated difficulties and ensure successful project completion, controls must be built in.

Organizing

When HRD professionals create a structure used in executing project plans, they are engaged in the process of organizing. Organizing is a set of activities, responsibilities, and authoritative relationships used in implementing the project plan. According to Gilley and Coffern (1994), organizing includes determining who is responsible for what activities, objectives, and results; who reports to whom; what activities are carried out where in the organization; and who is authorized to make critical project decisions.

Project management entails assembling necessary material and financial resources to carry out work defined in the project plan. Additionally, span of control most appropriate for the project must be identified. That is, too many or too few activities or people can prevent achievement of the desired results.

HRD professionals must identify a principal project manager who is ultimately responsible for achieving project objectives. This individual is accountable for identifying work divisions based on the tasks and activities to be achieved, balancing the authority and responsibility necessary to complete the project, and delegating work to other project team members.

Directing

Communicating, motivating, coaching, supervising, and providing performance feedback for project team members is a process known as directing. Directing is an ongoing activity, not a singular event. In certain circumstances, directing requires both formal and informal communication that can include memos, directives, meetings, reports, e-mail, phone and informal conversations with project team members.

Project managers are like orchestra conductors, who, at all times, know where they are in the plan and direct each team member in order to produce a quality performance. One of their chief responsibilities is to build synergy around project outcomes, encouraging participation and ownership during the process.

Controlling

Once human and material resources have been identified and assembled into a workable structure, it will be necessary to observe, monitor, and control that structure as the project progresses. Actual results must be compared to plan results, and their discrepancies isolated. Based on the feedback obtained, HRD professionals must make decisions necessary to narrow the gap between expectations and performance.

In order to minimize discrepancies between actual and desired performance, HRD professionals must possess knowledge of performance measurement and have a clear, specific understanding of their client's expectations. Establishment of proper reporting relationships at specific points throughout the project will provide an early warning of discrepancies that may threaten project outcomes. These controls allow the time necessary to redesign and/or adjust the project and its activities in order to produce deliverables on time, within budget, and at quality specifications. Project success depends greatly on the quality and quantity of checks and balances during execution. Checks and balances guarantee the continuous improvement of HRD professionals, project team members, and others involved in planning and controlling the project.

The project management process involves complete and specific identification of expected operations and results. It also includes systematic measurement of actual progress compared to expectations in order to identify deviations, and decision-making activities used in correcting and redirecting the project.

Project management differs from regular management in several ways. First, it is a comprehensive approach to planning and directing complex activities. Planning is the cornerstone of successful project management, while it is not as critical to regular management. Project management emphasizes results—getting the job done on time, within budget, and with specific controls to gauge progress and provide feedback. Regular management incorporates planning, organizing, directing, and controlling as part of the process of managing people, work flows, and achieving results. Project management uses systems analysis and measurement to make certain that expected results are achieved.

WHAT IS A PROJECT?

One of the best ways to understand project management is to identify the characteristics of a project. In HRD, projects vary in size and scope, from a simple one-day performance improvement intervention to a comprehensive organizational development redesign. A project is an organized effort with planned activities and schedules; it has specific timebound results, multiple tasks and roles, a series of specific yet interdependent tasks, and is a one-time effort that involves many people, usually across functional areas in the organization.

According to Gilley and Coffern (1994), successful projects exhibit certain characteristics. First, there should be a solid, conceptual plan leading toward the production of desired results. This means the thinking behind the project makes sense and is easily conveyed to other project team members. Second, successful projects contain goal and objective statements that should be specific, measurable, agreed upon, realistic, and timely (SMART). Third, project steps should be broken down, measurable, and clear, which helps HRD professionals reduce large projects to micro projects that are much easier to manage and control. Fourth, each step of a project should be discrete, with observable results. Projects are easier to control and quality easier to maintain when observable results have been established. Fifth, sufficient resources (material, financial, and human) should always be available to accomplish the desired objectives. Sixth, every member of the assembled project team should be focused on the desired outcomes. No team member should question or resist the methods chosen to complete the project or meet its objectives. Seventh, the human resources assembled should be competent, qualified, and cooperative. These resources will insure higher quality, promptness, efficiency, and cost control. Finally, successful projects require constant monitoring of outcomes, with proper feedback given to project team members. To monitor outcomes project controls must be identified from the beginning (pp. 129–30).

Projects are constrained by the organization's need to maintain service, quality, and positive human relations within the firm. Obviously, constraints can hinder progress and/or achievement of desired outcomes. Consequently, HRD professionals must guard against overzealousness, always realizing that internal political pressure and politics must be understood and managed.

IDENTIFYING PROJECT MANAGERS' RESPONSIBILITIES

Selecting a project manager requires consideration of an individual's experience, capabilities, qualifications, and competence in achieving project results in a timely fashion, within budget, and according to quality specifications.

Project managers must be able to motivate, inspire, and coach their team members. Active listening skills, as well as the ability to provide meaningful performance feedback, help ensure successful project completion. Managers should be assertive, not aggressive or submissive, in their interactions with team members and project support groups. That is, they must be able to confront poor performance while maintaining the self-esteem of team members or support personnel. Communicating tough decisions while being sensitive to the needs of team members and staff is an effective approach. Interpersonal conflicts over financial and material resources waste precious time and, thus, should be minimized. Finally, project managers should remain flexible while performing their multiple roles.

To ensure success, project managers must possess the technical expertise necessary to complete complex projects. While no project manager holds all the expertise necessary to execute every project, each must have the experience and competence to direct, evaluate, and make sound decisions on technical alternatives related to a project. Technical expertise includes an understanding of technology, product applications, technological trends, and relationships among supporting technologies (Kerzner, 1982).

Because project managers direct the project, they must have the leadership and strategic expertise to design, coordinate, control, and implement plans. Expertise includes the ability to envision and communicate the big picture to all members of the project team. As project leaders, project managers must have the ability to ask thought-provoking questions that help team members understand their roles and responsibilities. They must, therefore, delegate the appropriate responsibility and authority to team members to ensure successful project completion. Creation of reporting and control systems will alert team members to potential problems, and should allow them the time necessary to take corrective action when projects appear to be out of control.

TEN MAJOR REASONS WHY PROJECTS FAIL

HRD professionals must constantly guard against project failure. According to Bienkowski (1989, p. 99), there are ten reasons why projects fail:

1. The project is a solution in search of a problem.
2. Only the project team is interested in the end result.
3. No one is in charge.
4. The project plan lacks structure.
5. The project plan lacks details.
6. The project is underbudgeted.
7. Insufficient resources are allocated.
8. The project is not tracked against its plan.
9. The project team is not communicating.
10. The project strays from its original goals.

The presence of any or all of these conditions dooms the project to failure. Each project failure negatively impacts the image and credibility of HRD programs and professionals. By implementing a systematic process designed to overcome these failures, projects will be delivered on time, within budget, and at desired levels of quality.

THE EIGHT PHASES OF PROJECT MANAGEMENT

An effective project management process consists of eight phases that include project definition, planning, visualization, leadership, implementation, controls, termination, and evaluation. Each phase helps break down large, unmanageable projects into small activities that can be more easily mastered. This eight-phase process also provides a means of visualizing project planning activities.

Project Definition

The first task facing an HRD professional is to separate the project into parts and subparts that form sets of interrelated "work packages." A work package is a group of tasks that are continuous activities, each of which is assignable to a single individual (Gilley & Coffern, 1994). Deliverables for each work package are clearly defined and measurable according to established standards and project controls. Each work package has a scheduled start and end date for each task included. Finally, work packages are designed in such a way that preceding and succeeding work packages are identified. In other words, a logical flow exists for completing activities.

Let us consider a common example: building a home. Home construction comprises literally thousands of activities and steps, each of which can be assigned to individual workers such as carpenters, bricklayers, electricians, plumbers, roofers, drywallers, painters, and finish carpenters. Each of these individuals is responsible for activities in their area of expertise (work packages). The building contractor (project manager) schedules and coordinates work activities in what is deemed a logical, efficient manner. In this way, a large, nearly unmanageable project (building a home) can be broken down into manageable subprojects assigned to specialized workers (subcontractors). If managed correctly, the project should be completed by the deadline, under or at budget, and at quality specifications. Simply put, work packages are groups of activities or tasks that, when linked together, produce a projected outcome.

Project Planning

Project planning includes all tasks and activities necessary to achieve project goals, and sets objectives relative to schedules, costs, and quality. With ultimate objectives in mind, alternatives are identified that could include different tasks or activities. Five pro-

ject planning tools and techniques are available to HRD professionals for use in transforming large, unmanageable projects into
smaller, more negotiable efforts. They include:

1. goal analysis
2. risk analysis
3. stakeholder analysis
4. input process and output analysis (IPO)
5. scheduling technologies

Goal Analysis

Every project contains one or several goals to be accomplished.
The goal is a global statement of purpose and direction toward
which all objectives, activities, and tasks will point. According to
Weiss and Wysocki (1992), goals serve the following functions: they
define outcomes in terms of end products or services, act as a con-
tinual point of reference for settling disputes and misunderstand-
ings about the project, and are the guides that keep all objectives
and other associated work on track. Gilley and Coffern (1994) add
two more functions: project goals enable HRD professionals, their
clients, and team members to stay focused on desired results, and
they create commitment and agreement about project outcomes.

One of the best ways to capture the project goal is to consider
the statement of results. Randolph and Posner (1992) believe that
goal statements help project managers, team members, and clients
know when the project is finished. That is, project goals tell everyone involved what the end will look like.

Effectively written project goals (discussed in greater detail in
chapter four) should be specific, measurable, attainable, realistic,
and time-based (SMART). Project goals that meet this SMART criteria will be more easily communicated to clients, and will serve to
better manage and control project outcomes. When goals are written in such a way that they can be measured, evaluating project
results will also be easier.

Project goals written with end results in mind, and meeting the
SMART criteria, help clients understand what is in it for them. End
user satisfaction remains a critical component in goal development. The first step in goal identification is consideration of clients'
expectations, which requires two-way communication between
HRD professionals and their clients. In fact, formulating project
goals is as much an excuse to develop a dialogue with end users
and project team members as it is to identify the ultimate outcome
of the project.

Risk Analysis

Every project, regardless of size and scope, has risk associated with it. HRD professionals must identify risks and contemplate what might go wrong, or what undesirable results might occur, by accomplishing the project goal. When completing this activity, three project constraints should be considered—schedule, cost, and quality—which serve as constant reminders of the most important criteria used in measuring a project's success.

Project managers are responsible for examining the effects of limited resources on project completion. Accordingly, they should identify the optimal resources needed to realistically complete a project, as well as consequences surrounding failure to secure those resources.

In addition, project managers should consider what problems or delays might jeopardize the project. As delays seriously affect project execution, including budget and scheduling quality, the impact of cost overruns or missed deadlines should not be discounted. These outcomes will negatively influence the personal and professional credibility of HRD professionals, and can severely impact current and future project outcomes.

By addressing these issues, HRD professionals are better prepared to identify backup strategies before the project begins. That way, adjustments may be made to project scheduling and budgeting, allowing for allocation of additional resources, or negotiation of additional time to complete the project. Such an analysis will help identify discrepancies between clients' expectations and actual performance before the project begins, promoting better project control. Consequently, HRD professionals can produce better quality deliverables within the budgets available.

Stakeholder Analysis

Stakeholder analysis is another decision-making tool HRD professionals can use to better plan projects, understand planning obligations and tactics when dealing with clients, and improve communications between project team members, clients, and those individuals who stand to gain or lose as a result of the project. Each of these groups are considered stakeholders. According to Weiss and Wysocki (1992), the aims of stakeholder analysis are to:

1. enable project managers to identify groups that must be interacted with in order to meet project goals.
2. develop strategies and tactics to effectively negotiate competing goals and interests among the different groups.

3. identify each group's strategic interest in the project in order to negotiate common interests.
4. help the project manager better allocate resources to deal with differing constituencies.

When conducting a stakeholder analysis, HRD professionals should first identify all parties who have something to gain or lose as a result of the project (stakeholders). Second, the interests or expectations of each stakeholder in the project must be identified, thereby providing a baseline for all future decision-making and action. Third, HRD professionals must identify the action sequences they plan to follow to meet the interests or expectations of each stakeholder. Stakeholder analysis is a powerful tool that helps maintain customer service focus during project management.

Input, Process, and Output Analysis (IPO)

Input, process, and output analysis helps HRD professionals name the resources needed to complete a task or activity, the process by which they will achieve its outcome, and a list of each intended outcome (Brinkerhoff, 1995). IPO analyses are designed for each major part and subpart of the project. They can be used to communicate to clients and project teams the steps required for project completion, which can be very helpful when training new employees.

According to Gilley and Coffern (1994), IPO analyses are the blueprint for the project and help break down large, unmanageable projects into smaller miniprojects. HRD professionals delegate tasks and activities to members of the project team, who become "miniproject managers" (p. 142). IPO analysis greatly enhances control and management of a project, and helps increase involvement of clients and team members. Using goal and risk analysis, stakeholder analysis, scheduling technologies, and IPO analysis helps HRD professionals accurately define the project before it begins. Such knowledge fosters planning of more effective, efficient projects, as well as communicating to clients and project team members the desired outcomes and activities of the project. These analyses also allow for corrections, additions, or deletions before allocation of expensive limited financial, material, and human resources. In combination, these four tools promote better project management.

Scheduling Technologies

One of the most difficult parts of project management is identifying all project activities and determining their task dependency, which is the primary purpose of creating a project schedule. Another equally important aim is to identify when resources are needed. When these two components have been determined, HRD professionals (project managers) can schedule tasks in their proper sequence and allocate resources for maximum efficiency (Gilley & Coffern, 1994).

The most common type of scheduling format is the Gantt (bar) chart. While simple to draw, they capture a great deal of information about the project plan. Gantt charts are useful when overviewing a project with clients, and are a quick management tool for use in checking project progress. Gantt charts consist of three parts: a timeline, a list of activities or tasks, and a bar for each activity (the length of which represents the time estimate for each activity or task). Each bar depicts the start and end times for a task or activity. The bar chart also demonstrates which tasks cannot start until other tasks are completed.

It is said that a picture is worth a thousand words, which is quite true of Gantt charts. On a single page, team members and clients can view the entire project at a glance. This project planning tool conveys a considerable amount of information about the project, its complexities, and possible problem areas.

Human and material resources can be utilized quite differently during the project. They can be used early in the project (front-loaded), late in a project (rear-loaded), or on a constant basis (level-loaded). Each of these represents a type of schedule that can be used when planning project outcomes.

When HRD professionals use front-loaded schedules, most of the material and human resources are consumed and tasks are completed in the early phases of the project. One risk associated with front-loaded scheduling is that tasks and activities are completed so early in the project that the information developed may need to be reviewed or revised later in the project. Front-loaded schedules can also cause project team members some concern, as they may be nervous about doing tasks too early in the life of the project. Another risk associated with front-loaded schedules is that team members who complete tasks early may feel disassociated or abandoned as the project moves forward (Gilley & Coffern, 1994).

Rear-loaded schedules provide for resource allocation and task completion at the very end of the project timeline, which fosters project synergy and energy. In other words, tremendous activity is occurring, and project team members are abuzz over the completion of the project. This type of schedule does, however, have several risks associated with it. The most notable is task slippage, which can jeopardize project outcomes. Consequently, HRD professionals must make certain that team members adhere strictly to project timelines as no additional time remains to complete tasks. Another risk associated with rear-loaded schedules is that they create a tremendous amount of stress among project team members. Stress results from a seemingly overwhelming number of tasks facing the team, as well as fear of reduced quality associated with completing so many tasks so late in the project. In addition, cost overruns are most common with this type of schedule because project managers may have failed to allocate sufficient resources and, therefore, must acquire additional ones to meet project deadlines. These allocations may entail paying overtime or increased bonuses in order to accomplish the same project objectives.

The most common type of project schedule is level-loaded. In practice, it is not the most realistic because resources are seldom available in a uniform fashion. However, it is most commonly used during project proposals to demonstrate how a project is to be completed. Level-loaded schedules use resources and complete tasks equally from the beginning to the end of the project. They allow project team members to complete tasks in a linear fashion, in what we call the *domino effect*. That is, human resources can be assigned to complete all tasks within the project from beginning to end.

When using front and rear-loaded schedules, project managers may need to allocate multiple resources to carry out multiple tasks simultaneously. When level-loaded schedules are used, it is almost impossible to complete multiple tasks at the same time; therefore, they are often considered unrealistic. The biggest advantage of level-loaded schedules, however, is that they provide project continuity from beginning to end.

On the surface, project scheduling seems relatively simple. Unfortunately, some constraints make the process difficult and often lead to less than ideal schedules. According to Gilley and Coffern (1994), scheduling constraints include:

- the unavailability of a particular resource during a project
- demands on resource needs for other, present, or future projects
- different or conflicting demands by project managers for other resources
- a desire to avoid extensive work overloads for a particular individual
- lack of resource availability to complete a particular task
- budgetary constraints
- desire to lessen write-offs or budget overruns
- integration and use of other projects using the same resources

- not enough time for doing activities that are uncertain
- technical constraints that may need extra time
- difficulties inherent in scheduling far in advance

Any or all of these constraints can prevent HRD professionals from producing projects on time, within budget, and up to quality standards. Consequently, these constraints should be taken into consideration prior to creating a project schedule.

Project Visualization

One of the most effective tools for helping HRD professionals think through a project is project visualization. It helps them consider the major components of a project and its corresponding subparts, and shows the relationships between the parts. Project visualization is a tool that creates a picture of project activities and tasks. We have used project visualization throughout this book. For example, in Chapter 10, Figure 10.1 is a representation of project visualization, depicting the relationships between multiple tasks, their interdependency, and task relationships from beginning to end of the project. The arrows represent functional dependencies, where one part relies on another for one or more of its necessary inputs. Project visualization can be used to help HRD professionals delegate various tasks and activities, so that a project takes the form of a series of miniprojects rather than one large, unmanageable undertaking.

Sometimes it is useful to diagram a project in greater detail to help identify the resources needed for completion. Project visualization allows this to occur. It allows HRD professionals to better communicate with team members about their responsibilities.

Project Leadership

To manage a project effectively, HRD professionals must adopt a leadership style that motivates and empowers project team members, and monitors and guides their progress. According to Bolton (1986), project managers must treat team members with respect, listening to their opinions and ideas until managers fully understand their team members' respective points of view.

When conflict arises, HRD professionals' views, needs, and feelings must be expressed assertively, not submissively or aggressively. When communicating assertively, project managers are exhibiting self-respect, while at the same time demonstrating understanding and acceptance of their team members. However, they also are being clear in their assertions, opinions, and requests for more and better performance. Assertive project managers stand up for their own rights, yet express their personal needs, values, concerns and ideas in a direct and appropriate way. While meeting their own needs (i.e., improved performance) they do not violate those of their team members. True assertiveness is a way of behaving that affirms the project manager's own individual worth and dignity while simultaneously confirming and maintaining the worth and dignity of project team members (Gilley & Boughton, 1996).

Raudsepp (1987) identifies twelve guidelines for effective project management leadership. They are:

1. Do not overdirect, overobserve, or overreport.
2. Recognize differences in individuals. Hold a keen appreciation for each person's unique characteristics.
3. Help subordinates see problems as change opportunities.
4. Encourage employees to think more creatively and consider the types of creative contributions they would most like to make during the project.
5. Encourage self-directed work teams and behaviors during the project.
6. Respond positively rather than negatively to ideas.
7. Accept mistakes and errors as learning opportunities.
8. Create positive work environments where failure is not punished, but viewed as a way of improving future performance.
9. Be a resource person rather than a controller—a helper rather than a boss.
10. Insulate your employees from outside problems or internal organizational politics.
11. Participate in professional development activities that enhance creative abilities.
12. Make certain that innovative ideas are forwarded to superiors within the organization with your full support and backing.

Communication

Clear communication is the key to successfully managing human resources. All project team members and managers must be fully aware of the project's purpose, plan of action, current status, expected results, and their own roles and responsibilities. Throughout the project, effective, timely communications may include team meetings, one-on-ones with various project members, memorandums, e-mail, voice-mail, and the like. Communications planning helps project managers schedule appropriate, timely communiques capable of keeping all participants well-informed.

Barriers to Effective Communications

Project communications are often blocked by barriers that can be avoided if recognized. Sometimes the most innocent, well-intended comments can backfire, preventing project team members from trying new skills, resolving conflicts, or solving problems. Furthermore, employee confidence suffers, along with self-esteem. Gilley and Boughton (1996) call such behavior the "twelve performance killers," as they negatively impact or shut down employee performance if used at the wrong time or in the wrong way. Bolton (1986) clustered them into three categories: judging, providing unwanted or unwelcome solutions, and avoiding team members' concerns. Judging can be defined as placing oneself in a superior position—making it difficult to build and maintain positive relationships with project team members.

Sometimes providing solutions for team members compounds the problem or creates a new problem without resolving the original dilemma. Some project managers believe that advising, ordering, moralizing, questioning, or threatening project team members improves their overall performance. In reality, these behaviors often backfire. At other times project managers use techniques that cause performance to decline. For example, limited emotional involvement while addressing employee performance problems or conflicts may communicate lack of concern for the well-being of the project team member. As a result, team members resist logical, well-thought out feedback, as well as reassurances that project outcomes will indeed be achieved.

Occasionally, project managers distract team members by diverting their attention to unrelated or unimportant issues, rather than dealing directly with performance concerns, feelings, or project issues. When any of these barriers to communications is present, open and honest interaction seldom exists. Consequently, team members are reluctant to discuss problems or concerns with project mangers, resulting in failure to achieve project outcomes.

Project Implementation

Project implementation is a straightforward process that includes execution of all project tasks and activities using the tools and techniques already discussed in the first four phases of project management. Project implementation is the "just do it" part of project management. However, project managers must guard against procrastination or other diversions that prevent completion of projects on time, and must make certain that project team members are performing in an acceptable manner.

Project Controls

Regardless of how complete and accurate project planning has been, there will always be a number of events that prevent the project from being completed as planned. Unforeseen contingencies typically occur at precisely the worst time. This threatens project success. The acid test of any project manager will be his or her ability to detect problems and take appropriate, corrective action, keeping the project on schedule, within budget, and completing it according to quality specifications.

Predicting or controlling unforeseen events is the purpose of project controls, which are designed to focus on one or more of three components of a project: performance levels, costs, and time schedules (Weiss & Wysocki, 1992). The primary reasons for project controls are to track project progress, detect variance from the project plan, and take corrective action.

Track Project Progress

In order to track progress, project managers will have to produce a periodic (weekly or monthly) reporting system that will help them identify the status of every activity in a project. Reports should summarize progress for a specified period of time as well as identify any areas of concern or difficulty. These reports can be used for part of the project or the entire project.

Detect Variance from the Project Plan

One of the most important functions of project control is to detect variances from the project plan—allowing project managers time to take corrective action. Figure 13.5 is a simple variance report that provides project team members the opportunity to work closely with project managers to identify proposed changes that impact schedules, costs, and quality. By using these reports, project managers are not encouraging variances in the original project plan, but are providing team members an opportunity to discuss unforeseen contingencies and unexpected changes, early enough so that appropriate actions can be taken. This tool is extremely important for large, complex projects that utilize a number of material and human resources, and which must be coordinated and controlled over an extended period of time. Finally, these reports help reduce the number of questions regarding the implementation or clarification of activities or tasks, and are a more formalized dialogue than random discussions in the hallways of one's organization.

Take Corrective Action

When a significant variance from the project plan occurs, project managers must determine whether corrective action is needed, then respond accordingly. The project's complexity will help determine the number of "what ifs" that must be taken into account. Taking corrective action is most acute when projects appear to be falling behind schedule, thus jeopardizing project budgeting and/or quality of the deliverable. In order to get the project back on schedule, human and material resources may require reallocation and alternatives must be identified.

PROPOSED SCHEDULE/PLAN CHANGE WORKSHEET

	Impact on ...		
Proposed Change	Schedule?	Cost?	Quality?

Figure 13.1   Change Worksheet

Regardless of the contingency or problem that surfaces, project managers must use project controls to make adjustments. Two types of controls can be used to ensure that projects remain on track. They are steering and go/no go controls.

When a project reaches a critical checkpoint, HRD professionals must compare the project's current status with its plan. If activities or tasks do not meet specifications, a set of corrective actions known as steering controls should be implemented. Steering controls are designed to redirect tasks and activities in such a way that they adhere to the project plan and its corresponding schedule. According to Gilley and Coffern (1994), they are used to answer the "what if" questions, and are most useful when critical decisions must be made at key points within the project. Steering controls should be identified before the project begins, and serve as soundings along the way.

As an example, when a ship captain sails from England to Australia a number of conditions must be taken into account prior to launching. These conditions may include water currents, wind conditions, future weather systems, weight and size of the vessel, number of passengers, cargo weight and placement, and geographic variations beneath the water's surface. Each of these conditions can greatly influence the captain's selected route. While sailing, the captain continuously adjusts his charted course, unlike automobile travel, which follows a linear connection from one point to another. At certain points along the route, the captain determines whether he or she is on schedule and is at the appropriate geographical point. Measurements are taken to determine whether the ship is on course. If off course, adjustments will be made to return the ship to the appropriate course, or an acceptable alternative will be chosen. These checkpoints may occur several times during the sailing excursion. As one might imagine, the more complex the route, the more checkpoints will be necessary. This is an excellent example of steering controls. The ship captain functions as the quintessential project manager. The project plan is the sailing course, which will include a number of activities. Soundings are project controls. No ship captain would set sail without establishing a course of action and identifying steering controls. Therefore, it makes tremendous sense that HRD professionals embark upon performance improvement and organizational development projects only after establishing the same kinds of safeguards.

A go/no go control is similar to a steering control; however, the corrective action involved is different. When a go/no go control is used, project managers must determine whether it makes sound financial and business sense to continue the project. Go/no go controls allow the reallocation of financial, material, and human resources to other projects with greater potential for success. The most important purpose of go/no go controls is to provide project managers the opportunity to terminate projects that do not have a high probability of success. In this way, personal and professional credibility is preserved.

Project Budgeting

While project budgets are typically developed during the project planning phase, they are so critical to the outcomes of a project that we believe they should be a type of project control. In this way, project budgets help determine whether or not project outcomes are on time and within quality specifications. Underfunded projects are destined to produce inferior results. Therefore, the project manager is responsible for negotiation of a budgeting level appropriate to achieve desired outcomes.

When developing a budget, project managers must consider all costs germane to completing the project. To maximize control, budgets should be built at the component level of the project, which ensures budgetary linkage to a part and its subparts. In other words, project budgets should be built from the inside out. When this approach is used, a more exacting accountability of costs can be realized, allowing the project manager to examine the budgetary costs at a micro level rather than at a macro level. By summarizing component-level budgets, project managers can identify the overall costs of the project.

When building a budget, project managers should consider five different types of costs:

1. Direct costs—all items directly attributable to the project, its parts, and subparts (i.e., equipment, travel expenses, supplies, tools, or dedicated human resources)
2. Indirect costs—items difficult to assign to specific projects, parts, or subparts (i.e., heating, electricity, insurance, or other overhead expenses)
3. Fixed costs—items that do not vary regardless of their use (i.e., rent, computer equipment, or certain types of human resources such as administrative assistants)
4. Variable costs—items that vary with their usage (i.e., long-distance telephone calls, copying, or other disposable materials)
5. Allocated costs—items already paid for by the organization (i.e., salaries and benefits)

Project budgeting remains one of the most critical elements of project management, and is used to determine whether or not a project has been completed successfully. Budgets should be carefully developed and adhered to strictly, with adjustments made only when the quality of project deliverables is in jeopardy.

Project Termination

While it makes sense to plan, implement, and control project outcomes, it also makes sense to properly terminate a project. In many situations, project termination will help determine how people feel about the project's outcomes.

According to Weiss and Wysocki (1992) terminating a project means:

1. To formally close outside contractual relationships with suppliers, customers, and other budgeted parties who expect an early, agreed-upon termination of their services.
2. To formally terminate project team members' assignments.
3. To obtain client acceptance of project outcomes and deliverables.
4. To ensure that all deliverables have been installed and implemented according to time, budget, and quality specifications.
5. To ensure that adequate project documentation and baseline information are in place to facilitate interactions or changes that may need to occur in the future.
6. To issue or obtain sign-offs on the final report or project status, which show that contracted deliverables have been satisfactorily implemented.
7. To terminate all interior and exterior relationships.

According to Meredith and Mantel (1989), the three types of project termination are extinction, inclusion, and integration. Each of these helps project managers determine the project's acceptance within the organization.

The most formal project termination is extinction, which implies that project activities as scheduled are either successfully or unsuccessfully completed, and the decision to terminate is agreed-upon by all parties. When a project has been extinguished prior to its completion, stress and feelings of inadequacy may result on the part of project team members, managers, and clients since their time and effort have, for all practical purposes, been undermined.

Project termination by inclusion means the project is a success and has been institutionalized into the organization (Weiss & Wysocki, 1992). Termination by inclusion implies that a transformation has occurred within the organization, and that significant changes are occurring or are scheduled to occur as a result.

Project termination by integration is a "business as usual" approach. In other words, the project simply ends and successful deliverables are shared within the organization. Project equipment, materials, and human resources are then redistributed back into the organization to be reassigned to new projects. Little fanfare or celebration occurs during this type of project termination, which is seen as an everyday occurrence.

It is extremely important to know when a project should be terminated, especially when there is a departure from the deadlines set forth in the original project plan. Meredith and Mantel (1989) have identified a number of important guidelines that serve as a checklist for project managers in determining when a project should be terminated. They include:

1. Has the project lost its key champion or internal advocate?
2. Is the project team enthusiastic about project deliverables?
3. Does it seem likely that the project will achieve the minimal goals set for it?
4. Could the project be outsourced without loss of quality or extensive financial costs?
5. Is the project team still innovative, or have they gone stale?
6. Is organizational support for project deliverables enthusiastic?
7. Is organizational support significant for project success?
8. Is the project still consistent with organizational strategic business goals and objectives?
9. Is management sufficiently enthusiastic about the project to support its implementation?
10. Does the project have the support of all departments needed to implement it (important during organizational development interventions)?
11. Is the current project team properly qualified to continue the project?
12. Does the organization have the required skills to achieve full implementation of the project?
13. Is the scope of the project consistent with the organization's vision, mission, and guiding principles?

Project Evaluation

In order to determine a project's success, project managers must ascertain how well project goals and activities have been achieved by measuring them against the original project plan, budget, deadlines, quality of deliverables specifications, and client satisfaction. The most important questions to be answered are:

- Was the project goal achieved?
- Was project work completed on time, within budget, and according to quality specifications?
- Was the client satisfied with project results (Weiss & Wysocki, 1992)?

These questions should drive the postimplementation evaluation in such a way that project managers and team members learn from their successes and failures. It is extremely important to have a final discussion about how well the project was managed, coordinated, and implemented. Such meetings should be informal affairs allowing individuals to share their opinions and ideas freely. In this way, assemblies will be perceived as learning experiences rather than fault-gathering activities, and will result in a great deal of shared learning. It is important to remember that people have dedicated many hours to the successful execution and completion of a project; therefore, it makes sense to celebrate its success or discuss its failures. Otherwise, team members will feel a sense of loss or inadequacy as a result of the lack of closure.

CONCLUSION

Project management is, indeed, one of the most important tools available to HRD professionals to improve the image and credibility of HRD programs, its professionals, interventions, and consulting services. Projects provide an opportunity to develop strategic business partnerships, performance improvement, and organizational development partnerships throughout the firm. HRD professionals must remember that the eyes of the organization are upon them during project management, especially when plans are being championed by senior management or key influencers within the organization. Consequently, project management and execution are crucial as HRD programs struggle to evolve to the strategically integrated level.

References

Baldwin, T. T., & Ford, J. K. (1988). Transfer of training: A review and direction for future research. *Personal Psychology, 41*(1), 65–105.

Barry, T. E. (1986). *Marketing: An integrated approach.* Chicago: Dryden Press.

Beer, M. (1983). In L. S. Baird, C. E. Schneier, & D. Laird (Eds.) *What is organizational development? Training and development sourcebook.* Amherst, MA: HRD Press.

Biekowski, D. (1989). Ten causes of project bust. *Computerworld,* 99.

Block, P. (1981). *Flawless consulting: A guide to getting your expertise used.* San Diego: Pfeiffer.

Bolton, R. (1986). *People skills: How to assert yourself, listen to others, and resolve conflicts.* New York: Simon & Schuster.

Bowers, D. G., & Franklin, J. L. (1977). *Survey-guided development I: Data-based organizational change.* San Diego: University Associates.

Bradshaw, P. (1981). *The management of self-esteem: How people can feel good about themselves and better about their organizations.* Englewood Cliffs, NJ: Prentice-Hall.

Brinkerhoff, R. O. (1995). Personal interview.

Brinkerhoff, R. O., & Gill, S. J. (1994). *The learning alliance.* San Francisco: Jossey-Bass.

Broad, M. L., & Newstrom, J. W. (1992). *Transfer of training: Action-packed strategies to ensure high payoff from training investments.* Reading, MA: Addison-Wesley.

Burke, W. W. (1992). *Organization development: A process of learning and changing.* Reading, MA: Addison-Wesley.

Cameron, K. (1980). Critical questions in assessing organizational effectiveness. *Organizational Dynamics, 9*(2), 66–80.

Dean, R. L., & Gilley, J. W. (1986). A production model for experiential learning. *Performance and Instruction Journal, 25*(3), 26–28.

Donaldson, L., & Scannell, E. E. (1986). *Human resource development: The new trainers guide.* Reading, MA: Addison-Wesley.

Dyer, W. G. (1989, Winter). Team building: A microcosm of the past, present, and future of OD. *Academy of Management OD Newsletter,* 7–8.

Fallon, T., & Brinkerhoff, R. O. (1996). *Framework for organizational effectiveness.* Paper presented at the American Society for Training and Development international conference.

French, W. L., & Bell, C. H., Jr. (1984). *Organizational development: Behavioral science interventions for organizational improvement.* Englewood Cliffs, NJ: Prentice-Hall.

Gibson, J. L., Ivancevich, J. M., & Donnelly, J. H. (1997). *Organizations: Behavior, structures, processes* (9th ed.). Chicago: Richard D. Irwin.

Gill, S. J. (1995). Shifting gears for high performance. *Training and Development Journal, 49*(5), 25–31.

Gilley, J. W. (1990). *How to collect data.* Alexandria, VA: ASTD Press.

Gilley, J. W. (1996). *Promoting your consulting business: Techniques for success.* Alexandria, VA: ASTD Press.

Gilley, J. W. (1998). *Improving HRD practice.* Malabar, FL: Krieger. Forthcoming.

Gilley, J. W., & Boughton, N. W. (1996). *Stop managing, start coaching: How performance coaching can enhance commitment and improve productivity.* New York: McGraw-Hill.

Gilley, J. W., & Coffern, A. J. (1994). *Internal consulting for HRD professionals: Tools, techniques, and strategies for improving organizational performance.* New York: McGraw-Hill.

Gilley, J. W., & Eggland, S. A. (1989). *Principles of HRD.* Reading, MA: Addison-Wesley.

Gilley, J. W., & Eggland, S. A. (1992). *Marketing HRD programs within the organization: Improving the visibility, credibility, and image of programs.* San Francisco: Jossey-Bass.

Hale, J., & Westgaard, O. (1991). Planning for action. *Data Training,* 18–24.

Hodges, K. A. (1995). *Needs assessment and training evaluation: Toolkit.* Kalamazoo, MI: Organizational Development Consultants.

Kaufman, R., Rojas, A. M., & Mayer, H. (1992). *Needs assessment: A user's guide.* Englewood Cliffs, NJ: Educational Technology Publications.

Kerzner, H. (1982). *Project management: A system approach to planning, scheduling and controlling.* New York: Van Nostrand Reinhold.

Kotler, P. (1992). *Marketing management: Analysis, planning, and control* (3rd ed.). Englewood Cliffs, NJ: Prentice-Hall.

LeBoeuf, M. (1985). *Getting results: The secret to motivating yourself and others.* New York: Berkeley Books.

Lewin, K. (1951). *Field theory in social science.* New York: Harper.

McLagan, P., & Bedrick, R. (1983). *Models for excellence.* Alexandria, VA: ASTD Press.

McLagan, P., & Suhadolnik, L. (1989). *Models for HRD practice.* Alexandria, VA: ASTD Press.

Mager, R., & Pipe, P. (1984). *Analyzing performance problems* (2nd ed.). Belmont, CA: Lake Publishing Company.

Meredith, J. R., & Mantel, S. J. (1989). *Project management: A managerial approach.* New York: Wiley.

Michael, D. N. (1973). *On learning to plan—and planning to learn: The social psychology of changing toward future-responsive social learning.* San Francisco: Jossey-Bass.

Michalak, D. F., & Yager, E. G. (1979). *Making the training process work.* New York: Harper & Row.

Neilsen, E. H. (1984). *Becoming an OD practitioner.* Englewood Cliffs, NJ: Prentice-Hall.

Patterson, J. (1997). *Coming clean about organizational change.* Arlington, VA: American Association of School Administrators.

Randolph, A., & Poner, B. (1992). *Effective project planning and management, getting the job done.* Englewood Cliffs, NJ: Prentice-Hall.

Raudsepp, E. (1987). In R. L. Kuhn (Ed.), *Handbook for creative managers* (pp. 173–182). New York: McGraw-Hill.

Robinson, D. G., & Robinson, J. (1996). *Performance consulting.* San Francisco: Berrett-Koehler.

Rossett, A. (1990). Analysis in human performance problems. In H. D. Stolovitch & E. J. Keeps (Eds.), *Handbook of human performance technology: A comprehensive guide for analyzing and solving performance problems in organizations* (pp. 50–65). San Francisco: Jossey-Base.

Rummler, G. A., & Brache, A. P. (1995). *Improving performance: How to manage the white spaces on the organizational chart.* San Francisco: Jossey-Bass.

Schwinn, D. (1996). *The interactive project learning model.* Concept paper. Transportation, Inc.

Senge, P. M. (1990). *The fifth discipline: The art and practice of the learning organization.* New York: Doubleday.

Silber, K. H. (1992). Intervening at different levels in organizations. In H. D. Stolovitch & E. J. Keeps (Eds.), *Handbook of human performance technology: A comprehensive guide for analyzing and solving performance problems in organizations* (pp. 50–65). San Francisco: Jossey-Bass.

Simerly, R. O. (1989). *Handbook for marketing in continuing education.* San Francisco: Jossey-Bass.

Simerly, R. O. (1987). *Strategic planning and leadership in continuing education.* San Francisco: Jossey-Bass.

Tichy, N. M. (1989). GE's crotonville: A staging ground for corporate revolution. *Academy of Management Executive,* 102.

Thiagarajan, A. J. (1980). *Experimental learning packages.* Englewood Cliffs, NJ: Educational Technology Publications.

Turner, A. N. (1983). Consulting is more than giving advice. *Harvard Business Review, 61*(5), 120–29.

Weiss, J. W., & Wysocki, R. K. (1992). *5-phase project management: A practical planning and implementation guide.* Reading, MA: Addison-Wesley.

Wilson, L. (1987). *Changing the game: The new way to sell.* New York: Fireside.

Index